Early Praise for *Seven Concurrency Models in Seven Weeks*

For decades, professional programmers have dealt with concurrency and parallelism using threads and locks. But this model is one of many, as *Seven Concurrency Models in Seven Weeks* vividly demonstrates. If you want to get ahead in a world where mainstream languages are scrambling to support actors, CSP, data parallelism, functional programming, and Clojure's unified succession model, read this book.

➤ **Stuart Halloway**
   Cofounder, Cognitect

As our machines get more and more cores, understanding concurrency is more important than ever before. You'll learn why functional programming matters for concurrency, how actors can be leveraged for writing distributed software, and how to explore parallel processing with GPUs and Big Data. This book will expand your toolbox for writing software so you're prepared for the years to come.

➤ **José Valim**
   Cofounder, Plataformatec

An eye-opening survey of different concurrency/parallelism techniques, *Seven Concurrency Models* strikes an excellent balance between providing explanations and encouraging experimentation.

➤ **Frederick Cheung**
   CTO, Dressipi

The world is changing, and every working programmer must learn to think about concurrent programming. Now when they say, "How shall I do that?" I will have a book that I can suggest they read. I learned a lot and am happy to recommend it.

➤ **Andrew Haley**
   Java lead engineer, Red Hat

As Amdahl's law starts to eclipse Moore's law, a transition from object-oriented programming to concurrency-oriented programming is taking place. As a result, the timing of this book could not be more appropriate. Paul does a fantastic job describing the most important concurrency models, giving you the necessary ammunition to decide which one of them best suits your needs. A must-read if you are developing software in the multicore era.

➤ **Francesco Cesarini**
   Founder and technical director, Erlang Solutions

With this book, Paul has delivered an excellent introduction to the thorny topics of concurrency and parallelism, covering the different approaches in a clear and engaging way.

➤ **Sean Ellis**
   GPU architect, ARM

A simple approach for a complex subject. I would love to have a university course about this with *Seven Concurrency Models in Seven Weeks* as a guide.

➤ **Carlos Sessa**
   Android developer, Groupon

Paul Butcher takes an issue that strikes fear into many developers and gives a clear exposition of practical programming paradigms they can use to handle and exploit concurrency in the software they create.

➤ **Páidí Creed**
   Software engineer, SwiftKey

Having worked with Paul on a number of occasions, I can recommend him as a genuine authority on programming-language design and structure. This book is a lucid exposition of an often-misunderstood but vital topic in modern software engineering.

➤ **Ben Medlock**
   Cofounder and CTO, SwiftKey

Seven Concurrency Models in Seven Weeks
When Threads Unravel

Paul Butcher

The Pragmatic Bookshelf

Dallas, Texas • Raleigh, North Carolina

Many of the designations used by manufacturers and sellers to distinguish their products are claimed as trademarks. Where those designations appear in this book, and The Pragmatic Programmers, LLC was aware of a trademark claim, the designations have been printed in initial capital letters or in all capitals. The Pragmatic Starter Kit, The Pragmatic Programmer, Pragmatic Programming, Pragmatic Bookshelf, PragProg and the linking *g* device are trademarks of The Pragmatic Programmers, LLC.

Every precaution was taken in the preparation of this book. However, the publisher assumes no responsibility for errors or omissions, or for damages that may result from the use of information (including program listings) contained herein.

Our Pragmatic courses, workshops, and other products can help you and your team create better software and have more fun. For more information, as well as the latest Pragmatic titles, please visit us at *http://pragprog.com*.

The team that produced this book includes:

Bruce A. Tate (series editor)
Jacquelyn Carter (editor)
Potomac Indexing, LLC (indexer)
Molly McBeath (copyeditor)
David J Kelly (typesetter)
Janet Furlow (producer)
Ellie Callahan (support)

For international rights, please contact *rights@pragprog.com*.

ISBN-13: 978-1-937785-65-9
Book version: P1.0—July 2014

Contents

Foreword

This book tells a story.

That sentence may seem like a strange first thought for a book, but the idea is important to me. You see, we turn away dozens of proposals for *Seven in Seven* books from authors who think they can throw together seven disjointed essays and call it a book. That's not what we're about.

The original *Seven Languages in Seven Weeks: A Pragmatic Guide to Learning Programming Languages [Tat10]* story was that object-oriented programming languages were good for their time, but as pressures built around software complexity and concurrency driven by multicore architectures, functional programming languages would begin to emerge and would shape the way we program. Paul Butcher was one of the most effective reviewers of that book. After a growing four-year relationship, I've come to understand why.

Paul has been right on the front lines of bringing highly scalable concurrency to real business applications. In the *Seven Languages* book, he saw hints of some of the language-level answers to an increasingly important and complicated problem space. A couple of years later, Paul approached us to write a book of his own. He argued that languages play an important part of the overall story, but they just scratch the surface. He wanted to tell a much more complete story to our readers and map out in layman's terms the most critical tools that modern applications use to solve big parallel problems in a scalable way.

At first we were skeptical. These books are hard to write—they take much longer than most other books and have a high failure rate—and Paul chose a huge dragon to slay. As a team, we fought and worked, eventually coaxing a good story out of the original table of contents. As the pages came together, it became increasingly clear that Paul had not only the technical ability but also the passion to attack this topic. We have come to understand that this is a special book, one that arrives at the right time. As you dig in, you'll see what I mean.

You'll cringe with us as we show threading and locking, the most widely used concurrency solution today. You'll see where that solution comes up short, and then you'll go to work. Paul will walk you through vastly different approaches, from the Lambda Architecture used in some of busiest social platforms to the actor-based model that powers many of the world's largest and most reliable telecoms. You will see the languages that the pros use, from Java to Clojure to the exciting, emerging Erlang-based Elixir language. Every step of the way, Paul will walk you through the complexities from an insider's perspective.

I am excited to present *Seven Concurrency Models in Seven Weeks*. I hope you will treasure it as much as I do.

Bruce A. Tate
CTO, icanmakeitbetter.com
Series editor of the *Seven in Seven* books
Austin, Texas

Acknowledgments

When I announced that I had signed the contract to write this book, a friend asked, "Has it been long enough that you've forgotten what writing the first one was like?" I guess I was naïve enough to imagine that writing a second book would be easier. Perhaps if I'd chosen an easier format than a *Seven in Seven* book, I would have been right.

It certainly wouldn't have been possible without the amazing support I've received from series editor Bruce Tate and development editor Jackie Carter. Thanks to both of you for sticking with me during this book's occasionally difficult gestation, and thanks to Dave and Andy for the opportunity to make another contribution to a great series.

Many people offered advice and feedback on early drafts, including (in no particular order) Simon Hardy-Francis, Sam Halliday, Mike Smith, Neil Eccles, Matthew Rudy Jacobs, Joe Osborne, Dave Strauss, Derek Law, Frederick Cheung, Hugo Tyson, Paul Gregory, Stephen Spencer, Alex Nixon, Ben Coppin, Kit Smithers, Andrew Eacott, Freeland Abbott, James Aley, Matthew Wilson, Simon Dobson, Doug Orr, Jonas Bonér, Stu Halloway, Rich Morin, David Whittaker, Bo Rydberg, Jake Goulding, Ari Gold, Juan Manuel Gimeno Illa, Steve Bassett, Norberto Ortigoza, Luciano Ramalho, Siva Jayaraman, Shaun Parry, and Joel VanderWerf.

I'm particularly grateful to the book's technical reviewers (again in no particular order): Carlos Sessa, Danny Woods, Venkat Subramaniam, Simon Wood, Páidí Creed, Ian Roughley, Andrew Thomson, Andrew Haley, Sean Ellis, Geoffrey Clements, Loren Sands-Ramshaw, and Paul Hudson.

Finally, I owe both thanks and an apology to friends, colleagues, and family. Thanks for your support and encouragement, and sorry for being so monomaniacal over the last eighteen months.

Preface

In 1989 I started a PhD in languages for parallel and distributed computing—I was convinced that concurrent programming was about to turn mainstream. A belated two decades later, I've finally been proven correct—the world is buzzing with talk of multiple cores and how to take advantage of them.

But there's more to concurrency than achieving better performance by exploiting multiple cores. Used correctly, concurrency is the key that unlocks responsiveness, fault tolerance, efficiency, and simplicity.

About This Book

This book follows the structure of The Pragmatic Bookshelf's existing *Seven in Seven* books, *Seven Languages in Seven Weeks [Tat10]*, *Seven Databases in Seven Weeks [RW12]*, and *Seven Web Frameworks in Seven Weeks [MD14]*. The seven approaches here have been chosen to give a broad overview of the concurrency landscape. We'll cover some approaches that are already mainstream, some that are rapidly becoming mainstream, and others that are unlikely to ever be mainstream but are fantastically powerful in their particular niches. It's my hope that, after reading this book, you'll know exactly which tool(s) to reach for when faced with a concurrency problem.

Each chapter is designed to be read over a long weekend, split up into three days. Each day ends with exercises that expand on that day's subject matter, and each chapter concludes with a wrap-up that summarizes the strengths and weaknesses of the approach under consideration.

Although a little philosophical hand-waving occurs along the way, the focus of the book is on practical working examples. I encourage you to work through these examples as you're reading—nothing is more convincing than real, working code.

What This Book Is Not

This book is not a reference manual. I'm going to be using languages that might be new to you, such as Elixir and Clojure. Because this is a book about concurrency, not languages, there are going to be some aspects of these languages that I'll use without explaining in detail. Hopefully everything will be clear from context, but I'm relying on you to persevere if you need to explore some language feature further to understand fully. You might want to read along with a web browser handy so you can consult the language's documentation if you need to.

Nor is this an installation manual. To run the example code, you're going to need to install and run various tools—the README files included in the example code contain hints, but broadly speaking you're on your own here. I've used mainstream toolchains for all the examples, so there's plenty of help available on the Internet if you find yourself stuck.

Finally, this book is not comprehensive—there isn't space to cover every topic in detail. I mention some aspects only in passing or don't discuss them at all. On occasion, I've deliberately used slightly nonidiomatic code because doing so makes it easier for someone new to the language to follow along. If you decide to explore one or more of the technologies used here in more depth, check out one of the more definitive books referenced in the text.

Example Code

All the code discussed in the book can be downloaded from the book's website.[1] Each example includes not only source but also a build system. For each language, I've chosen the most popular build system for that language (Maven for Java, Leiningen for Clojure, Mix for Elixir, sbt for Scala, and GNU Make for C).

In most cases, these build systems will not only build the example but also automatically download any additional dependencies. In the case of sbt and Leiningen, they will even download the appropriate version of the Scala or Clojure compiler, so all you need to do is successfully install the relevant build tool, instructions for which are readily available on the Internet.

The primary exception to this is the C code used in Chapter 7, *Data Parallelism*, on page 189, for which you will need to install the relevant OpenCL toolkit for your particular operating system and graphics card (unless you're on a Mac, that is, for which Xcode comes with everything built in).

---

1. http://pragprog.com/book/pb7con/

A Note to IDE Users

The build systems have all been tested from the command line. If you're a hardcore IDE user, you should be able to import the build system into your IDE—most IDEs are Maven-aware already, and plugins for sbt and Leiningen can create projects for most mainstream IDEs. But this isn't something I've tested, so you might find it easier to stick to using the command line.

A Note to Windows Users

All the examples have been tested on both OS X and Linux. They should all run just fine on Windows, but they haven't been tested there.

The exception is the C code used in Chapter 7, *Data Parallelism*, on page 189, which uses GNU Make and GCC. It should be relatively easy to move the code over to Visual C++, but again this isn't something I've tested.

Online Resources

The apps and examples shown in this book can be found at the Pragmatic Programmers website for this book.[2] You'll also find the community forum and the errata-submission form, where you can report problems with the text or make suggestions for future versions.

Paul Butcher
Ten Tenths Consulting
paul@tententhsconsulting.com
Cambridge, UK, June 2014

---

2. http://pragprog.com/book/pb7con

CHAPTER 1

Introduction

Concurrent programming is nothing new, but it's recently become a hot topic. Languages like Erlang, Haskell, Go, Scala, and Clojure are gaining mindshare, in part thanks to their excellent support for concurrency.

The primary driver behind this resurgence of interest is what's become known as the "multicore crisis." Moore's law continues to deliver more transistors per chip,[1] but instead of those transistors being used to make a single CPU faster, we're seeing computers with more and more cores.

As Herb Sutter said, "The free lunch is over."[2] You can no longer make your code run faster by simply waiting for faster hardware. These days if you need more performance, you need to exploit multiple cores, and that means exploiting parallelism.

Concurrent or Parallel?

This is a book about concurrency, so why are we talking about parallelism? Although they're often used interchangeably, *concurrent* and *parallel* refer to related but different things.

Related but Different

A *concurrent* program has multiple logical *threads of control*. These threads may or may not run in parallel.

A *parallel* program potentially runs more quickly than a sequential program by executing different parts of the computation simultaneously (in parallel). It may or may not have more than one logical thread of control.

---

1. http://en.wikipedia.org/wiki/Moore's_law
2. http://www.gotw.ca/publications/concurrency-ddj.htm

An alternative way of thinking about this is that concurrency is an aspect of the problem domain—your program needs to handle multiple simultaneous (or near-simultaneous) events. Parallelism, by contrast, is an aspect of the solution domain—you want to make your program faster by processing different portions of the problem in parallel.

As Rob Pike puts it,[3]

> Concurrency is about dealing with lots of things at once.

> Parallelism is about doing lots of things at once.

So is this book about concurrency or parallelism?

Joe asks:

Concurrent or Parallel?

My wife is a teacher. Like most teachers, she's a master of multitasking. At any one instant, she's only doing one thing, but she's having to deal with many things concurrently. While listening to one child read, she might break off to calm down a rowdy classroom or answer a question. This is concurrent, but it's not parallel (there's only one of her).

If she's joined by an assistant (one of them listening to an individual reader, the other answering questions), we now have something that's both concurrent and parallel.

Imagine that the class has designed its own greeting cards and wants to mass-produce them. One way to do so would be to give each child the task of making five cards. This is parallel but not (viewed from a high enough level) concurrent—only one task is underway.

Beyond Sequential Programming

What parallelism and concurrency have in common is that they both go beyond the traditional sequential programming model in which things happen one at a time, one after the other. We're going to cover both concurrency and parallelism in this book (if I were a pedant, the title would have been *Seven Concurrent and/or Parallel Programming Models in Seven Weeks*, but that wouldn't have fit on the cover).

Concurrency and parallelism are often confused because traditional threads and locks don't provide any direct support for parallelism. If you want to

---

3.   http://concur.rspace.googlecode.com/hg/talk/concur.html

exploit multiple cores with threads and locks, your only choice is to create a concurrent program and then run it on parallel hardware.

This is unfortunate because concurrent programs are often *nondeterministic* —they will give different results depending on the precise timing of events. If you're working on a genuinely concurrent problem, nondeterminism is natural and to be expected. Parallelism, by contrast, doesn't necessarily imply nondeterminism—doubling every number in an array doesn't (or at least, shouldn't) become nondeterministic just because you double half the numbers on one core and half on another. Languages with explicit support for parallelism allow you to write parallel code without introducing the specter of nondeterminism.

Parallel Architecture

Although there's a tendency to think that parallelism means multiple cores, modern computers are parallel on many different levels. The reason why individual cores have been able to get faster every year, until recently, is that they've been using all those extra transistors predicted by Moore's law in parallel, both at the bit and at the instruction level.

Bit-Level Parallelism

Why is a 32-bit computer faster than an 8-bit one? Parallelism. If an 8-bit computer wants to add two 32-bit numbers, it has to do it as a sequence of 8-bit operations. By contrast, a 32-bit computer can do it in one step, handling each of the 4 bytes within the 32-bit numbers in parallel.

That's why the history of computing has seen us move from 8- to 16-, 32-, and now 64-bit architectures. The total amount of benefit we'll see from this kind of parallelism has its limits, though, which is why we're unlikely to see 128-bit computers soon.

Instruction-Level Parallelism

Modern CPUs are highly parallel, using techniques like *pipelining*, *out-of-order execution*, and *speculative execution*.

As programmers, we've mostly been able to ignore this because, despite the fact that the processor has been doing things in parallel under our feet, it's carefully maintained the illusion that everything is happening sequentially.

This illusion is breaking down, however. Processor designers are no longer able to find ways to increase the speed of an individual core. As we move into a multicore world, we need to start worrying about the fact that instructions aren't handled sequentially. We'll talk about this more in *Memory Visibility*, on page 15.

Data Parallelism

Data-parallel (sometimes called SIMD, for "single instruction, multiple data") architectures are capable of performing the same operations on a large quantity of data in parallel. They're not suitable for every type of problem, but they can be extremely effective in the right circumstances.

One of the applications that's most amenable to data parallelism is image processing. To increase the brightness of an image, for example, we increase the brightness of each pixel. For this reason, modern GPUs (graphics processing units) have evolved into extremely powerful data-parallel processors.

Task-Level Parallelism

Finally, we reach what most people think of as parallelism—multiple processors. From a programmer's point of view, the most important distinguishing feature of a multiprocessor architecture is the memory model, specifically whether it's shared or distributed.

In a *shared-memory* multiprocessor, each processor can access any memory location, and interprocessor communication is primarily through memory, as you can see in Figure 1, *Shared memory*, on page 5.

Figure 2, *Distributed memory*, on page 5 shows a *distributed-memory* system, where each processor has its own local memory and where interprocessor communication is primarily via the network.

Because communicating via memory is typically faster and simpler than doing so over the network, writing code for shared memory-multiprocessors is generally easier. But beyond a certain number of processors, shared memory becomes a bottleneck—to scale beyond that point, you're going to have to tackle distributed memory. Distributed memory is also unavoidable if you want to write fault-tolerant systems that use multiple machines to cope with hardware failures.

Concurrency: Beyond Multiple Cores

Concurrency is about a great deal more than just exploiting parallelism—used correctly, it allows your software to be responsive, fault tolerant, efficient, and simple.

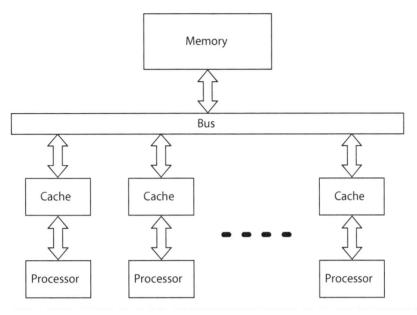

Figure 1—Shared memory

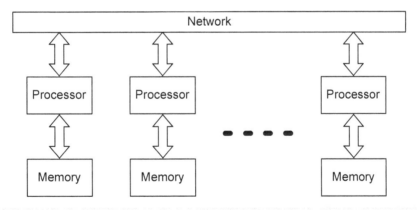

Figure 2—Distributed memory

Concurrent Software for a Concurrent World

The world is concurrent, and so should your software be if it wants to interact effectively.

Your mobile phone can play music, talk to the network, and pay attention to your finger poking its screen, all at the same time. Your IDE checks the syntax of your code in the background while you continue to type. The flight system in an airplane simultaneously monitors sensors, displays information to the pilot, obeys commands, and moves control surfaces.

Concurrency is the key to *responsive* systems. By downloading files in the background, you avoid frustrated users having to stare at an hourglass cursor. By handling multiple connections concurrently, a web server ensures that a single slow request doesn't hold up others.

Distributed Software for a Distributed World

Sometimes geographical distribution is a key element of the problem you're solving. Whenever software is distributed on multiple computers that aren't running in lockstep, it's intrinsically concurrent.

Among other things, distributing software helps it handle failure. You might locate half your servers in a data center in Europe and the others in the United States, so that a power outage at one site doesn't result in global downtime. This brings us to the subject of resilience.

Resilient Software for an Unpredictable World

Software contains bugs, and programs crash. Even if you could somehow produce perfectly bug-free code, the hardware that it's running on will sometimes fail.

Concurrency enables resilient, or fault-tolerant, software through *independence* and *fault detection*. Independence is important because a failure in one task should not be able to bring down another. And fault detection is critical so that when a task fails (because it crashes or becomes unresponsive, or because the hardware it's running on dies), a separate task is notified so that it can take remedial action.

Sequential software can never be as resilient as concurrent software.

Simple Software in a Complex World

If you've spent hours wrestling with difficult-to-diagnose threading bugs, it might be hard to believe, but a concurrent solution can be simpler and clearer than its sequential equivalent when written in the right language with the right tools.

This is particularly true whenever you're dealing with an intrinsically concurrent real-world problem. The extra work required to translate from the concurrent problem to its sequential solution clouds the issue. You can avoid this extra work by creating a solution with the same structure as the problem:

rather than a single complex thread that tries to handle multiple tasks when they need it, create one simple thread for each.

The Seven Models

The seven models covered in this book have been chosen to provide a broad view of the concurrency and parallelism landscape.

Threads and locks: Threads-and-locks programming has many well-understood problems, but it's the technology that underlies many of the other models we'll be covering and it is still the default choice for much concurrent software.

Functional programming: Functional programming is becoming increasingly prominent for many reasons, not the least of which is its excellent support for concurrency and parallelism. Because they eliminate mutable state, functional programs are intrinsically thread-safe and easily parallelized.

The Clojure Way—separating identity and state: The Clojure language has popularized a particularly effective hybrid of imperative and functional programming, allowing the strengths of both approaches to be leveraged in concert.

Actors: The actor model is a general-purpose concurrent programming model with particularly wide applicability. It can target both shared- and distributed-memory architectures and facilitate geographical distribution, and it provides particularly strong support for fault tolerance and resilience.

Communicating Sequential Processes: On the face of things, Communicating Sequential Processes (CSP) has much in common with the actor model, both being based on message passing. Its emphasis on the channels used for communication, rather than the entities between which communication takes place, leads to CSP-based programs having a very different flavor, however.

Data parallelism: You have a supercomputer hidden inside your laptop. The GPU utilizes data parallelism to speed up graphics processing, but it can be brought to bear on a much wider range of tasks. If you're writing code to perform finite element analysis, computational fluid dynamics, or anything else that involves significant number-crunching, its performance will eclipse almost anything else.

The Lambda Architecture: Big Data would not be possible without parallelism—only by bringing multiple computing resources to bear can we contemplate processing terabytes of data. The Lambda Architecture combines the strengths of MapReduce and stream processing to create an architecture that can tackle a wide variety of Big Data problems.

Each of these models has a different sweet spot. As you read through each chapter, bear the following questions in mind:

- Is this model applicable to solving concurrent problems, parallel problems, or both?

- Which parallel architecture or architectures can this model target?

- Does this model provide tools to help you write resilient or geographically distributed code?

In the next chapter we'll look at the first model, Threads and Locks.

CHAPTER 2

Threads and Locks

Threads-and-locks programming is like a Ford Model T. It will get you from point A to point B, but it is primitive, difficult to drive, and both unreliable and dangerous compared to newer technology.

Despite their well-known problems, threads and locks are still the default choice for writing much concurrent software, and they underpin many of the other technologies we'll be covering. Even if you don't plan to use them directly, you should understand how they work.

The Simplest Thing That Could Possibly Work

Threads and locks are little more than a formalization of what the underlying hardware actually does. That's both their great strength and their great weakness.

Because they're so simple, almost all languages support them in one form or another, and they impose very few constraints on what can be achieved through their use. But they also provide almost no help to the poor programmer, making programs very difficult to get right in the first place and even more difficult to maintain.

We'll cover threads-and-locks programming in Java, but the principles apply to any language that supports threads. On day 1 we'll cover the basics of multithreaded code in Java, the primary pitfalls you'll encounter, and some rules that will help you avoid them. On day 2 we'll go beyond these basics and investigate the facilities provided by the java.util.concurrent package. Finally, on day 3 we'll look at some of the concurrent data structures provided by the standard library and use them to solve a realistic real-world problem.

A Word About Best Practices

We're going to start by looking at Java's low-level thread and lock primitives. Well-written modern code should rarely use these primitives directly, using the higher-level services we'll talk about in days 2 and 3 instead. Understanding these higher-level services depends upon an appreciation of the underlying basics, so that's what we'll cover first, but be aware that you probably shouldn't be using the Thread class directly within your production code.

Day 1: Mutual Exclusion and Memory Models

If you've done any concurrent programming at all, you're probably already familiar with the concept of *mutual exclusion*—using locks to ensure that only one thread can access data at a time. And you'll also be familiar with the ways in which mutual exclusion can go wrong, including *race conditions* and *deadlocks* (don't worry if these terms mean nothing to you yet—we'll cover them all very soon).

These are real problems, and we'll spend plenty of time talking about them, but it turns out that there's something even more basic you need to worry about when dealing with shared memory—the Memory Model. And if you think that race conditions and deadlocks can cause weird behavior, just wait until you see how bizarre shared memory can be.

We're getting ahead of ourselves, though—let's start by seeing how to create a thread.

Creating a Thread

The basic unit of concurrency in Java is the *thread*, which, as its name suggests, encapsulates a single *thread of control*. Threads communicate with each other via shared memory.

No programming book is complete without a "Hello, World!" example, so without further ado here's a multithreaded version:

ThreadsLocks/HelloWorld/src/main/java/com/paulbutcher/HelloWorld.java
```java
public class HelloWorld {

  public static void main(String[] args) throws InterruptedException {
    Thread myThread = new Thread() {
      public void run() {
        System.out.println("Hello from new thread");
      }
    };
```

```
    myThread.start();
    Thread.yield();
    System.out.println("Hello from main thread");
    myThread.join();
  }
}
```

This code creates an instance of Thread and then starts it. From this point on, the thread's run() method executes concurrently with the remainder of main(). Finally join() waits for the thread to terminate (which happens when run() returns).

When you run this, you might get this output:

```
Hello from main thread
Hello from new thread
```

Or you might get this instead:

```
Hello from new thread
Hello from main thread
```

Which of these you see depends on which thread gets to its println() first (in my tests, I saw each approximately 50% of the time). This kind of dependence on timing is one of the things that makes multithreaded programming tough—just because you see one behavior one time you run your code doesn't mean that you'll see it consistently.

> \\//   **Joe asks:**
> ᵛⁿᶠ   # Why the Thread.yield?
>
> Our multithreaded "Hello, World!" includes the following line:
>
> ```
> Thread.yield();
> ```
>
> According to the Java documentation, yield() is:
>
> > a hint to the scheduler that the current thread is willing to yield its current use of a processor.
>
> Without this call, the startup overhead of the new thread would mean that the main thread would almost certainly get to its println() first (although this isn't guaranteed to be the case—and as we'll see, in concurrent programming if something *can* happen, then sooner or later it will, probably at the most inconvenient moment).
>
> Try commenting this method out and see what happens. What happens if you change it to Thread.sleep(1)?

Our First Lock

When multiple threads access shared memory, they can end up stepping on each others' toes. We avoid this through *mutual exclusion* via *locks*, which can be held by only a single thread at a time.

Let's create a couple of threads that interact with each other:

ThreadsLocks/Counting/src/main/java/com/paulbutcher/Counting.java

```java
public class Counting {
  public static void main(String[] args) throws InterruptedException {
    class Counter {
      private int count = 0;
      public void increment() { ++count; }
      public int getCount() { return count; }
    }
    final Counter counter = new Counter();
    class CountingThread extends Thread {
      public void run() {
        for(int x = 0; x < 10000; ++x)
          counter.increment();
      }
    }

    CountingThread t1 = new CountingThread();
    CountingThread t2 = new CountingThread();
    t1.start(); t2.start();
    t1.join(); t2.join();
    System.out.println(counter.getCount());
  }
}
```

Here we have a very simple Counter class and two threads, each of which call its increment() method 10,000 times. Very simple, and very broken.

Try running this code, and you'll get a different answer each time. The last three times I ran it, I got 13850, 11867, then 12616. The reason is a *race condition* (behavior that depends on the relative timing of operations) in the two threads' use of the count member of Counter.

If this surprises you, think about what the Java compiler generates for ++count. Here are the bytecodes:

```
getfield #2
iconst_1
iadd
putfield #2
```

Even if you're not familiar with JVM bytecodes, it's clear what's going on here: getfield #2 retrieves the value of count, iconst_1 followed by iadd adds 1 to it, and then putfield #2 writes the result back to count. This pattern is commonly known as *read-modify-write*.

Imagine that both threads call increment() simultaneously. Thread 1 executes getfield #2, retrieving the value 42. Before it gets a chance to do anything else, thread 2 also executes getfield #2, also retrieving 42. Now we're in trouble because both of them will increment 42 by 1, and both of them will write the result, 43, back to count. The effect is as though count had been incremented once instead of twice.

The solution is to *synchronize* access to count. One way to do so is to use the *intrinsic lock* that comes built into every Java object (you'll sometimes hear it referred to as a *mutex, monitor,* or *critical section*) by making increment() synchronized:

ThreadsLocks/CountingFixed/src/main/java/com/paulbutcher/Counting.java

```
class Counter {
  private int count = 0;
  public synchronized void increment() { ++count; }
  public int getCount() { return count; }
}
```

Now increment() claims the Counter object's lock when it's called and releases it when it returns, so only one thread can execute its body at a time. Any other thread that calls it will *block* until the lock becomes free (later in this chapter we'll see that, for simple cases like this where only one variable is involved, the java.util.concurrent.atomic package provides good alternatives to using a lock).

Sure enough, when we execute this new version, we get the result 20000 every time.

But all is not rosy—our new code still contains a subtle bug, the cause of which we'll cover next.

Mysterious Memory

Let's spice things up with a puzzle. What will this code output?

ThreadsLocks/Puzzle/src/main/java/com/paulbutcher/Puzzle.java

```
Line 1  public class Puzzle {
          static boolean answerReady = false;
          static int answer = 0;
          static Thread t1 = new Thread() {
      5      public void run() {
                answer = 42;
                answerReady = true;
             }
          };
```

```
10  static Thread t2 = new Thread() {
      public void run() {
        if (answerReady)
          System.out.println("The meaning of life is: " + answer);
        else
15        System.out.println("I don't know the answer");
      }
    };

    public static void main(String[] args) throws InterruptedException {
20    t1.start(); t2.start();
      t1.join(); t2.join();
    }
}
```

If you're thinking "race condition!" you're absolutely right. We might see the answer to the meaning of life or a disappointing admission that our computer doesn't know it, depending on the order in which the threads happen to run. But that's not all—there's one other result we might see:

```
The meaning of life is: 0
```

What?! How can answer possibly be zero if answerReady is true? It's almost as if something switched lines 6 and 7 around underneath our feet.

Well, it turns out that it's entirely possible for something to do exactly that. Several somethings, in fact:

- The compiler is allowed to statically optimize your code by reordering things.

- The JVM is allowed to dynamically optimize your code by reordering things.

- The hardware you're running on is allowed to optimize performance by reordering things.

It goes further than just reordering. Sometimes effects don't become visible to other threads at all. Imagine that we rewrote run() as follows:

```
public void run() {
  while (!answerReady)
    Thread.sleep(100);
  System.out.println("The meaning of life is: " + answer);
}
```

Our program may never exit because answerReady may never appear to become true.

If your first reaction to this is that the compiler, JVM, and hardware should keep their sticky fingers out of your code, that's understandable. Unfortunately, it's also unachievable—much of the increased performance we've seen over the last few years has come from exactly these optimizations. Shared-memory parallel computers, in particular, depend on them. So we're stuck with having to deal with the consequences.

Clearly, this can't be a free-for-all—we need something to tell us what we can and cannot rely on. That's where the Java memory model comes in.

Memory Visibility

The Java memory model defines when changes to memory made by one thread become *visible* to another thread.[1] The bottom line is that there are no guarantees unless both the reading and the writing threads use synchronization.

We've already seen one example of synchronization—obtaining an object's intrinsic lock. Others include starting a thread, detecting that a thread is stopped with join(), and using many of the classes in the java.util.concurrent package.

An important point that's easily missed is that *both* threads need to use synchronization. It's not enough for just the thread making changes to do so. This is the cause of a subtle bug still remaining in the code on page 13. Making increment() synchronized isn't enough—getCount() needs to be synchronized as well. If it isn't, a thread calling getCount() may see a stale value (as it happens, the way that getCount() is used in the code on page 12 is thread-safe, because it's called after a call to join(), but it's a ticking time bomb waiting for anyone who uses Counter).

We've spoken about race conditions and memory visibility, two common ways that multithreaded programs can go wrong. Now we'll move on to the third: deadlock.

Multiple Locks

You would be forgiven if, after reading the preceding text, you thought that the only way to be safe in a multithreaded world was to make every method synchronized. Unfortunately, it's not that easy.

Firstly, this would be dreadfully inefficient. If every method were synchronized, most threads would probably spend most of their time blocked, defeating the point of making your code concurrent in the first place. But this is the least of your worries—as soon as you have more than one lock (remember, in Java every object has its own lock), you create the opportunity for threads to become deadlocked.

---

1. http://docs.oracle.com/javase/specs/jls/se7/html/jls-17.html#jls-17.4

We'll demonstrate deadlock with a nice little example commonly used in academic papers on concurrency—the "dining philosophers" problem. Imagine that five philosophers are sitting around a table, with five (not ten) chopsticks arranged like this:

A philosopher is either thinking or hungry. If he's hungry, he picks up the chopsticks on either side of him and eats for a while (yes, our philosophers are male—women would behave more sensibly). When he's done, he puts them down.

Here's how we might implement one of our philosophers:

ThreadsLocks/DiningPhilosophers/src/main/java/com/paulbutcher/Philosopher.java

```
Line 1  class Philosopher extends Thread {
          private Chopstick left, right;
          private Random random;

     5    public Philosopher(Chopstick left, Chopstick right) {
            this.left = left; this.right = right;
            random = new Random();
          }

    10    public void run() {
            try {
              while(true) {
                Thread.sleep(random.nextInt(1000));    // Think for a while
                synchronized(left) {                   // Grab left chopstick //
    15            synchronized(right) {                 // Grab right chopstick //
                    Thread.sleep(random.nextInt(1000)); // Eat for a while
                  }
                }
              }
    20      } catch(InterruptedException e) {}
          }
        }
```

Lines 14 and 15 demonstrate an alternative way of claiming an object's intrinsic lock: synchronized(object).

On my machine, if I set five of these going simultaneously, they typically run very happily for hours on end (my record is over a week). Then, all of a sudden, everything grinds to a halt.

After a little thought, it's obvious what's going on—if all the philosophers decide to eat at the same time, they all grab their left chopstick and then find themselves stuck—each has one chopstick, and each is blocked waiting for the philosopher on his right. Deadlock.

Deadlock is a danger whenever a thread tries to hold more than one lock. Happily, there is a simple rule that guarantees you will never deadlock—always acquire locks in a fixed, global order.

Here's one way we can achieve this:

ThreadsLocks/DiningPhilosophersFixed/src/main/java/com/paulbutcher/Philosopher.java

```java
class Philosopher extends Thread {
  private Chopstick first, second;
  private Random random;

  public Philosopher(Chopstick left, Chopstick right) {
    if(left.getId() < right.getId()) {
      first = left; second = right;
    } else {
      first = right; second = left;
    }
    random = new Random();
  }

  public void run() {
    try {
      while(true) {
        Thread.sleep(random.nextInt(1000));      // Think for a while
        synchronized(first) {                    // Grab first chopstick
          synchronized(second) {                 // Grab second chopstick
            Thread.sleep(random.nextInt(1000)); // Eat for a while
          }
        }
      }
    } catch(InterruptedException e) {}
  }
}
```

Instead of holding on to left and right chopsticks, we now hold on to first and second, using Chopstick's id member to ensure that we always lock chopsticks in increasing ID order (we don't actually care what IDs chopsticks have—just

> ### Joe asks:
> ### Can I Use an Object's Hash to Order Locks?
>
> One piece of advice you'll often see is to use an object's hash code to order lock acquisition, such as shown here:
>
> ```
> if(System.identityHashCode(left) < System.identityHashCode(right)) {
>   first = left; second = right;
> } else {
>   first = right; second = left;
> }
> ```
>
> This technique has the advantage of working for any object, and it avoids having to add a means of ordering your objects if they don't already define one. But hash codes aren't guaranteed to be unique (two objects are very unlikely to have the same hash code, but it does happen). So personally speaking, I wouldn't use this approach unless I really had no choice.

that they're unique and ordered). And sure enough, now things will happily run forever without locking up.

It's easy to see how to stick to the global ordering rule when the code to acquire locks is all in one place. It gets much harder in a large program, where a global understanding of what all the code is doing is impractical.

The Perils of Alien Methods

Large programs often make use of *listeners* to decouple modules. Here, for example, is a class that downloads from a URL and allows ProgressListeners to be registered:

ThreadsLocks/HttpDownload/src/main/java/com/paulbutcher/Downloader.java
```java
class Downloader extends Thread {
  private InputStream in;
  private OutputStream out;
  private ArrayList<ProgressListener> listeners;

  public Downloader(URL url, String outputFilename) throws IOException {
    in = url.openConnection().getInputStream();
    out = new FileOutputStream(outputFilename);
    listeners = new ArrayList<ProgressListener>();
  }
  public synchronized void addListener(ProgressListener listener) {
    listeners.add(listener);
  }
  public synchronized void removeListener(ProgressListener listener) {
    listeners.remove(listener);
  }
```

```
  private synchronized void updateProgress(int n) {
    for (ProgressListener listener: listeners)
      listener.onProgress(n);
  }

  public void run() {
    int n = 0, total = 0;
    byte[] buffer = new byte[1024];

    try {
      while((n = in.read(buffer)) != -1) {
        out.write(buffer, 0, n);
        total += n;
        updateProgress(total);
      }
      out.flush();
    } catch (IOException e) { }
  }
}
```

Because addListener(), removeListener(), and updateProgress() are all synchronized, multiple threads can call them without stepping on one another's toes. But a trap lurks in this code that could lead to deadlock even though there's only a single lock in use.

The problem is that updateProgress() calls an *alien method*—a method it knows nothing about. That method could do anything, including acquiring another lock. If it does, then we've acquired two locks without knowing whether we've done so in the right order. As we've just seen, that can lead to deadlock.

The only solution is to avoid calling alien methods while holding a lock. One way to achieve this is to make a *defensive copy* of listeners before iterating through it:

ThreadsLocks/HttpDownloadFixed/src/main/java/com/paulbutcher/Downloader.java
```
private void updateProgress(int n) {
  ArrayList<ProgressListener> listenersCopy;
  synchronized(this) {
    listenersCopy = (ArrayList<ProgressListener>)listeners.clone();
  }
  for (ProgressListener listener: listenersCopy)
    listener.onProgress(n);
}
```

This change kills several birds with one stone. Not only does it avoid calling an alien method with a lock held, it also minimizes the period during which we hold the lock. Holding locks for longer than necessary both hurts performance (by restricting the degree of achievable concurrency) and increases the danger of deadlock. This change also fixes another bug that isn't related to concurrency—a listener can now call removeListener() within its onProgress() method without modifying the copy of listeners that's mid-iteration.

Day 1 Wrap-Up

This brings us to the end of day 1. We've covered the basics of multithreaded code in Java, but as we'll see in day 2, the standard library provides alternatives that are often a better choice.

What We Learned in Day 1

We covered how to create threads and use the intrinsic locks built into every Java object to enforce mutual exclusion between them. We also saw the three primary perils of threads and locks—race conditions, deadlock, and memory visibility, and we discussed some rules that help us avoid them:

- Synchronize all access to shared variables.
- Both the writing and the reading threads need to use synchronization.
- Acquire multiple locks in a fixed, global order.
- Don't call alien methods while holding a lock.
- Hold locks for the shortest possible amount of time.

Day 1 Self-Study

Find

- Check out William Pugh's "Java memory model" website.

- Acquaint yourself with the JSR 133 (Java memory model) FAQ.

- What guarantees does the Java memory model make regarding initialization safety? Is it always necessary to use locks to safely publish objects between threads?

- What is the double-checked locking anti-pattern? Why is it an anti-pattern?

Do

- Experiment with the original, broken "dining philosophers" example. Try modifying the length of time that philosophers think and eat and the number of philosophers. What effect does this have on how long it takes until deadlock? Imagine that you were trying to debug this and wanted to increase the likelihood of reproducing the deadlock—what would you do?

- (Hard) Create a program that demonstrates writes to memory appearing to be reordered in the absence of synchronization. This is difficult because although the Java memory model allows things to be reordered, most simple examples won't be optimized to the point of actually demonstrating the problem.

Day 2: Beyond Intrinsic Locks

Day 1 covered Java's Thread class and the intrinsic locks built into every Java object. For a long time this was pretty much all the support that Java provided for concurrent programming. Java 5 changed all that with the introduction of java.util.concurrent. Today we'll look at the enhanced locking mechanisms it provides.

Intrinsic locks are convenient but limited.

- There is no way to interrupt a thread that's blocked as a result of trying to acquire an intrinsic lock.

- There is no way to time out while trying to acquire an intrinsic lock.

- There's exactly one way to acquire an intrinsic lock: a synchronized block.

```
synchronized(object) {
  «use shared resources»
}
```

This means that lock acquisition and release have to take place in the same method and have to be strictly nested. Note that declaring a method as synchronized is just syntactic sugar for surrounding the method's body with the following:

```
synchronized(this) {
  «method body»
}
```

ReentrantLock allows us to transcend these restrictions by providing explicit lock and unlock methods instead of using synchronized.

Before we go into how it improves upon intrinsic locks, here's how ReentrantLock can be used as a straight replacement for synchronized:

```
Lock lock = new ReentrantLock();
lock.lock();
try {
  «use shared resources»
} finally {
  lock.unlock();
}
```

The try ... finally is good practice to ensure that the lock is always released, no matter what happens in the code the lock is protecting.

Now let's see how it lifts the restrictions of intrinsic locks.

Interruptible Locking

Because a thread that's blocked on an intrinsic lock is not interruptible, we have no way to recover from a deadlock. We can see this with a small example that manufactures a deadlock and then tries to interrupt the threads:

ThreadsLocks/Uninterruptible/src/main/java/com/paulbutcher/Uninterruptible.java
```java
public class Uninterruptible {

  public static void main(String[] args) throws InterruptedException {

    final Object o1 = new Object(); final Object o2 = new Object();

    Thread t1 = new Thread() {
      public void run() {
        try {
          synchronized(o1) {
            Thread.sleep(1000);
            synchronized(o2) {}
          }
        } catch (InterruptedException e) { System.out.println("t1 interrupted"); }
      }
    };

    Thread t2 = new Thread() {
      public void run() {
        try {
          synchronized(o2) {
            Thread.sleep(1000);
            synchronized(o1) {}
          }
        } catch (InterruptedException e) { System.out.println("t2 interrupted"); }
      }
    };

    t1.start(); t2.start();
    Thread.sleep(2000);
    t1.interrupt(); t2.interrupt();
    t1.join(); t2.join();
  }
}
```

This program will deadlock forever—the only way to exit it is to kill the JVM running it.

There is a solution, however. We can reimplement our threads using Reentrant-Lock instead of intrinsic locks, and we can use its lockInterruptibly() method:

ThreadsLocks/Interruptible/src/main/java/com/paulbutcher/Interruptible.java

```
final ReentrantLock l1 = new ReentrantLock();
final ReentrantLock l2 = new ReentrantLock();

Thread t1 = new Thread() {
  public void run() {
    try {
      l1.lockInterruptibly();
      Thread.sleep(1000);
      l2.lockInterruptibly();
    } catch (InterruptedException e) { System.out.println("t1 interrupted"); }
  }
};
```

This version exits cleanly when Thread.interrupt() is called. The slightly noisier syntax of this version seems a small price to pay for the ability to interrupt a deadlocked thread.

Timeouts

ReentrantLock lifts another limitation of intrinsic locks: it allows us to time out while trying to acquire a lock. This provides us with an alternative way to solve the "dining philosophers" problem from day 1.

Here's a Philosopher that times out if it fails to get both chopsticks:

ThreadsLocks/DiningPhilosophersTimeout/src/main/java/com/paulbutcher/Philosopher.java

```java
class Philosopher extends Thread {
  private ReentrantLock leftChopstick, rightChopstick;
  private Random random;

  public Philosopher(ReentrantLock leftChopstick, ReentrantLock rightChopstick) {
    this.leftChopstick = leftChopstick; this.rightChopstick = rightChopstick;
    random = new Random();
  }

  public void run() {
    try {
      while(true) {
        Thread.sleep(random.nextInt(1000)); // Think for a while
        leftChopstick.lock();
        try {
          if (rightChopstick.tryLock(1000, TimeUnit.MILLISECONDS)) {
            // Got the right chopstick
            try {
              Thread.sleep(random.nextInt(1000)); // Eat for a while
            } finally { rightChopstick.unlock(); }
          } else {
            // Didn't get the right chopstick - give up and go back to thinking
          }
        } finally { leftChopstick.unlock(); }
      }
    } catch(InterruptedException e) {}
  }
}
```

Instead of using lock(), this code uses tryLock(), which times out if it fails to acquire the lock. This means that, even though we don't follow the "acquire multiple locks in a fixed, global order" rule, this version will not deadlock (or at least, will not deadlock forever).

Livelock

Although the tryLock() solution avoids infinite deadlock, that doesn't mean it's a good solution. Firstly, it doesn't avoid deadlock—it simply provides a way to recover when it happens. Secondly, it's susceptible to a phenomenon known as *livelock*—if all the threads time out at the same time, it's quite possible for them to immediately deadlock again. Although the deadlock doesn't last forever, no progress is made either.

This situation can be mitigated by having each thread use a different timeout value, for example, to minimize the chances that they will all time out simultaneously. But the bottom line is that timeouts are rarely a good solution—it's far better to avoid deadlock in the first place.

Hand-over-Hand Locking

Imagine that we want to insert an entry into a linked list. One approach would be to have a single lock protecting the whole list, but this would mean that nobody else could access it while we held the lock. *Hand-over-hand* locking is an alternative in which we lock only a small portion of the list, allowing other threads unfettered access as long as they're not looking at the particular nodes we've got locked. Here's a graphical representation:

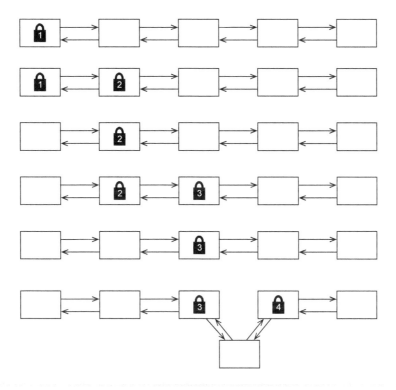

Figure 3—Hand-over-hand locking

To insert a node, we need to lock the two nodes on either side of the point we're going to insert. We start by locking the first two nodes of the list. If this isn't the right place to insert the new node, we unlock the first node and lock the third. If this still isn't the right place, we unlock the second and lock the fourth. This continues until we find the appropriate place, insert the new node, and finally unlock the nodes on either side.

This sequence of locks and unlocks is impossible with intrinsic locks, but it is possible with ReentrantLock because we can call lock() and unlock() whenever we like. Here is a class that implements a sorted linked list using this approach:

ThreadsLocks/LinkedList/src/main/java/com/paulbutcher/ConcurrentSortedList.java

```
Line 1  class ConcurrentSortedList {

          private class Node {
            int value;
    5       Node prev;
            Node next;
            ReentrantLock lock = new ReentrantLock();

            Node() {}
    10
            Node(int value, Node prev, Node next) {
              this.value = value; this.prev = prev; this.next = next;
            }
          }
    15
          private final Node head;
          private final Node tail;

          public ConcurrentSortedList() {
    20      head = new Node(); tail = new Node();
            head.next = tail; tail.prev = head;
          }

          public void insert(int value) {
    25      Node current = head;
            current.lock.lock();
            Node next = current.next;
            try {
              while (true) {
    30          next.lock.lock();
                try {
                  if (next == tail || next.value < value) {
                    Node node = new Node(value, current, next);
                    next.prev = node;
    35              current.next = node;
                    return;
                  }
                } finally { current.lock.unlock(); }
                current = next;
    40          next = current.next;
              }
            } finally { next.lock.unlock(); }
          }
        }
```

The insert() method ensures that the list is always sorted by searching until it finds the first entry that's less than the new one. When it does, it inserts the new node just before.

Line 26 locks the head of the list, and line 30 locks the next node. We then check to see if we've found the right place to insert our new node. If not, the current node is unlocked on line 38 and we loop. If we have found the right place, lines 33–36 create the new node, insert it into the list, and return. The locks are released in the two finally blocks (lines 38 and 42).

Not only can several threads insert entries concurrently using this scheme, but other operations can also safely take place on the list. Here, for example, is a method that counts how many elements are in the list—and just for kicks it iterates backward through the list:

ThreadsLocks/LinkedList/src/main/java/com/paulbutcher/ConcurrentSortedList.java

```java
public int size() {
  Node current = tail;
  int count = 0;

  while (current.prev != head) {
    ReentrantLock lock = current.lock;
    lock.lock();
    try {
      ++count;
      current = current.prev;
    } finally { lock.unlock(); }
  }

  return count;
}
```

We'll look at one further feature of ReentrantLock today—condition variables.

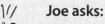

Joe asks:
Doesn't This Break the "Global Ordering" Rule?

ConcurrentSortedList's insert() method acquires locks starting at the head of the list and moving toward the tail. The size() method above acquires them from the tail of the list, moving toward the head. Doesn't this violate the "Always acquire multiple locks in a fixed, global order" rule?

It doesn't, because the size() method never holds *multiple* locks—it never holds more than a single lock at a time.

Condition Variables

Concurrent programming often involves waiting for something to happen. Perhaps we need to wait for a queue to become nonempty before removing an element from it. Or we need to wait for space to be available in a buffer before adding something to it. This type of situation is what condition variables are designed to address.

To use a condition variable effectively, we need to follow a very specific pattern:

```
ReentrantLock lock = new ReentrantLock();
Condition condition = lock.newCondition();

lock.lock();
try {
  while (!«condition is true»)
    condition.await();
  «use shared resources»
} finally { lock.unlock(); }
```

A condition variable is associated with a lock, and a thread must hold that lock before being able to wait on the condition. Once it holds the lock, it checks to see if the condition that it's interested in is already true. If it is, then it continues with whatever it wants to do and unlocks the lock.

If, however, the condition is not true, it calls await(), which *atomically* unlocks the lock and blocks on the condition variable. An operation is *atomic* if, from the point of view of another thread, it appears to be a single operation that has either happened or not—it never appears to be halfway through.

When another thread calls signal() or signalAll() to indicate that the condition might now be true, await() unblocks and automatically reacquires the lock. An important point is that when await() returns, it only indicates that the condition *might* be true. This is why await() is called within a loop—we need to go back, recheck whether the condition is true, and potentially block on await() again if necessary.

This gives us yet another solution to the "dining philosophers" problem:

ThreadsLocks/DiningPhilosophersCondition/src/main/java/com/paulbutcher/Philosopher.java
```
class Philosopher extends Thread {

  private boolean eating;
  private Philosopher left;
  private Philosopher right;
  private ReentrantLock table;
  private Condition condition;
  private Random random;
```

```
  public Philosopher(ReentrantLock table) {
    eating = false;
    this.table = table;
    condition = table.newCondition();
    random = new Random();
  }

  public void setLeft(Philosopher left) { this.left = left; }
  public void setRight(Philosopher right) { this.right = right; }

  public void run() {
    try {
      while (true) {
        think();
        eat();
      }
    } catch (InterruptedException e) {}
  }

  private void think() throws InterruptedException {
    table.lock();
    try {
      eating = false;
      left.condition.signal();
      right.condition.signal();
    } finally { table.unlock(); }
    Thread.sleep(1000);
  }

  private void eat() throws InterruptedException {
    table.lock();
    try {
      while (left.eating || right.eating)
        condition.await();
      eating = true;
    } finally { table.unlock(); }
    Thread.sleep(1000);
  }
}
```

This solution differs from those we've already seen by using only a single lock (table) and not having an explicit Chopstick class. Instead we make use of the fact that a philosopher can eat if neither of his neighbors is currently eating. In other words, a hungry philosopher is waiting for this condition:

```
!(left.eating || right.eating)
```

When a philosopher is hungry, he first locks the table so no other philosophers can change state, and then he checks to see if his neighbors are currently eating. If they aren't, he can start to eat and release the table. Otherwise, he calls await() (which unlocks the table).

When a philosopher has finished eating and wants to start thinking, he first locks the table and sets eating to false. Then he signals both of his neighbors to let them know that they might be able to start eating and releases the table. If those neighbors are currently waiting, they'll be woken, reacquire the lock on the table, and check again to see if they can eat.

Although this code is more complex than the other solutions we've seen, the payoff is that it results in significantly better concurrency. With the previous solutions, it's often the case that only a single hungry philosopher can eat, because the others all have a single chopstick and are waiting for the other to become available. With this solution, whenever it's theoretically possible for a philosopher to eat (when neither of his neighbors are eating), he will be able to do so.

That's it for ReentrantLock, but there's another alternative to intrinsic locks that we'll cover next—atomic variables.

Atomic Variables

On day 1, we fixed our multithreaded counter by making the increment() method synchronized (see the code on page 13). It turns out that java.util.concurrent.atomic provides a better option:

ThreadsLocks/CountingBetter/src/main/java/com/paulbutcher/Counting.java
```java
public class Counting {
  public static void main(String[] args) throws InterruptedException {

    final AtomicInteger counter = new AtomicInteger();

    class CountingThread extends Thread {
      public void run() {
        for(int x = 0; x < 10000; ++x)
          counter.incrementAndGet();
      }
    }

    CountingThread t1 = new CountingThread();
    CountingThread t2 = new CountingThread();

    t1.start(); t2.start();
    t1.join(); t2.join();

    System.out.println(counter.get());
  }
}
```

AtomicInteger's incrementAndGet() method is functionally equivalent to ++count (it also supports getAndIncrement, which is equivalent to count++). Unlike ++count, however, it's atomic.

Using an atomic variable instead of locks has a number of benefits. First, it's not possible to forget to acquire the lock when necessary. For example, the memory-visibility problem in Counter, which arose because getCount() wasn't synchronized, cannot occur with this code. Second, because no locks are involved, it's impossible for an operation on an atomic variable to deadlock.

Finally, atomic variables are the foundation of *non-blocking, lock-free* algorithms, which achieve synchronization without locks or blocking. If you think that programming with locks is tricky, then just wait until you try writing lock-free code. Happily, the classes in java.util.concurrent make use of lock-free code where possible, so you can take advantage painlessly. We'll cover these classes in day 3, but for now this brings us to the end of day 2.

Joe asks:
What About Volatile?

Java allows us to mark a variable as *volatile*. Doing so guarantees that reads and writes to that variable will not be reordered. We could fix Puzzle (see the code on page 13) by making answerReady volatile.

Volatile is a very weak form of synchronization. It would not help us fix Counter, for example, because making count volatile would not ensure that count++ is atomic.

These days, with highly optimized JVMs that have very low-overhead locks, valid use cases for volatile variables are rare. If you find yourself considering volatile, you should probably use one of the java.util.concurrent.atomic classes instead.

Day 2 Wrap-Up

We've built upon the basics introduced in day 1 to cover the more sophisticated and flexible mechanisms provided by java.util.concurrent.locks and java.util.concurrent.atomic. Although it's important to understand these mechanisms, you'll rarely use locks directly in practice, as we'll see in day 3.

What We Learned in Day 2

We saw how ReentrantLock and java.util.concurrent.atomic can overcome the limitations of intrinsic locks so that our threads can do the following:

- Be interrupted while trying to acquire a lock
- Time out while acquiring a lock
- Acquire and release locks in any order
- Use condition variables to wait for arbitrary conditions to become true
- Avoid locks entirely by using atomic variables

Day 2 Self-Study

Find

- ReentrantLock supports a fairness parameter. What does it mean for a lock to be "fair"? Why might you choose to use a fair lock? Why might you not?

- What is ReentrantReadWriteLock? How does it differ from ReentrantLock? When might you use it?

- What is a "spurious wakeup"? When can one happen and why doesn't a well-written program care if one does?

- What is AtomicIntegerFieldUpdater? How does it differ from AtomicInteger? When might you use it?

Do

- What would happen if the loop within the "dining philosophers" implementation that uses condition variables was replaced with a simple if statement? What failure modes might you see? What would happen if the call to signal() was replaced by signalAll()? What problems (if any) would this cause?

- Just as intrinsic locks are more limited than ReentrantLock, they also support a more limited type of condition variable. Rewrite the dining philosophers to use an intrinsic lock plus the wait() and notify() or notifyAll() methods. Why is it less efficient than using ReentrantLock?

- Write a version of ConcurrentSortedList that uses a single lock instead of hand-over-hand locking. Benchmark it against the other version. Does hand-over-hand locking provide any performance advantage? When might it be a good choice? When might it not?

Day 3: On the Shoulders of Giants

As well as the enhanced locks we covered in day 2, java.util.concurrent contains a collection of general-purpose, high-performance, and thoroughly debugged concurrent data structures and utilities. Today we'll see that more often than not, these prove to be a better choice than rolling our own solution.

Thread-Creation Redux

In day 1 we saw how to start threads, but it turns out that it rarely makes sense to create threads directly. Here, for example, is a very simple server that echoes whatever it's sent:

ThreadsLocks/EchoServer/src/main/java/com/paulbutcher/EchoServer.java

```java
public class EchoServer {

  public static void main(String[] args) throws IOException {

    class ConnectionHandler implements Runnable {
      InputStream in; OutputStream out;
      ConnectionHandler(Socket socket) throws IOException {
        in = socket.getInputStream();
        out = socket.getOutputStream();
      }

      public void run() {
        try {
          int n;
          byte[] buffer = new byte[1024];
          while((n = in.read(buffer)) != -1) {
            out.write(buffer, 0, n);
            out.flush();
          }
        } catch (IOException e) {}
      }
    }

    ServerSocket server = new ServerSocket(4567);
    while (true) {
      Socket socket = server.accept();
      Thread handler = new Thread(new ConnectionHandler(socket));
      handler.start();
    }
  }
}
```

The highlighted lines follow the common pattern of accepting an incoming connection and then immediately creating a new thread to handle it. This works fine, but it suffers from a couple of issues. First, although thread creation is cheap, it's not free, and this design will pay that price for each connection. Second, it creates as many threads as connections—if connections are coming in faster than they can be handled, then the number of threads will increase and the server will grind to a halt and possibly even crash. This is a perfect opening for anyone who wants to subject your server to a denial-of-service attack.

We can avoid these problems by using a thread pool:

ThreadsLocks/EchoServerBetter/src/main/java/com/paulbutcher/EchoServer.java
```
int threadPoolSize = Runtime.getRuntime().availableProcessors() * 2;
ExecutorService executor = Executors.newFixedThreadPool(threadPoolSize);
while (true) {
  Socket socket = server.accept();
  executor.execute(new ConnectionHandler(socket));
}
```

This code creates a thread pool with twice as many threads as there are available processors. If more than this number of execute() requests are active at a time, they will be queued until a thread becomes free. Not only does this mean that we don't incur the overhead of thread creation for each connection, but it also ensures that our server will continue to make progress in the face of high load (not that it will service the incoming requests quickly enough to keep up, but at least some of them will be serviced).

Copy on Write

On day 1 we looked at how to call listeners safely in a concurrent program. If you recall, we modified updateProgress() to make a defensive copy (see the code on page 19). It turns out that the Java standard library provides a more elegant, ready-made solution in CopyOnWriteArrayList:

ThreadsLocks/HttpDownloadBetter/src/main/java/com/paulbutcher/Downloader.java
```
private CopyOnWriteArrayList<ProgressListener> listeners;

public void addListener(ProgressListener listener) {
  listeners.add(listener);
}
public void removeListener(ProgressListener listener) {
  listeners.remove(listener);
}
private void updateProgress(int n) {
  for (ProgressListener listener: listeners)
    listener.onProgress(n);
}
```

As its name suggests, CopyOnWriteArrayList turns our previous defensive copy strategy on its head. Instead of making a copy before iterating through the list, it makes a copy whenever it's changed. Any existing iterators will continue to refer to the previous copy. This isn't an approach that would be appropriate for many use cases, but it's perfect for this one.

First, as you can see, it results in very clear and concise code. In fact, apart from the definition of listeners, it's identical to the naïve, non-thread-safe version we first came up with in the code on page 18. Second, it's more efficient

Joe asks:

How Large Should My Thread Pool Be?

The optimum number of threads will vary according to the hardware you're running on, whether your threads are IO or CPU bound, what else the machine is doing at the same time, and a host of other factors.

Having said that, a good rule of thumb is that for computation-intensive tasks, you probably want to have approximately the same number of threads as available cores. Larger numbers are appropriate for IO-intensive tasks.

Beyond this rule of thumb, your best bet is to create a realistic load test and break out the stopwatch.

because we don't have to make a copy each time updateProgress() is called, but only when listeners is modified (which is likely to happen much less often).

A Complete Program

Up until now, we've looked at individual tools in isolation. For the remainder of today, we'll look at solving a small but realistic problem: What's the most commonly used word on Wikipedia?

It should be easy enough to find out—just download an XML dump and write a program to parse it and count the words.[2] Given that the dump weighs in at around 40 GiB, it's going to take a while; perhaps we can speed it up by parallelizing things?

Let's start by getting a baseline—how long does a simple sequential program take to count the words in the first 100,000 pages?

ThreadsLocks/WordCount/src/main/java/com/paulbutcher/WordCount.java
```java
public class WordCount {
  private static final HashMap<String, Integer> counts =
    new HashMap<String, Integer>();

  public static void main(String[] args) throws Exception {
    Iterable<Page> pages = new Pages(100000, "enwiki.xml");
    for(Page page: pages) {
      Iterable<String> words = new Words(page.getText());
      for (String word: words)
        countWord(word);
    }
  }
}
```

---

2. http://dumps.wikimedia.org/enwiki/

```
  private static void countWord(String word) {
    Integer currentCount = counts.get(word);
    if (currentCount == null)
      counts.put(word, 1);
    else
      counts.put(word, currentCount + 1);
  }
}
```

On my MacBook Pro, this runs in just under 105 seconds.

So where do we start with a parallel version? Each iteration of the main loop performs two tasks—first it parses enough of the XML to produce a Page, and then it consumes that page by counting the words in its text.

There is a classic pattern that can be applied to this kind of problem—the *producer-consumer* pattern. Instead of a single thread that alternates between producing values and then consuming them, we create two threads, a producer and a consumer.

Here's a Parser implemented as a producer:

ThreadsLocks/WordCountProducerConsumer/src/main/java/com/paulbutcher/Parser.java
```
class Parser implements Runnable {
  private BlockingQueue<Page> queue;

  public Parser(BlockingQueue<Page> queue) {
    this.queue = queue;
  }

  public void run() {
    try {
      Iterable<Page> pages = new Pages(100000, "enwiki.xml");
      for (Page page: pages)
        queue.put(page);
    } catch (Exception e) { e.printStackTrace(); }
  }
}
```

The run() method contains the outer loop of our sequential solution, but instead of counting the words in the newly parsed page, it adds it to the tail of a queue.

Here's the corresponding consumer:

ThreadsLocks/WordCountProducerConsumer/src/main/java/com/paulbutcher/Counter.java
```
class Counter implements Runnable {
  private BlockingQueue<Page> queue;
  private Map<String, Integer> counts;
```

```
  public Counter(BlockingQueue<Page> queue,
                 Map<String, Integer> counts) {
    this.queue = queue;
    this.counts = counts;
  }

  public void run() {
    try {
      while(true) {
        Page page = queue.take();
        if (page.isPoisonPill())
          break;

        Iterable<String> words = new Words(page.getText());
        for (String word: words)
          countWord(word);
      }
    } catch (Exception e) { e.printStackTrace(); }
  }
}
```

As you might expect, it contains the inner loop of our sequential solution, taking its input from the queue.

Finally, here's a modified version of our main loop that creates these two threads:

ThreadsLocks/WordCountProducerConsumer/src/main/java/com/paulbutcher/WordCount.java
```
ArrayBlockingQueue<Page> queue = new ArrayBlockingQueue<Page>(100);
HashMap<String, Integer> counts = new HashMap<String, Integer>();

Thread counter = new Thread(new Counter(queue, counts));
Thread parser = new Thread(new Parser(queue));

counter.start();
parser.start();
parser.join();
queue.put(new PoisonPill());
counter.join();
```

ArrayBlockingQueue from java.util.concurrent is a concurrent queue that's ideal for implementing the producer-consumer pattern. Not only does it provide efficient concurrent put() and take() methods, but these methods will block when necessary. Trying to take() from an empty queue will block until the queue is nonempty, and trying to put() into a full queue will block until the queue has space available.

Joe asks:
Why a Blocking Queue?

As well as blocking queues, java.util.concurrent provides ConcurrentLinkedQueue, an unbounded, wait-free, and nonblocking queue. That sounds like a very desirable set of attributes, so why isn't it a good choice for this problem?

The issue is that the producer and consumer may not (almost certainly will not) run at the same speed. In particular, if the producer runs faster than the consumer, the queue will get larger and larger. Given that the Wikipedia dump we're parsing is around 40 GiB, that could easily result in the queue becoming too large to fit in memory.

Using a blocking queue, by contrast, will allow the producer to get ahead of the consumer, but not too far.

One other interesting aspect of this solution is how the consumer knows when to exit:

ThreadsLocks/WordCountProducerConsumer/src/main/java/com/paulbutcher/Counter.java

```
if (page.isPoisonPill())
  break;
```

As its name suggests, a *poison pill* is a special token that indicates that the end of the available data has been reached and that the consumer should therefore exit. It's very similar to the way that C/C++ uses a null character to indicate the end of a string.

The good news is that this has sped things up—instead of running in 105 seconds, this version runs in 95.

That's great, but we can do better. The beauty of the producer-consumer pattern is that it allows us not only to produce and consume values in parallel, but also to have multiple producers and/or multiple consumers.

But should we concentrate on speeding up the producer or the consumer? Where is the code spending its time? If I temporarily modify the code so that only the producer runs and I get my stopwatch out, I find that I can parse the first 100,000 pages in around 10 seconds.

This isn't surprising if you think about it for a moment. The original, sequential version of the code ran in 105 seconds, and the producer-consumer version ran in 95. Clearly parsing takes 10 seconds, and counting the words takes 95. By parsing and counting in parallel, we can reduce the total to whichever is the longest of these—in this case, 95 seconds.

So to improve performance further, we need to parallelize the counting process and have multiple consumers. The following figure shows where we're heading:

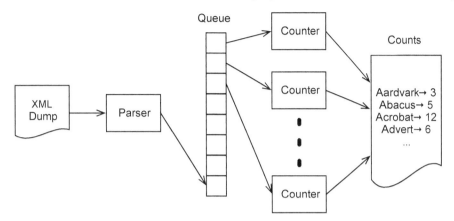

If we're going to have multiple threads counting words simultaneously, we're going to have to find a way to synchronize access to the counts map.

The first thing we might consider is using a *synchronized map*, returned by the synchronizedMap() method in Collections. Unfortunately, synchronized collections don't provide atomic read-modify-write methods, so this isn't going to help us. If we want to use a HashMap, we're going to have to synchronize access to it ourselves.

Here's a modified countWord() method that does exactly this:

ThreadsLocks/WordCountSynchronizedHashMap/src/main/java/com/paulbutcher/Counter.java

```
private void countWord(String word) {
    lock.lock();
    try {
        Integer currentCount = counts.get(word);
        if (currentCount == null)
            counts.put(word, 1);
        else
            counts.put(word, currentCount + 1);
    } finally { lock.unlock(); }
}
```

And here's a modified main loop that runs multiple consumers:

ThreadsLocks/WordCountSynchronizedHashMap/src/main/java/com/paulbutcher/WordCount.java

```
ArrayBlockingQueue<Page> queue = new ArrayBlockingQueue<Page>(100);
HashMap<String, Integer> counts = new HashMap<String, Integer>();
ExecutorService executor = Executors.newCachedThreadPool();
for (int i = 0; i < NUM_COUNTERS; ++i)
    executor.execute(new Counter(queue, counts));
Thread parser = new Thread(new Parser(queue));
parser.start();
```

```
parser.join();
for (int i = 0; i < NUM_COUNTERS; ++i)
  queue.put(new PoisonPill());
executor.shutdown();
executor.awaitTermination(10L, TimeUnit.MINUTES);
```

This is very similar to what we had before, except we've switched to using a thread pool, which is more convenient than managing multiple threads ourselves. And we need to make sure that we add the right number of poison pills to the queue to shut down cleanly.

This all looks great, but our hopes are about to be dashed. Here's how long it takes to run with one and two consumers (speedup is relative to the sequential version):

Consumers	Time (s)	Speedup
1	101	1.04
2	212	0.49

Why does adding another consumer make things slower? And not just slightly slower, but more than twice as slow?

The answer is excessive *contention*—too many threads are trying to access a single shared resource simultaneously. In our case, the consumers are spending so much of their time with the counts map locked that they spend more time waiting for the other to unlock it than they spend actually doing useful work, which leads to horrid performance.

Happily, we're not beaten yet. ConcurrentHashMap in java.util.concurrent looks like exactly what we need. Not only does it provide atomic read-modify-write methods, but it's been designed to support high levels of concurrent access (via a technique called *lock striping*).

Here's a modified countWord() that uses ConcurrentHashMap:

ThreadsLocks/WordCountConcurrentHashMap/src/main/java/com/paulbutcher/Counter.java
```java
private void countWord(String word) {
  while (true) {
    Integer currentCount = counts.get(word);
    if (currentCount == null) {
      if (counts.putIfAbsent(word, 1) == null)
        break;
    } else if (counts.replace(word, currentCount, currentCount + 1)) {
      break;
    }
  }
}
```

It's worth spending a little time understanding exactly how this works. Instead of put(), we're now using a combination of putIfAbsent() and replace(). Here's the documentation for putIfAbsent():

> If the specified key is not already associated with a value, associate it with the given value. This is equivalent to
>
> ```
> if (!map.containsKey(key))
>   return map.put(key, value);
> else
>   return map.get(key);
> ```
>
> except that the action is performed atomically.

And for replace():

> Replaces the entry for a key only if currently mapped to a given value. This is equivalent to
>
> ```
> if (map.containsKey(key) && map.get(key).equals(oldValue)) {
>   map.put(key, newValue);
>   return true;
> } else return false;
> ```
>
> except that the action is performed atomically.

So whenever we call either of these functions, we need to check their return value to work out whether they have successfully made the change we expected. If not, we need to loop around and try again.

With this version, the stopwatch is much kinder to us:

Consumers	Time (s)	Speedup
1	120	0.87
2	83	1.26
3	65	1.61
4	63	1.67
5	70	1.50
6	79	1.33

Success! This time, adding more consumers makes us go faster, at least until we have more than four consumers, after which things get slower again.

Having said that, although 63 seconds is certainly faster than the 105 seconds taken by the sequential version of the code, it's not even twice as fast. My MacBook has four cores—surely we should be able to get closer to a 4x speedup?

With a little thought, it's clear that our solution is creating far more contention for the counts map than it has to. Instead of each consumer updating a shared set of counts concurrently, each should maintain its own local set of counts. All we need to do is merge these local counts before we exit:

ThreadsLocks/WordCountBatchConcurrentHashMap/src/main/java/com/paulbutcher/Counter.java

```java
private void mergeCounts() {
  for (Map.Entry<String, Integer> e: localCounts.entrySet()) {
    String word = e.getKey();
    Integer count = e.getValue();
    while (true) {
      Integer currentCount = counts.get(word);
      if (currentCount == null) {
        if (counts.putIfAbsent(word, count) == null)
          break;
      } else if (counts.replace(word, currentCount, currentCount + count)) {
        break;
      }
    }
  }
}
```

This gets us much closer to our ideal 4x speedup:

Consumers	Time (s)	Speedup
1	95	1.10
2	57	1.83
3	40	2.62
4	39	2.69
5	35	2.96
6	33	3.14
7	41	2.55

Not only does this version increase in performance more quickly as we add consumers, but it even continues to improve in performance beyond four consumers. This is possible because each of the cores in my MacBook supports two "hyperthreads"—availableProcessors() actually returns eight, even though there are only four physical cores.

Figure 4, *Word Count Performance by Number of Consumers*, on page 43 shows a graph that shows the performance of the three different versions.

You'll see this curve again and again when working with parallel programs. The performance initially increases linearly and is then followed by a period

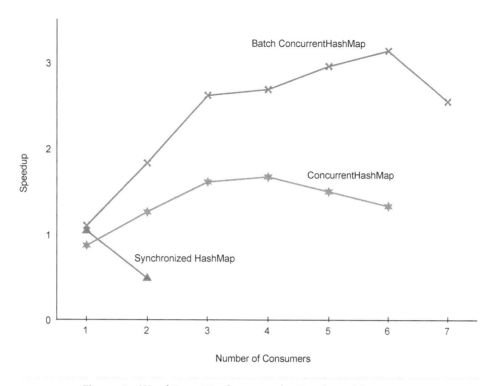

Figure 4—Word Count Performance by Number of Consumers

where performance continues to increase, but more slowly. Eventually performance will peak, and adding more threads will only make things slower.

It's worth taking a moment to reflect on what we've just done. We've created a relatively sophisticated producer-consumer program, with multiple consumers coordinating with one another via a concurrent queue and a concurrent map. And we did all of this without any explicit locking because we built on top of the facilities provided in the standard library.

Day 3 Wrap-Up

This brings us to the end of day 3 and the end of our discussion of programming with threads and locks.

What We Learned in Day 3

We saw how the facilities provided by java.util.concurrent not only make it easier to create concurrent programs, but also make those programs safer and more efficient by doing the following:

- Using thread pools instead of creating threads directly

- Creating simpler and more efficient listener-management code with
  CopyOnWriteArrayList

- Allowing producers and consumers to communicate efficiently with
  ArrayBlockingQueue

- Supporting highly concurrent access to a map with ConcurrentHashMap

Day 3 Self-Study

Find

- The documentation for ForkJoinPool—how does a fork/join pool differ from
  a thread pool? When might you prefer one, and when the other?

- What is *work-stealing* and when might it be useful? How would you
  implement work-stealing with the facilities provided by java.util.concurrent?

- What is the difference between a CountDownLatch and a CyclicBarrier? When
  might you use one, and when the other?

- What is Amdahl's law? What does it say about the maximum theoretical
  speedup we might be able to get for our word-counting algorithm?

Do

- Rewrite the producer-consumer code to use a separate "end of data" flag
  instead of a poison pill. Make sure that your solution correctly handles
  the cases where the producer runs faster than the consumer and vice
  versa. What will happen if the consumer has already tried to remove
  something from the queue when the "end of data" flag is set? Why do you
  think that the poison-pill approach is so commonly used?

- Run the different versions of the word-count program on your computer,
  as well as any others you can get access to. How do the performance
  graphs differ from one computer to another? If you could run it on a
  computer with 32 cores, do you think you would see anything close to a
  32x speedup?

Wrap-Up

Threads-and-locks programming probably divides opinion more than any of
the other techniques we'll cover. It has a reputation for being fiendishly difficult
to get right, and plenty of programmers shrink from it, avoiding multithreaded
programming at all costs. Others don't understand the fuss—a few simple

rules need to be followed, and if you follow them it's no harder than any other form of programming.

Let's look at its strengths and weaknesses.

Strengths

The primary strength of threads and locks is the model's broad applicability. As you might expect, given that they're the basis upon which many of the approaches we'll cover later are built, they can be applied to a very wide range of problems. Because they are "close to the metal"—little more than a formalization of what the underlying hardware does anyway—they can be very efficient when used correctly. This means that they can be used to tackle problems of a wide range of granularities, from fine to coarse.

In addition, they can easily be integrated into most programming languages. Language designers can add threads and locks to an existing imperative or object-oriented language with little effort.

Weaknesses

Threads and locks provide no direct support for parallelism (recall that concurrency and parallelism are related but different things—see *Concurrent or Parallel?*, on page 1. As we've seen with the word-counting example, they can be used to parallelize a sequential algorithm, but this has to be constructed out of concurrent primitives, which introduces the specter of nondeterminism.

Outside of a few experimental distributed shared-memory research systems, threads and locks support only shared-memory architectures. If you need to support distributed memory (and, by extension, either geographical distribution or resilience), you will need to look elsewhere. This also means that threads and locks cannot be used to solve problems that are too large to fit on a single system.

The greatest weakness of the approach, however, is that threads-and-locks programming is *hard*. It may be easy for a language designer to add them to a language, but they provide us, the poor programmers, with very little help.

The Elephant in the Room

To my mind, what makes multithreaded programming difficult is not that writing it is hard, but that *testing* it is hard. It's not the pitfalls that you can fall into; it's the fact that you don't necessarily know whether you've fallen into one of them.

Let's take the memory model as an example. As we saw in *Memory Visibility*, on page 15, all sorts of odd things can happen if two threads access a memory location without synchronization. But how do you know if you've got it wrong? How would you write a test to prove that you never access memory without appropriate synchronization?

Sadly, there isn't any way to do so. You can certainly write something to stress-test your code, but passing those tests doesn't mean that it's correct. We know, for example, that the solution to the "dining philosophers" problem in the code on page 16 is wrong and might deadlock, but I've seen it run for more than a week without doing so.

The fact that threading bugs tend to happen infrequently is a large part of the problem—more than once, I've been woken in the small hours of the morning to be told that a server has locked up after running without problem for months on end. If it happened every ten minutes, I'm sure we'd quickly find the problem, but if you need to run the server for months before the problem recurs, it's virtually impossible to debug.

Worse than this, it's quite possible to write programs that contain threading bugs that will *never* fail no matter how thoroughly or for how long we test them. Just because they access memory in a way that might result in accesses being reordered doesn't mean that they actually will be. So we'll be completely unaware of the problem until we upgrade the JVM or move to different hardware, when we'll suddenly be faced with a mysterious failure that no one understands.

Maintenance

All these problems are bad enough when you're creating code, but code rarely stands still. It's one thing to make sure that everything's synchronized correctly, locks are acquired in the right order, and no foreign functions are called with locks held. It's quite another to guarantee that it will remain that way after twelve months of maintenance by ten different programmers. In the last decade, we've learned how to use automated testing to help us refactor with confidence, but if you can't reliably test for threading problems, you can't reliably refactor multithreaded code.

The upshot is that our only recourse is to think very carefully about our multithreaded code. And then when we've done that, think about it very carefully some more. Needless to say, this is neither easy nor scalable.

Picking Through the Wreckage

Diagnosing a threading problem can be similar to how I imagine Formula 1 engineers must feel when trying to diagnose an engine failure. The engine runs flawlessly for hours and then suddenly, with little or no warning, fails spectacularly, showering following cars with oil and lumps of crankcase.

When the car is dragged back to the workshop, the poor engineers are faced with a pile of wreckage and somehow need to figure out what caused the failure. The problem was probably something tiny—a failed oil-pump bearing or broken valve, but how can they tell what it was from the mess on the bench?

What tends to happen is that they put as much data logging in place as possible and send the driver back out with a new engine. Hopefully the data will contain something informative the next time a failure happens.

Other Languages

If you want to go deeper into threads-and-locks programming on the JVM, an excellent starting point is *Java Concurrency in Practice [Goe06]*, which was written by the authors of the java.util.concurrent package. The details of multithreaded programming vary between languages, but the general principles we covered in this chapter are broadly applicable. The rules about using synchronization to access shared variables; acquiring locks in a fixed, global order; and avoiding alien method calls while holding a lock are applicable to any language with threads and locks.

In particular, although we spoke about only the Java memory model, reordered memory accesses in concurrent code are not unique to Java. The difference is that most languages don't have a well-defined memory model that constrains how and when such reorderings are allowed. Java was the pioneer, the first major language to have a well-defined memory model. C and C++ only recently caught up when a memory model was added to the C11 and C++ 11 standards.

Final Thoughts

For all its challenges, multithreaded programming is going to be with us for the foreseeable future. But we'll cover other options that you should have in your toolbox in the rest of this book.

In the next chapter we'll look at functional programming, which avoids many of the problems with threads and locks by avoiding mutable state. Even if you never write any functional code, understanding the principles behind functional programming is valuable—as you'll see, they underlie many of the other concurrency models we'll cover.

CHAPTER 3

Functional Programming

Functional Programming is like a car powered by hydrogen fuel cells—advanced, futuristic, and not yet widely used, but it's what we'll all rely on in twenty years.

In contrast to an imperative program, which consists of a series of statements that change global state when executed, a *functional program* models computation as the evaluation of expressions. Those expressions are built from pure mathematical functions that are both first-class (can be manipulated like any other value) and side effect–free. It's particularly useful when dealing with concurrency because the lack of side effects makes reasoning about thread safety much easier. It is also the first model we'll look at that allows parallelism to be represented directly.

If It Hurts, Stop Doing It

The rules about locking that we discussed in Chapter 2, *Threads and Locks*, on page 9, apply only to data that is both shared between threads and might change—in other words *shared mutable state.* Data that doesn't change (is *immutable*) can be accessed by multiple threads without any kind of locking.

This is what makes functional programming so compelling when it comes to concurrency and parallelism—functional programs have no mutable state, so they cannot suffer from any of the problems associated with shared mutable state.

In this chapter we're going to look at functional programming in Clojure,[1] a dialect of Lisp that runs on the JVM. Clojure is dynamically typed; and if you're a Ruby or Python programmer, you'll feel right at home once you get used to the unfamiliar syntax. Clojure is not a pure functional language, but

---

1. http://clojure.org

in this chapter we'll be concentrating on its purely functional subset. I'll introduce the bits of Clojure that we'll be using along the way, but if you want to learn more about the language I recommend Stuart Halloway and Aaron Bedra's *Programming Clojure [HB12]*.

In day 1 we'll look at the basics of functional programming and see how it's trivial to parallelize a functional algorithm. In day 2 we'll dig deeper into Clojure's reducers framework and see how this parallelization works under the hood. Finally, in day 3, we'll switch our focus from parallelism to concurrency and create a concurrent functional web service with futures and promises.

Day 1: Programming Without Mutable State

When programmers first encounter functional programming, their reaction is often one of disbelief—that it can't be possible to write nontrivial programs without modifying variables. We'll see that it is not only possible but very often simpler and easier than creating normal imperative code.

The Perils of Mutable State

Today we're going to concentrate on parallelism. We'll construct a simple functional program and then show how, because it's functional, it's almost trivially easy to parallelize.

But first let's look at a couple of examples in Java that show why it's so helpful to avoid mutable state.

Hidden Mutable State

Here's a class that doesn't have any mutable state and should therefore be perfectly thread-safe:

FunctionalProgramming/DateFormatBug/src/main/java/com/paulbutcher/DateParser.java
```java
class DateParser {
  private final DateFormat format = new SimpleDateFormat("yyyy-MM-dd");

  public Date parse(String s) throws ParseException {
    return format.parse(s);
  }
}
```

When I run a small example program that uses this class from multiple threads (you can see the source in the code that accompanies the book), I get the following:

```
Caught: java.lang.NumberFormatException: For input string: ".12012E4.12012E4"
Expected: Sun Jan 01 00:00:00 GMT 2012, got: Wed Apr 15 00:00:00 BST 2015
```

The next time I run it, I get this:

```
Caught: java.lang.ArrayIndexOutOfBoundsException: -1
```

And the next time, I get this:

```
Caught: java.lang.NumberFormatException: multiple points
Caught: java.lang.NumberFormatException: multiple points
```

Clearly the code isn't thread-safe at all, but why? It only has a single member variable, and that's immutable because it's final.

The reason is that SimpleDateFormat has mutable state buried deep within. You can argue that this is a bug,[2] but for our purposes it doesn't matter. The problem is that languages like Java make it both easy to write code with hidden mutable state like this and virtually impossible to tell when it happens—there's no way to tell from its API that SimpleDateFormat isn't thread-safe.

Hidden mutable state isn't the only thing you need to be careful about, as we'll see next.

Escapologist Mutable State

Imagine that you're creating a web service that manages a tournament. Among other things, it's going to need to manage a list of players, which you might be tempted to implement along these lines:

```java
public class Tournament {
  private List<Player> players = new LinkedList<Player>();

  public synchronized void addPlayer(Player p) {
    players.add(p);
  }

  public synchronized Iterator<Player> getPlayerIterator() {
    return players.iterator();
  }
}
```

At first glance, this looks like it should be thread-safe—players is private and accessed only via the addPlayer() and getPlayerIterator() methods, both of which are synchronized. Unfortunately, it is not thread-safe because the iterator returned by getPlayerIterator() still references the mutable state contained within players—if another thread calls addPlayer() while the iterator is in use, we'll see a ConcurrentModificationException or worse. The state has *escaped* from the protection provided by Tournament.

---

2. http://bugs.sun.com/bugdatabase/view_bug.do?bug_id=4228335

Hidden and escaped state are just two of the dangers of mutable state in concurrent programs—there are plenty of others. These dangers would disappear if we could find a way to avoid mutable state entirely, which is exactly what functional programming enables us to do.

A Whirlwind Tour of Clojure

It takes only a few minutes to get the hang of Clojure's Lisp syntax.

The easiest way to experiment with Clojure is through its REPL (read-evaluate-print loop), which you can start with lein repl (lein is the standard Clojure build tool). This allows you to type code and have it evaluated immediately without having to create source files and compile them, which can be amazingly helpful when experimenting with unfamiliar code. When the REPL starts, you should see the following prompt:

```
user=>
```

Any Clojure code you type at this prompt will be evaluated immediately.

Clojure code is almost entirely constructed from parenthesized lists called *s-expressions.* A function call that in most languages would be written max(3, 5) is written like this:

```
user=> (max 3 5)
5
```

The same is true of mathematical operators. Here's 1 + 2 * 3, for example:

```
user=> (+ 1 (* 2 3))
7
```

Defining a constant is achieved with def:

```
user=> (def meaning-of-life 42)
#'user/meaning-of-life
user=> meaning-of-life
42
```

Even control structures are *s*-expressions:

```
user=> (if (< meaning-of-life 0) "negative" "non-negative")
"non-negative"
```

Although almost everything in Clojure is an *s*-expression, there are a few exceptions. Vector (array) literals are surrounded by square brackets:

```
user=> (def droids ["Huey" "Dewey" "Louie"])
#'user/droids
user=> (count droids)
3
```

```
user=> (droids 0)
"Huey"
user=> (droids 2)
"Louie"
```

And map literals are surrounded by curly brackets:

```
user=> (def me {:name "Paul" :age 45 :sex :male})
#'user/me
user=> (:age me)
45
```

Keys in maps are often *keywords*, which start with a colon and are very similar to symbols in Ruby or interned strings in Java.

Finally, a function is defined with defn, with arguments specified as a vector:

```
user=> (defn percentage [x p] (* x (/ p 100.0)))
#'user/percentage
user=> (percentage 200 10)
20.0
```

That concludes our whirlwind tour of Clojure. I'll introduce other aspects of the language as we go.

Our First Functional Program

I've said that the most interesting thing about functional programming is that it avoids mutable state, but we haven't actually seen an example yet. Let's rectify that now.

Imagine that you want to find the sum of a sequence of numbers. In an imperative language like Java, you would probably write something like this:

```
public int sum(int[] numbers) {
  int accumulator = 0;
  for (int n: numbers)
    accumulator += n;
  return accumulator;
}
```

That isn't functional because accumulator is mutable: it changes after each iteration of the for loop. By contrast, this Clojure solution has no mutable variables:

FunctionalProgramming/Sum/src/sum/core.clj
```
(defn recursive-sum [numbers]
  (if (empty? numbers)
    0
    (+ (first numbers) (recursive-sum (rest numbers)))))
```

This is a *recursive* solution—recursive-sum calls itself (recurses). If numbers is empty, it simply returns zero. Otherwise, it returns the result of adding the first (head) element of numbers to the sum of the rest (tail) of the sequence.

Although our recursive solution works, we can do better. Here is a solution that's both simpler and more efficient:

FunctionalProgramming/Sum/src/sum/core.clj
```
(defn reduce-sum [numbers]
  (reduce (fn [acc x] (+ acc x)) 0 numbers))
```

This uses Clojure's reduce function, which takes three arguments—a function, an initial value, and a collection.

In this instance, we're passing it an anonymous function defined with fn that takes two arguments and returns their sum. It's called once by reduce for each element in the collection—the first time, it's passed the initial value (0 in this case) together with the first item in the collection; the second time, it's passed the result of the first invocation together with the second item in the collection; and so on.

We're not quite done yet—we can make this code better still by noticing that + is already a function that, when given two arguments, returns their sum. We can pass it directly to reduce without creating an anonymous function:

FunctionalProgramming/Sum/src/sum/core.clj
```
(defn sum [numbers]
  (reduce + numbers))
```

So we've arrived at a solution that is both simpler and more concise than the imperative one. You'll find that this is a common experience when converting imperative code to functional.

Effortless Parallelism

So we've seen some functional code, but what about parallelism? What would we need to do to convert our sum function to operate in parallel? Very little, it turns out:

FunctionalProgramming/Sum/src/sum/core.clj
```
(ns sum.core
  (:require [clojure.core.reducers :as r]))

(defn parallel-sum [numbers]
  (r/fold + numbers))
```

Joe asks:
What If We Pass an Empty Collection to reduce?

Our final version of sum doesn't pass an initial value to reduce:

```
(reduce + numbers)
```

This might make you wonder what happens if we give it an empty collection. The answer is that it does the right thing and returns zero:

```
sum.core=> (sum [])
0
```

But how does reduce know that zero (and not, say, 1 or nil) is the right thing to return? This relies on an interesting feature of many of Clojure's operators—they know what their identity values are. The + function, for example, can take any number of arguments, including zero:

```
user=> (+ 1 2)
3
user=> (+ 1 2 3 4)
10
user=> (+ 42)
42
user=> (+)
0
```

When called with no arguments, it returns the additive identity, 0.

Similarly, * knows that the multiplicative identity is 1:

```
user=> (*)
1
```

If we don't pass an initial value to reduce, it uses the result of calling the function it's given with no arguments.

Incidentally, because + can take any number of arguments, this also means that we can implement sum with apply, which takes a function together with an vector and calls the function with the vector as arguments:

```
FunctionalProgramming/Sum/src/sum/core.clj
(defn apply-sum [numbers]
  (apply + numbers))
```

But unlike the version that uses reduce, this can't easily be parallelized.

The only difference is that we're now using the fold function from the clojure.core.reducers package (which we alias to r to save typing) instead of using reduce.

Here's a REPL session that shows what this buys us in terms of performance:

```
sum.core=> (def numbers (into [] (range 0 10000000)))
#'sum.core/numbers
sum.core=> (time (sum numbers))
"Elapsed time: 1099.154 msecs"
49999995000000
sum.core=> (time (sum numbers))
"Elapsed time: 125.349 msecs"
49999995000000
sum.core=> (time (parallel-sum numbers))
"Elapsed time: 236.609 msecs"
49999995000000
sum.core=> (time (parallel-sum numbers))
"Elapsed time: 49.835 msecs"
49999995000000
```

We start by creating a vector that contains all the integers between zero and ten million by inserting the result of (range 0 10000000) into an empty vector with into. Then we use the time macro, which prints the time taken by whatever code it's given. As is often the case with code running on the JVM, we have to run more than once to give the just-in-time optimizer a chance to kick in and get a representative time.

So, on my four-core Mac, fold takes us from 125 ms to 50 ms, a 2.5x speedup. We'll see how fold achieves this tomorrow, but before then let's look at a functional version of our Wikipedia word-count example.

Counting Words Functionally

Today we'll create a sequential implementation of word count—we'll parallelize it tomorrow. We're going to need to have three things:

- A function that, given a Wikipedia XML dump, returns a sequence of the pages contained within that dump

- A function that, given a page, returns a sequence of the words on that page

- A function that, given a sequence of words, returns a map containing the frequencies of those words

We're not going to cover the first two of these in any detail—this is a book about concurrency, not string processing or XML (see the accompanying code if you're interested in the details). We will look at how to count words, however, as that's what we'll be parallelizing.

Functional Maps

Because we want to return a map of word frequencies, we'll need to understand a couple of Clojure's map functions—get and assoc:

```
user=> (def counts {"apple" 2 "orange" 1})
#'user/counts
user=> (get counts "apple" 0)
2
user=> (get counts "banana" 0)
0
user=> (assoc counts "banana" 1)
{"banana" 1, "orange" 1, "apple" 2}
user=> (assoc counts "apple" 3)
{"orange" 1, "apple" 3}
```

So get simply looks up a key in the map and either returns its value or returns a default if the key isn't in the map. And assoc takes a map together with a key and value and returns a new map with the key mapped to the value.

Frequencies

We now know enough to write a function that takes a sequence of words and returns a map in which each word is associated with the number of times it appears:

FunctionalProgramming/WordCount/src/wordcount/word_frequencies.clj
```
(defn word-frequencies [words]
  (reduce
    (fn [counts word] (assoc counts word (inc (get counts word 0))))
    {} words))
```

This time we're passing an empty map {} as the initial value to reduce. And then for each word in words, we add one more than the current count for that word. Here's an example of it in use:

```
user=> (word-frequencies ["one" "potato" "two" "potato" "three" "potato" "four"])
{"four" 1, "three" 1, "two" 1, "potato" 3, "one" 1}
```

It turns out that the Clojure standard library has beaten us to it—there's a standard function called frequencies that takes any collection and returns a map of the frequencies of its members:

```
user=> (frequencies ["one" "potato" "two" "potato" "three" "potato" "four"])
{"one" 1, "potato" 3, "two" 1, "three" 1, "four" 1}
```

Now that we can count words, all that remains is to wire things up with the XML processing.

More Sequence Functions

To see how to do that, we need to introduce a little more machinery. First, here's the map function:

```
user=> (map inc [0 1 2 3 4 5])
(1 2 3 4 5 6)
user=> (map (fn [x] (* 2 x)) [0 1 2 3 4 5])
(0 2 4 6 8 10)
```

Given a function and a sequence, map returns a new sequence that contains the result of applying the function to each element of the sequence in turn.

We can simplify the second version slightly by using partial, which takes a function together with one or more arguments and returns a partially applied function:

```
user=> (def multiply-by-2 (partial * 2))
#'user/multiply-by-2
user=> (multiply-by-2 3)
6
user=> (map (partial * 2) [0 1 2 3 4 5])
(0 2 4 6 8 10)
```

Finally, imagine that you have a function that returns a sequence, such as using a regular expression to break a string into a sequence of words:

```
user=> (defn get-words [text] (re-seq #"\w+" text))
#'user/get-words
user=> (get-words "one two three four")
("one" "two" "three" "four")
```

As you would expect, mapping this function over a sequence of strings will give you a sequence of sequences:

```
user=> (map get-words ["one two three" "four five six" "seven eight nine"])
(("one" "two" "three") ("four" "five" "six") ("seven" "eight" "nine"))
```

If you want a single sequence that consists of all the subsequences concatenated, you can use mapcat:

```
user=> (mapcat get-words ["one two three" "four five six" "seven eight nine"])
("one" "two" "three" "four" "five" "six" "seven" "eight" "nine")
```

We now have all the tools we need to create our word-counting function.

Putting It All Together

Here's count-words-sequential. Given a sequence of pages, it returns a map of the frequencies of the words on those pages:

FunctionalProgramming/WordCount/src/wordcount/core.clj

```
(defn count-words-sequential [pages]
  (frequencies (mapcat get-words pages)))
```

It starts by converting the sequence of pages into a sequence of words with (mapcat get-words pages). This sequence of words is then passed to frequencies.

It's worth comparing this to the imperative version in the code on page 35. Again, the functional solution turns out to be significantly simpler, clearer, and more concise than its imperative equivalent.

It's Good to Be Lazy

Something might be bothering you—a Wikipedia dump runs to around 40 GiB. If count-words starts by collating every word into a single huge sequence, surely we're going to end up running out of memory.

We don't, and the reason for that is that sequences in Clojure are *lazy*—elements of a lazy sequence are generated only when they're needed. Let's see what this means in practice.

Clojure's range function produces a sequence of numbers:

```
user=> (range 0 10)
(0 1 2 3 4 5 6 7 8 9)
```

In the preceding code, the REPL *realizes* (fully evaluates) the sequence and then prints it.

There's nothing to stop you from realizing really big ranges, but doing so can turn your computer into an expensive room heater. Try the following, for example, and you'll have to wait a long time before seeing a result (assuming that you don't run out of memory first):

```
user=> (range 0 100000000)
```

Try this, on the other hand, and you'll get the answer immediately:

```
user=> (take 10 (range 0 100000000))
(0 1 2 3 4 5 6 7 8 9)
```

Because take is only interested in the first ten elements of its sequence argument, range only needs to generate the first ten elements. This works across any level of function-call nesting:

```
user=> (take 10 (map (partial * 2) (range 0 100000000)))
(0 2 4 6 8 10 12 14 16 18)
```

We can even program with infinite sequences. Clojure's iterate function, for example, generates an infinite sequence by repeatedly applying a function to an initial value, then the returned value, and so on:

```
user=> (take 10 (iterate inc 0))
(0 1 2 3 4 5 6 7 8 9)
user=> (take 10 (iterate (partial + 2) 0))
(0 2 4 6 8 10 12 14 16 18)
```

One final aspect of lazy sequences is that not only do we not need to generate the elements at the end of a sequence until we need them (which might be never), but we can discard the elements at the front if we've finished with them (if we don't "hold on to our head"). The following, for example, might take a while to complete, but you won't run out of memory:

```
user=> (take-last 5 (range 0 100000000))
(99999995 99999996 99999997 99999998 99999999)
```

Because the sequence of pages returned by get-pages is lazy, count-words can handle a 40 GiB Wikipedia dump without problem. And the bonus is that it's very easy to parallelize, as we'll see tomorrow.

Day 1 Wrap-Up

That brings us to the end of day 1. In day 2 we'll parallelize our word count and look into fold in more detail.

What We Learned in Day 1

Concurrent programming in imperative languages is difficult because of the prevalence of shared mutable state. Functional programming makes concurrency easier and safer by eliminating shared mutable state. We saw how to do the following:

- Apply a function to every element of a sequence with map or mapcat
- Use laziness to handle large, or even infinite, sequences
- Reduce a sequence to a single (possibly complex) value with reduce
- Parallelize a reduce operation with fold

Day 1 Self-Study

Find

- The Clojure "cheat sheet," which contains a quick reference to the most commonly used functions

- The documentation for lazy-seq, which enables you to create your own lazy sequences

Do

- Unlike many functional languages, Clojure does not provide tail-call elimination, so idiomatic Clojure makes very little use of recursion. Rewrite the recursive-sum function (see the code on page 53) to use Clojure's loop and recur special forms instead.

- Rewrite reduce-sum (see the code on page 54) to use the #() reader macro instead of (fn …).

Day 2: Functional Parallelism

Today we'll continue our discussion of how functional programming helps with parallelism by looking at fold in more detail. But before we do that, we'll look at parallelizing our Wikipedia word count.

One Page at a Time

In day 1 we saw that the map function creates a sequence by applying a function to each element of an input sequence in turn. But there's no reason this has to happen serially—Clojure's pmap function operates just like map, except that the function is applied in parallel. It's *semi-lazy*, in that the parallel computation stays ahead of the consumption, but it won't realize the entire result unless required.

We could, for example, convert our sequence of Wikipedia pages to a sequence of maps of word counts within those pages in parallel with this:

```
(pmap #(frequencies (get-words %)) pages)
```

In this case, we're defining the function passed to pmap using the #(…) *reader macro*, which is a shorthand way to write an anonymous function. Arguments are specified with %1, %2, and so on, which can be further shortened to a single % if it takes only a single argument:

```
#(frequencies (get-words %))
```

The preceding code is equivalent to this:

```
(fn [page] (frequencies (get-words page)))
```

Here it is in action:

```
wordcount.core=> (def pages ["one potato two potato three potato four"
          #_=>                "five potato six potato seven potato more"])
#'wordcount.core/pages
wordcount.core=> (pmap #(frequencies (get-words %)) pages)
({"one" 1, "potato" 3, "two" 1, "three" 1, "four" 1}
 {"five" 1, "potato" 3, "six" 1, "seven" 1, "more" 1})
```

We can then get the total word counts we're looking for by reducing this sequence to a single map. Our reducing function will need to take two maps and merge them so that

- the keys in the resulting map are the union of the keys in the two input maps, and;

- if the key exists in only one of the two input maps, that value is associated with the key in the result map, or;

- if the key exists in both of the input maps, the value associated with that key is the sum of the values from the two input maps.

The following diagram shows what we're aiming for:

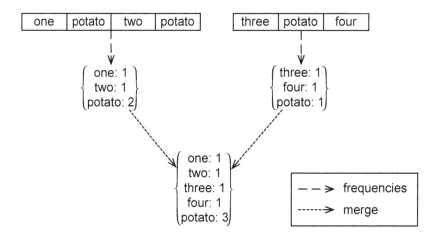

We could write this reducing function ourselves, but (as is so often the case) a function in the standard library does what we need. Here's the documentation:

(merge-with f & maps)

Returns a map that consists of the rest of the maps conj-ed onto the first—if a key occurs in more than one map, the mapping(s) from the latter (left-to-right) will be combined with the mapping in the result by calling (f val-in-result val-in-latter).

Recall that partial returns a partially applied function, so (partial merge-with +) will give us a function that takes two maps and merges them using + to combine values if the same key appears in both:

```
user=> (def merge-counts (partial merge-with +))
#'user/merge-counts
user=> (merge-counts {:x 1 :y 2} {:y 1 :z 1})
{:z 1, :y 3, :x 1}
```

Putting this all together, here's a parallel word count:

FunctionalProgramming/WordCount/src/wordcount/core.clj

```clojure
(defn count-words-parallel [pages]
  (reduce (partial merge-with +)
    (pmap #(frequencies (get-words %)) pages)))
```

Now that we've got a parallel word count, let's see how well it performs.

Batching for Performance

On my MacBook Pro, the sequential version takes 140 seconds to count the words in the first 100,000 pages of Wikipedia. The parallel version takes 94 s, a 1.5x speedup. So we're getting some performance benefit from parallelism, but not as much as we might like.

The reason is exactly the same as we saw last week in our threads and locks–based solution (see the code on page 40). We're counting and merging on a page-by-page basis, which results in a large number of merges. We can reduce those merges by counting batches of pages instead of a single page at a time:

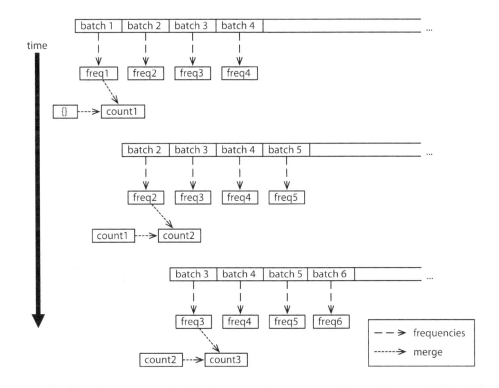

Figure 5—Batched word count

Here, for example, is an implementation of word-count that processes batches of 100 pages at a time:

FunctionalProgramming/WordCount/src/wordcount/core.clj
```
(defn count-words [pages]
  (reduce (partial merge-with +)
    (pmap count-words-sequential (partition-all 100 pages))))
```

This uses partition-all, which batches (partitions) a sequence into multiple sequences:

```
user=> (partition-all 4 [1 2 3 4 5 6 7 8 9 10])
((1 2 3 4) (5 6 7 8) (9 10))
```

We then count the words within each batch with word-count-sequential and merge them as before. And sure enough, this version counts the words in the first 100,000 pages of Wikipedia in forty-four seconds, a 3.2x speedup.

Reducers

In day 1 we saw that switching from reduce to fold could deliver dramatic performance improvements. To understand how fold achieves this, we need to understand Clojure's reducers library.

A *reducer* is a recipe that describes how to reduce a collection. The normal version of map takes a function and a (possibly lazy) sequence and returns another (possibly lazy) sequence:

```
user=> (map (partial * 2) [1 2 3 4])
(2 4 6 8)
```

Given the same arguments, the version from clojure.core.reducers, in contrast, returns a *reducible*:

```
user=> (require '[clojure.core.reducers :as r])
nil
user=> (r/map (partial * 2) [1 2 3 4])
#<reducers$folder$reify__1599 clojure.core.reducers$folder$reify__1599@151964cd>
```

A reducible isn't a directly usable value—it's just something that can subsequently be passed to reduce:

```
user=> (reduce conj [] (r/map (partial * 2) [1 2 3 4]))
[2 4 6 8]
```

The anonymous function we're passing to reduce in the preceding code takes a collection as its first argument (initially an empty vector, []) and uses conj to add its second argument to it. The result, therefore, is a collection representing the result of the mapping.

The following is equivalent to the preceding code because into uses reduce internally:

```
user=> (into [] (r/map (partial * 2) [1 2 3 4]))
[2 4 6 8]
```

As well as map and mapcat, which we've already seen, there are reducer versions of most of the sequence-handling functions in clojure.core. And just like their clojure.core equivalents, they can be chained:

```
user=> (into [] (r/map (partial + 1) (r/filter even? [1 2 3 4])))
[3 5]
```

A reducer, instead of returning a result, returns a *recipe* for creating a result—a recipe that isn't executed until it's passed to either reduce or fold. This has two primary benefits:

- It's more efficient than a chain of functions returning lazy sequences, because no intermediate sequences need to be created.

- It allows fold to parallelize the entire chain of operations on the underlying collection.

Reducers' Internals

To understand how reducers work, we're going to create our own slightly simplified, but still very effective, version of clojure.core.reducers. To do so, we first need to know about Clojure's *protocols*. A protocol is very similar to an interface in Java—it's a collection of methods that together define an abstraction. Clojure's collections support reduce via the CollReduce protocol:

```
(defprotocol CollReduce
  (coll-reduce [coll f] [coll f init]))
```

CollReduce defines a single function called coll-reduce with multiple *arities*—it can take either two arguments (coll and f) or three (coll, f, and init). The first argument performs the same role as Java's this reference, allowing *polymorphic dispatch*. Look at this Clojure code:

```
(coll-reduce coll f)
```

This Clojure code is equivalent to this Java:

```
coll.collReduce(f);
```

The reduce function simply calls through to coll-reduce, delegating the task of reducing to the collection itself. We can see this by implementing our own version of reduce:

FunctionalProgramming/Reducers/src/reducers/core.clj
```
(defn my-reduce
  ([f coll] (coll-reduce coll f))
  ([f init coll] (coll-reduce coll f init)))
```

This shows a feature of defn we've not seen before—it can be used to define functions that take varying numbers of arguments (in this case either two or three). In both cases, it simply forwards its arguments to coll-reduce. Let's prove that it works:

```
reducers.core=> (my-reduce + [1 2 3 4])
10
reducers.core=> (my-reduce + 10 [1 2 3 4])
20
```

Next, let's see how to implement our own version of map:

FunctionalProgramming/Reducers/src/reducers/core.clj
```
(defn make-reducer [reducible transformf]
  (reify
    CollReduce
    (coll-reduce [_ f1]
      (coll-reduce reducible (transformf f1) (f1)))
    (coll-reduce [_ f1 init]
      (coll-reduce reducible (transformf f1) init))))

(defn my-map [mapf reducible]
  (make-reducer reducible
    (fn [reducef]
      (fn [acc v]
        (reducef acc (mapf v))))))
```

We're using a function called make-reducer that takes a reducible and a transform function and returns a *reification* of the CollReduce protocol. Reifying a protocol is similar to using new in Java to create an anonymous instance of an interface.

This instance of CollReduce calls the coll-reduce method on the reducible, using the transform function to transform its f1 argument.

> ### Joe asks:
> ### What Does an Underscore Mean?
>
> It's common Clojure style to use an underscore ("_") as the name of an unused function parameter. We could have written this:
>
> ```
> (coll-reduce [this f1]
>   (coll-reduce reducible (transformf f1) (f1)))
> ```
>
> But using the underscore makes it clear that this is unused.

The transform function that's passed to make-reducer is a function that takes a function as an argument and returns a transformed version of that function. Here's my-map's transformation function:

```
(fn [reducef]
  (fn [acc v]
    (reducef acc (mapf v))))
```

Recall that the reducing function is called once for each element of the collection, with an accumulator (acc) as its first argument and the value from the collection (v) as its second. So, given a reducing function reducef, we're returning a function that calls reducef with its second argument modified by mapf (the function passed to my-map). Let's prove that this works as expected:

```
reducers.core=> (into [] (my-map (partial * 2) [1 2 3 4]))
[2 4 6 8]
reducers.core=> (into [] (my-map (partial + 1) [1 2 3 4]))
[2 3 4 5]
```

As you would hope, we can also chain multiple mappings:

```
reducers.core=> (into [] (my-map (partial * 2) (my-map (partial + 1) [1 2 3 4])))
[4 6 8 10]
```

If you work through what this is doing, you'll see that it performs a single reduce, using a single reducing function created by composing (partial * 2) with (partial + 1).

We've seen how reducers support reduce. Next, we'll look at how fold parallelizes reductions.

Divide and Conquer

Instead of reducing a collection serially, fold uses a *binary chop*. It starts by dividing the collection into two halves, then halving those halves, and so on until the collection has been divided into groups that are smaller than some limit (by default, 512). It then runs a set of sequential reduce operations over each group and combines the results pairwise until only a single result is left. This results in a binary tree like Figure 6, *A fold Tree*, on page 68.

The reduce and combine operations run in parallel because fold creates a matching tree of parallel tasks (using Java 7's Fork/Join framework). The tasks at the leaves of the tree run the reduce operations. The tasks at the next level wait for the results of those reduce operations to be ready and, when they are, it combines them and the process continues until only a single result is left at the root of the tree.

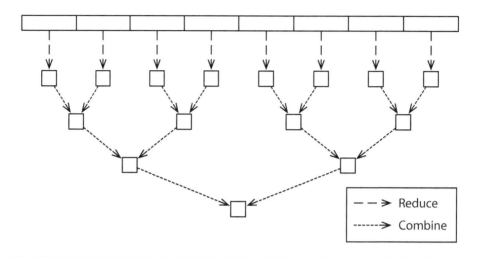

Figure 6—A fold Tree

If fold is given a single function (+ in our example), that function is used for both the reduce and combine operations. As we'll soon see, however, it sometimes makes sense to use one function for the reductions and another for the combinations.

Supporting Fold

In addition to CollReduce, collections that can be folded also support CollFold:

```
(defprotocol CollFold
  (coll-fold [coll n combinef reducef]))
```

Just as reduce delegates to coll-reduce, fold delegates to coll-fold:

FunctionalProgramming/Reducers/src/reducers/core.clj
```
(defn my-fold
  ([reducef coll]
    (my-fold reducef reducef coll))
  ([combinef reducef coll]
    (my-fold 512 combinef reducef coll))
  ([n combinef reducef coll]
    (coll-fold coll n combinef reducef)))
```

The two- and three-argument versions just call my-fold recursively, providing defaults for combinef and n if they're not provided. The four-argument version calls the collection's coll-fold implementation.

The only modification we need to make to our code to support parallel fold operations is to have make-reducer reify CollFold in addition to CollReduce:

FunctionalProgramming/Reducers/src/reducers/core.clj

```
(defn make-reducer [reducible transformf]
  (reify
    CollFold
    (coll-fold [_ n combinef reducef]
      (coll-fold reducible n combinef (transformf reducef)))

    CollReduce
    (coll-reduce [_ f1]
      (coll-reduce reducible (transformf f1) (f1)))
    (coll-reduce [_ f1 init]
      (coll-reduce reducible (transformf f1) init))))
```

The implementation is very similar to CollReduce—we transform the reducing function and pass the rest of the arguments through to coll-fold. Let's prove that it works as expected:

```
reducers.core=> (def v (into [] (range 10000)))
#'reducers.core/v
reducers.core=> (my-fold + v)
49995000
reducers.core=> (my-fold + (my-map (partial * 2) v))
99990000
```

Next, we'll see an example of passing a different reduce and combine function to fold.

Frequencies with Fold

Our old friend, the frequencies function, is an excellent example of requiring different reduce and combine functions when implemented with fold:

FunctionalProgramming/Reducers/src/reducers/parallel_frequencies.clj

```
(defn parallel-frequencies [coll]
  (r/fold
    (partial merge-with +)
    (fn [counts x] (assoc counts x (inc (get counts x 0))))
    coll))
```

This should remind you strongly of the batched parallel implementation of word-count we saw earlier today (see the code on page 64)—each batch is reduced to a map that is then merged with (partial merge-with +).

We can't try this out on our Wikipedia page count, because fold doesn't work on a lazy sequence (there's no way to perform a binary chop on a lazy sequence). But we can check that it works on, say, a large vector of random integers.

The repeatedly function creates an infinite lazy sequence by repeatedly calling the function it's given as an argument. In this case, we're using it to call rand-int, which returns a different random integer each time it's called:

```
user=> (take 10 (repeatedly #(rand-int 10)))
(2 6 2 8 8 5 9 2 5 5)
```

We can use this to create a large vector of random integers as follows:

```
reducers.core=> (def numbers (into [] (take 10000000 (repeatedly #(rand-int 10)))))
#'reducers.core/numbers
```

And then we can count the occurrences of each number in that vector with frequencies and parallel-frequencies:

```
reducers.core=> (require ['reducers.parallel-frequencies :refer :all])
nil
reducers.core=> (time (frequencies numbers))
"Elapsed time: 1500.306 msecs"
{0 1000983, 1 999528, 2 1000515, 3 1000283, 4 997717, 5 1000101, 6 999993, …
reducers.core=> (time (parallel-frequencies numbers))
"Elapsed time: 436.691 msecs"
{0 1000983, 1 999528, 2 1000515, 3 1000283, 4 997717, 5 1000101, 6 999993, …
```

So the sequential version of frequencies takes around 1500 ms, and the parallel version a little over 400 ms, a 3.5x speedup.

Day 2 Wrap-Up

That brings us to the end of day 2 and our discussion of parallelism in Clojure. Tomorrow we'll move on to concurrency with futures and promises, and we'll see how they enable the dataflow style of programming.

What We Learned in Day 2

Clojure allows operations on sequences to be easily and naturally parallelized.

- A map operation can be parallelized with pmap, yielding a semi-lazy parallel map.

- Such a parallel map can be batched for efficiency with partition-all.

- Alternatively, fold parallelizes reduce operations with an eager divide-and-conquer strategy.

- Instead of returning an intermediate sequence, the clojure.core.reducers versions of functions like map, mapcat, and filter return reducibles, which can be thought of as recipes for how to reduce a sequence.

Day 2 Self-Study

Find

- The video of Rich Hickey presenting reducers at QCon 2012

- The documentation for pcalls and pvalues—how do they differ from pmap? Is it possible to implement them in terms of pmap?

Do

- Create my-flatten and my-mapcat along the lines of my-map (see the code on page 66). Note that these will both be more complex than my-map because they will need to expand a single input sequence element into one or more elements of the resulting sequence. If you get stuck, see the implementation in the code that accompanies this book.

- Create my-filter. Again, this will be more complex than my-map because it will need to reduce the number of elements in the input sequence.

Day 3: Functional Concurrency

Over the previous two days, we've concentrated on parallelism. Today we're going to change focus and look at concurrency. But before we do so, we'll look deeper into why functional programming allows us to parallelize code so easily.

Same Structure, Different Evaluation Order

A common theme runs through everything we've seen over the last couple of days—functional programming allows us to play games with the order in which things are evaluated. If two calculations are independent, we can run them in any order we like, including in parallel.

The following code snippets all perform the same calculation, return the same result, and have almost identical structure, but they execute their component operations in very different orders:

```
(reduce + (map (partial * 2) (range 10000)))
```
Reduces a lazy sequence built on top of a lazy sequence—elements in each lazy sequence are generated on an as-needed basis.

```
(reduce + (doall (map (partial * 2) (range 10000))))
```
First generates the entirety of the mapped sequence (doall forces a lazy sequence to be fully realized) and then reduces it.

(reduce + (pmap (partial * 2) (range 10000))))

> Reduces a semi-lazy sequence, which is generated in parallel.

(reduce + (r/map (partial * 2) (range 10000))))

> Reduces a single lazy sequence with a single reducing function constructed by combining + with (partial * 2).

(r/fold + (r/map (partial * 2) (into [] (range 10000)))))

> Generates the entirety of the range first and then reduces that in parallel by creating a tree of reduce and combine operations.

In an imperative language like Java, the order in which things happen is tightly bound to the order in which statements appear in the source code. The compiler and runtime can move things around somewhat (something we have to be careful of when using threads and locks, as we saw in *Mysterious Memory*, on page 13), but broadly speaking things happen in the same order as we write them down.

Functional languages have a much more *declarative* feel. Instead of writing a set of instructions for *how* to perform an operation, a functional program is more a statement of *what* the result should be. How the various calculations are ordered to achieve that result is much more fluid—this freedom to reorder calculations is what allows functional code to be parallelized so easily.

In the next section we'll see why functional languages can play these kinds of games with evaluation order and why imperative languages cannot.

Referential Transparency

Pure functions are *referentially transparent*—anywhere an invocation of the function appears, we can replace it with its result without changing the behavior of the program. Look at this example:

(+ 1 (+ 2 3))

This is exactly equivalent to the following:

(+ 1 5)

Indeed, one way to think about what executing functional code means is to think of it as repeatedly replacing function invocations with their results until you reach the final result. For example, we could evaluate (+ (+ 1 2) (+ 3 4)) like this:

(+ (+ 1 2) (+ 3 4)) → (+ (+ 1 2) 7) → (+ 3 7) → 10

Or like this:

(+ (+ 1 2) (+ 3 4)) → (+ 3 (+ 3 4)) → (+ 3 7) → 10

Of course, the same is true for the + operator in Java, but in a functional program *every* function is referentially transparent. It is this fact that enables us to safely make the radical changes to evaluation order we've seen so far.

> \|/   **Joe asks:**
> ᠄ᢩᢔ   **But Isn't Clojure Impure?**
>
> As we'll see in the next chapter, Clojure is an *impure* functional language—it is possible to write functions with side effects in Clojure, and any such functions will not be referentially transparent.
>
> This turns out to make little difference in practice because side effects are both very rare in idiomatic Clojure code and obvious when they do exist. There are a few simple rules about where side effects can safely appear, and as long as you follow those rules you're unlikely to hit problems with evaluation order.

Dataflow

It's interesting to think about how data flows between functions. Here is a graph of the data flows within (+ (+ 1 2) (+ 3 4)):

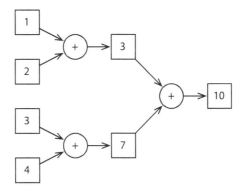

There are no dependencies between (+ 1 2) and (+ 3 4), so these two evaluations could theoretically happen in any order, including concurrently with each other. The final addition, however, can't take place until the results of both the subcalculations are available.

Theoretically, the language runtime could start at the left side of this graph and "push" data toward the right side. Whenever the data associated with a function's inputs becomes available, that function is executed. And each function could (theoretically, at least) execute concurrently. This style of execution is called *dataflow* programming. Clojure allows us to use this execution strategy through futures and promises.

Futures

A *future* takes a body of code and executes it in another thread. Its return value is a future object:

```
user=> (def sum (future (+ 1 2 3 4 5)))
#'user/sum
user=> sum
#<core$future_call$reify__6110@5d4ee7d0: 15>
```

We can retrieve the value of a future by dereferencing it with either deref or the shorthand @:

```
user=> (deref sum)
15
user=> @sum
15
```

Dereferencing a future will block until the value is available (or *realized*). We can use this to create exactly the dataflow graph we saw before:

```
user=> (let [a (future (+ 1 2))
  #_=>       b (future (+ 3 4))]
  #_=>    (+ @a @b))
10
```

In that code, we're using let to bind a to (future (+ 1 2)) and b to (future (+ 3 4)). The evaluation of (+ 1 2) takes place in one thread and (+ 3 4) in another. Finally, the outer addition blocks until both the inner additions have completed.

Of course, it makes no sense to use futures for such tiny operations as adding two numbers—we'll see a more realistic example soon. Before then, we'll look at Clojure's promises.

Promises

A *promise* is very similar to a future in that it's a value that's realized asynchronously and accessed with deref or @, which will block until it's realized. The difference is that creating a promise does not cause any code to run—instead its value is set with deliver. Here's a REPL session that illustrates this:

```
user=> (def meaning-of-life (promise))
#'user/meaning-of-life
user=> (future (println "The meaning of life is:" @meaning-of-life))
#<core$future_call$reify__6110@224e59d9: :pending>
user=> (deliver meaning-of-life 42)
#<core$promise$reify__6153@52c9f3c7: 42>
The meaning of life is: 42
```

We start by creating a promise called meaning-of-life and then use future to create a thread that prints its value (using future to create a thread like this is a common Clojure idiom). Finally we use deliver to set the value of our promise, which unblocks the thread we created earlier.

Now that we've seen how futures and promises work, let's see them in a real application.

A Functional Web Service

We're going to create a web service that accepts real-time transcript data (for example, the transcript of a television program) and translates it. The transcript is divided into "snippets," where each snippet has a sequence number. Here, for example, is how the first stanza of Lewis Carroll's poem *Jabberwocky* (from *Through the Looking-Glass*) might be divided into snippets:

0   Twas brillig, and the slithy toves

1   Did gyre and gimble in the wabe:

2   All mimsy were the borogoves,

3   And the mome raths outgrabe.

To deliver snippet 0 to our web service, we make a PUT request to */snippet/0* with the body, "Twas brillig, and the slithy toves." Snippet 1 is delivered to */snippet/1*, and so on.

This is a very simple API, but it's not as simple to implement as it might at first appearance. First, because it's going to run within a concurrent web server, our code will need to be thread-safe. Second, networks being what they are, it will have to handle snippets being lost and retried, delivered more than once, and arriving out of order.

If we want to process snippets sequentially (independent of the order they arrive in), we're going to have to keep track of which snippets we've already received and which we've processed. And, whenever we receive a new snippet, we'll need to check to see which (if any) are now available to be handled. Implementing this sequentially isn't easy—we're going to show how concurrency can be used to create a simple solution.

Figure 7, *The Structure of the Transcript Handler*, on page 76 shows the structure of the solution we're heading for.

On the left are the threads created by our web server to handle incoming requests. On the right is a thread that processes incoming snippets sequentially, waiting until the next snippet is available. In the next section we'll talk

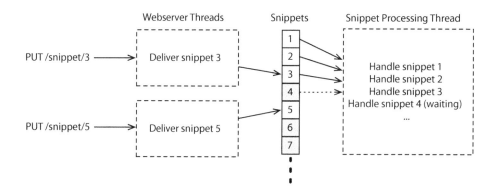

Figure 7—The Structure of the Transcript Handler

about snippets, the data structure that mediates the communication between these threads.

Accepting Snippets

Here's how we're going to keep track of the snippets we've received:

FunctionalProgramming/TranscriptHandler/src/server/core.clj
```
(def snippets (repeatedly promise))
```

So snippets is an infinite lazy sequence of promises (insert your own software-engineer-versus-sales, infinite-sequence-of-undelivered-promises-related joke here). These promises are realized by accept-snippet when snippets become available:

FunctionalProgramming/TranscriptHandler/src/server/core.clj
```
(defn accept-snippet [n text]
  (deliver (nth snippets n) text))
```

To handle snippets sequentially, we simply need to create a thread that dereferences each promise in turn. As an illustration, here's one that simply prints out the value of each snippet as it becomes available:

FunctionalProgramming/TranscriptHandler/src/server/core.clj
```
(future
  (doseq [snippet (map deref snippets)]
    (println snippet)))
```

This uses doseq, which processes a sequence sequentially. In this case, the sequence it's processing is a lazy sequence of dereferenced promises, each one of which is bound to snippet.

All that remains is to wire this all up into a web service. Here's code that uses the Compojure library to do so:[3]

FunctionalProgramming/TranscriptHandler/src/server/core.clj
```
(defroutes app-routes
  (PUT "/snippet/:n" [n :as {:keys [body]}]
    (accept-snippet (edn/read-string n) (slurp body))
    (response "OK")))

(defn -main [& args]
  (run-jetty (site app-routes) {:port 3000}))
```

This defines a single PUT route that calls our accept-snippet function. We're using an embedded Jetty web server[4]—like most web servers, Jetty is multithreaded, so our code needs to be thread-safe.

If we start the server (with lein run), we can use curl to prove to ourselves that this all works as we expect. Send snippet 0, for example:

```
$ curl -X put -d "Twas brillig, and the slithy toves" \
-H "Content-Type: text/plain" localhost:3000/snippet/0
OK
```

And it's immediately printed:

```
Twas brillig, and the slithy toves
```

But nothing will be printed if we send snippet 2 before snippet 1 has been sent:

```
$ curl -X put -d "All mimsy were the borogoves," \
-H "Content-Type: text/plain" localhost:3000/snippet/2
OK
```

Send snippet 1, however:

```
$ curl -X put -d "Did gyre and gimble in the wabe:" \
-H "Content-Type: text/plain" localhost:3000/snippet/1
OK
```

And both it and snippet 2 are printed:

```
Did gyre and gimble in the wabe:
All mimsy were the borogoves,
```

Delivering a snippet more than once causes no problems, because deliver is a no-op if called on a promise that's already been realized. So the following results in no error and nothing being printed:

---

3.   https://github.com/weavejester/compojure

4.   http://www.eclipse.org/jetty/

```
$ curl -X put -d "Did gyre and gimble in the wabe:" \
-H "Content-Type: text/plain" localhost:3000/snippet/1
OK
```

Now that we've demonstrated that we can handle snippets, let's do something more interesting with them. Imagine that we have another web service that translates any sentences it's given. We're going to modify our transcript handler to use this web service to translate whatever it's given.

Sentences

Before we look at how to call our translation service, we first need to implement code to turn our sequence of snippets into a sequence of sentences. Sentence boundaries might appear anywhere within a snippet, so we might need to either split or join snippets to obtain sentences.

Let's start by looking at how to split on sentence boundaries:

FunctionalProgramming/TranscriptHandler2/src/server/sentences.clj
```
(defn sentence-split [text]
  (map trim (re-seq #"[^\.!\?:;]+[\.!\?:;]*" text)))
```

This passes a regular expression that matches sentences to re-seq, which returns a sequence of matches and uses trim to get rid of any extraneous spaces:

```
server.core=> (sentence-split "This is a sentence. Is this?! A fragment")
("This is a sentence." "Is this?!" "A fragment")
```

Next, a little more regular-expression magic gives us a function that allows us to tell whether a string is a sentence:

FunctionalProgramming/TranscriptHandler2/src/server/sentences.clj
```
(defn is-sentence? [text]
  (re-matches #"^.*[\.!\?:;]$" text))
```

```
server.core=> (is-sentence? "This is a sentence.")
"This is a sentence."
server.core=> (is-sentence? "A sentence doesn't end with a comma,")
nil
```

Finally, we can wire this all up to create strings->sentences, a function that takes a sequence of strings and returns a sequence of sentences:

FunctionalProgramming/TranscriptHandler2/src/server/sentences.clj
```
(defn sentence-join [x y]
  (if (is-sentence? x) y (str x " " y)))

(defn strings->sentences [strings]
  (filter is-sentence?
    (reductions sentence-join
```

```
(mapcat sentence-split strings))))
```

This makes use of reductions. As its name suggests, this behaves like reduce; but instead of returning a single value, it returns a sequence of each of the intermediate values:

```
server.core=> (reduce + [1 2 3 4])
10
server.core=> (reductions + [1 2 3 4])
(1 3 6 10)
```

In our case, we're using sentence-join as the reducing function. If its first argument is a sentence, this just returns its second argument. But if its first argument is not, it returns the two concatenated (with an intervening space):

```
server.core=> (sentence-join "A complete sentence." "Start of another")
"Start of another"
server.core=> (sentence-join "This is" "a sentence.")
"This is a sentence."
```

So with reductions, this gives us the following:

```
server.core=> (def fragments ["A" "sentence." "And another." "Last" "sentence."])
#'server.core/fragments
server.core=> (reductions sentence-join fragments)
("A" "A sentence." "And another." "Last" "Last sentence.")
```

Finally, we filter the result with is-sentence?:

```
server.core=> (filter is-sentence? (reductions sentence-join fragments))
("A sentence." "And another." "Last sentence.")
```

Now that we've got a sequence of sentences, we can pass them to our translation server.

Translating Sentences

A classic use case for futures is talking to another web service. A future allows computation, such as network access, to take place on another thread while the main thread continues. Here's translate, a function that returns a future that will, when realized, contain the translation of its argument:

FunctionalProgramming/TranscriptHandler2/src/server/core.clj
```
(def translator "http://localhost:3001/translate")

(defn translate [text]
  (future
    (:body (client/post translator {:body text}))))
```

This uses client/post from the clj-http library to make a POST request and retrieve the response.[5] We can use this to transform the result of the strings->sentences function we created earlier into a set of translations:

FunctionalProgramming/TranscriptHandler2/src/server/core.clj

```
(def translations
  (delay
    (map translate (strings->sentences (map deref snippets)))))
```

This introduces the delay function, which creates a lazy value that isn't realized until it's dereferenced.

Putting It All Together

Here's the complete source of our web service:

FunctionalProgramming/TranscriptHandler2/src/server/core.clj

```
Line 1 (def snippets (repeatedly promise))

       (def translator "http://localhost:3001/translate")

   5   (defn translate [text]
         (future
           (:body (client/post translator {:body text}))))

       (def translations
  10       (delay
           (map translate (strings->sentences (map deref snippets)))))

       (defn accept-snippet [n text]
         (deliver (nth snippets n) text))
  15
       (defn get-translation [n]
         @(nth @translations n))

       (defroutes app-routes
  20       (PUT "/snippet/:n" [n :as {:keys [body]}]
           (accept-snippet (edn/read-string n) (slurp body))
           (response "OK"))
         (GET "/translation/:n" [n]
           (response (get-translation (edn/read-string n)))))
  25
       (defn -main [& args]
         (run-jetty (wrap-charset (api app-routes)) {:port 3000}))
```

As well as the code to translate sentences, we've added a new GET endpoint to allow translations to be retrieved (line 23). This makes use of get-translation (line 16), which accesses the translations sequence we created earlier.

---

5.   https://github.com/dakrone/clj-http

If you want to see this all in action, start the server, together with the translator server that's included in the accompanying code. Then run the TranscriptTest application (also in the accompanying code) and you should see a sentence-by-sentence French translation of Jabberwocky:

```
$ lein run
Il brilgue, les tôves lubricilleux Se gyrent en vrillant dans le guave:
Enmîmés sont les gougebosqueux Et le mômerade horsgrave.
Garde-toi du Jaseroque, mon fils!
La gueule qui mord; la griffe qui prend!
Garde-toi de l'oiseau Jube, évite Le frumieux Band-à-prend!
«...»
```

So there we have it—a complete concurrent web service that uses a combination of laziness, futures, and promises. It has no mutable state and no locks, and it's considerably simpler and easier to read than an equivalent service implemented in an imperative language is likely to be.

Joe asks:
Aren't We Holding Onto Our Head?

Our web service makes use of two lazy sequences, snippets and translations. In both cases, we hold on to the head of these sequences (see *It's Good to Be Lazy*, on page 59), meaning that they will grow forever. Over time, they will consume more and more memory.

In the next chapter we'll see how to use Clojure's reference types to fix this problem and enhance this web service to handle more than one transcript.

Day 3 Wrap-Up

This brings us to the end of day 3 and our discussion of how functional programming facilitates concurrency and parallelism.

What We Learned in Day 3

Functions in a functional program are referentially transparent. This allows us to safely modify the order in which those functions are called without affecting the behavior of the program. In particular, this facilitates the dataflow style of programming (supported in Clojure with futures and promises), in which code executes when the data it depends on becomes available. We saw an example of how concurrent dataflow programming can simplify the implementation of a web service.

Day 3 Self-Study

Find

- What is the difference between future and future-call? How would you implement one in terms of the other?

- How do you tell if a future has been realized without blocking? How do you cancel a future?

Do

- Modify the transcript server so that a GET request to */translation/:n* doesn't block if the translation isn't yet available, but returns an HTTP 409 status code instead.

- Implement the transcript server in an imperative language. Is your solution as simple as the functional Clojure implementation? How confident are you that it contains no race conditions?

Wrap-Up

There's a common misconception about parallelism—many people believe that parallel programming necessarily raises the specter of nondeterminism. If things aren't proceeding sequentially, the reasoning goes, and we can no longer rely on effects happening in a specific order, we're always going to have to worry about race conditions.

Certainly, there are some concurrent programs that will always be nondeterministic. And this is unavoidable—some problems require solutions that are intrinsically dependent on the details of timing. But it's not the case that all parallel programs are necessarily nondeterministic. The value of the sum of the numbers between 0 and 10,000 won't change just because we add those numbers together in parallel instead of sequentially. The frequencies of the words in a particular Wikipedia dump is and always will be the same, no matter how many threads we use to count them.

Most of the potential race conditions in traditional threads and locks–based parallel programs are accidental, arising from the details of the solution rather than any intrinsic nondeterminism in the problem.

Because functional code is referentially transparent, we can modify the order in which it's executed, safe in the knowledge that we will not change the final result by doing so. This includes evaluating mutually independent functions in parallel—as we've seen, this allows us to parallelize functional code almost trivially easily.

> \\// **Joe asks:**
> ːʏ̆ **Where Are the Monads and the Monoids?**
>
> Introductions to functional programming tend to involve descriptions of mathematical concepts like monads, monoids, and category theory. We've just had a whole chapter on functional programming, with no mention of any of these. What gives?
>
> One of the biggest influences on the flavor of any programming language is its type system. Writing code in a statically typed language like Java or Scala feels very different from writing code in a dynamically typed language like Ruby or Python.
>
> Static type systems place an up-front burden on the programmer to get the types right. The payoff is that doing so enables the compiler to make guarantees that certain types of errors will not occur at runtime and to improve efficiency by making optimizations guided by the type system.
>
> A programmer using a dynamically typed language avoids this up-front burden but accepts the risks that some errors will happen at runtime and that compiled code may be less efficient.
>
> The same distinction is present in the world of functional programming. A statically typed functional language like Haskell uses concepts like monads and monoids to allow its type system to accurately encode restrictions on where particular functions and values can be used and to keep track of side effects while remaining functional.
>
> Although an understanding of these mathematical concepts is undoubtedly helpful when writing Clojure code, no static type system needs to be told about them. The downside is that this places an additional burden on the programmer to make sure that functions and values are used in appropriate contexts—the compiler won't warn you if you fail to do so.

Strengths

The primary benefit of functional programming is confidence, confidence that your program does what you think it does. Once you've got into thinking functionally (which can take a while, especially if you have years of experience with imperative programming), functional programs tend to be simpler, easier to reason about, and easier to test than their imperative equivalents.

Once you have a working functional solution, referential transparency allows you to parallelize it, or operate in a concurrent environment, with very little effort. Because functional code eliminates mutable state, the majority of the concurrency bugs that can show up in traditional threads and locks–based programs are impossible.

Weaknesses

Many people expect that functional code will be less efficient than its imperative equivalent. Although there are performance implications for some types of problem, the penalty is likely to be less than you fear. And any small performance hit is likely to be more than worth it for the payoff of increased robustness and scalability.

Other Languages

Java 8 has recently added a number of features that make it easier to write code in a functional style, most notably *lambda expressions* and *streams*.[6,7] Streams support *aggregate operations* that can process streams in parallel in a manner very similar to Clojure's reducers.

No description of functional programming would be complete without mentioning Haskell.[8] Haskell provides equivalents of everything we've seen in this chapter and more. For an excellent introduction to parallel and concurrent programming in Haskell, see Simon Marlow's tutorial.[9]

Final Thoughts

There's a great deal more to functional programming than we've seen in this chapter—above and beyond its excellent support for concurrency and parallelism. It seems inevitable that functional programming will play an increasingly important role in the future.

Having said that, mutable state is going to be with us for the foreseeable future. In the next chapter we'll see how Clojure supports side effects without compromising its support for concurrency.

---

6. http://docs.oracle.com/javase/tutorial/java/javaOO/lambdaexpressions.html
7. http://docs.oracle.com/javase/tutorial/collections/streams/index.html
8. http://haskell.org/
9. http://community.haskell.org/~simonmar/par-tutorial.pdf

CHAPTER 4

The Clojure Way—
Separating Identity from State

A modern hybrid passenger car combines the strengths of an internal combustion engine with those of an electric motor. Depending on context, it sometimes runs on electric power only, sometimes on gasoline only, and sometimes both simultaneously. Clojure provides a similar hybrid of functional programming and mutable state—the "Clojure Way" leverages the strengths of both to provide a particularly powerful approach to concurrent programming.

The Best of Both Worlds

While functional programming works incredibly well for some problems, some have modifying state as a fundamental element of the solution. Although it may be possible to create a functional solution to such problems, they are easier to think of in a more traditional manner. In this chapter we'll stray beyond the pure functional subset of Clojure we looked at previously and see how it helps us create concurrent solutions to such problems.

In day 1 we'll discuss atoms, the simplest of Clojure's concurrency-aware mutable datatypes, and show how, in concert with persistent data structures, they allow us to separate identity from state. In day 2 we'll explore Clojure's other mutable data structures: agents and software transactional memory. Finally, in day 3 we'll implement an algorithm using both atoms and STM and discuss the trade-offs between the two solutions.

Day 1: Atoms and Persistent Data Structures

A *pure* functional language provides no support for mutable data whatsoever. Clojure, by contrast, is *impure*—it provides a number of different types of concurrency-aware mutable variables, each of which is suitable for different use cases. These, in concert with Clojure's persistent data structures (we'll cover what *persistent* means in this context later) allow us to avoid many of the problems that traditionally afflict concurrent programs with shared mutable state.

The difference between an impure functional language and an imperative language is one of emphasis. In an imperative language, variables are mutable by default and idiomatic code modifies them frequently. In an impure functional language, variables are immutable by default and idiomatic code modifies those that aren't only when absolutely necessary. As we'll see, Clojure's mutable variables allow us to handle real-world side effects while remaining safe and consistent.

Today we'll see how Clojure's mutable variables work in concert with persistent data structures to separate identity from state. This allows multiple threads to access mutable variables concurrently without locks (and the associated danger of deadlock) and without any of the problems of escaped or hidden mutable state that we saw in *The Perils of Mutable State*, on page 50. We'll start by looking at what is arguably the simplest of Clojure's mutable variable types, the *atom*.

Atoms

An atom is an atomic variable, very similar to those we saw in *Atomic Variables*, on page 30 (in fact, Clojure's atoms are built on top of java.util.concurrent.atomic). Here's an example of creating and retrieving the value of an atom:

```
user=> (def my-atom (atom 42))
#'user/my-atom
user=> (deref my-atom)
42
user=> @my-atom
42
```

An atom is created with atom, which takes an initial value. We can find the current value of an atom with deref or @.

If you want to update an atom to a new value, use swap!:

```
user=> (swap! my-atom inc)
43
user=> @my-atom
43
```

This takes a function and passes it the current value of the atom. The new value of the atom becomes the return value from the function. We can also pass additional arguments to the function, as in this example:

```
user=> (swap! my-atom + 2)
45
```

The first argument passed to the function will be the current value of the atom, and then any additional arguments given to swap!. So in this case, the new value becomes the result of (+ 43 2).

Rarely, you might want to set an atom to a value that doesn't depend on its current value, in which case you can use reset!:

```
user=> (reset! my-atom 0)
0
user=> @my-atom
0
```

Atoms can be any type—many web applications use an atomic map to store session data, as in this example:

```
user=> (def session (atom {}))
#'user/session
user=> (swap! session assoc :username "paul")
{:username "paul"}
user=> (swap! session assoc :session-id 1234)
{:session-id 1234, :username "paul"}
```

Now that we've played with them in the REPL, let's see an example of an atom in an application.

A Multithreaded Web Service with Mutable State

In *Escapologist Mutable State*, on page 51, we discussed a hypothetical web service that managed a list of players in a tournament. In this section we'll look at the complete Clojure code for such a web service and show how Clojure's persistent data structures mean that mutable state cannot escape as it can in Java.

Clojure/TournamentServer/src/server/core.clj
```
(def players (atom ()))

(defn list-players []
  (response (json/encode @players)))

(defn create-player [player-name]
  (swap! players conj player-name)
  (status (response "") 201))
```

```
10 (defroutes app-routes
     (GET "/players" [] (list-players))
     (PUT "/players/:player-name" [player-name] (create-player player-name)))
   (defn -main [& args]
     (run-jetty (site app-routes) {:port 3000}))
```

This defines a couple of routes—a GET request to */players* will retrieve a list of the current players (in JSON format), and a PUT request to */players/name* will add a player to that list. As with the web service we saw in the last chapter, the embedded Jetty server is multithreaded, so our code will need to be thread-safe.

We'll talk about how the code works in a moment, but let's see it in action first. We can exercise it from the command line with curl:

```
$ curl localhost:3000/players
[]

$ curl -X put localhost:3000/players/john
$ curl localhost:3000/players
["john"]

$ curl -X put localhost:3000/players/paul
$ curl -X put localhost:3000/players/george
$ curl -X put localhost:3000/players/ringo
$ curl localhost:3000/players
["ringo","george","paul","john"]
```

Now let's see how this code works. The players atom (line 1) is initialized to the empty list (). A new player is added to the list with conj (line 7), and an empty response is returned with an HTTP 201 (created) status. The list of players is returned by JSON-encoding the result of fetching the value of players with @ (line 4).

This all seems very simple (and it is), but something might be worrying you about it. Both the list-players and create-player functions access players—why doesn't this code suffer from the same problem as the Java code on page 51? What happens if one thread adds an entry to the players list while another is iterating over it, converting it to JSON?

This code is thread-safe because Clojure's data structures are *persistent.*

Persistent Data Structures

Persistence in this case doesn't have anything to do with persistence on disk or within a database. Instead it refers to a data structure that always preserves its previous version when it's modified, which allows code to have a consistent view of the data in the face of modifications. We can see this easily in the REPL:

```
user=> (def mapv1 {:name "paul" :age 45})
#'user/mapv1
user=> (def mapv2 (assoc mapv1 :sex :male))
#'user/mapv2
user=> mapv1
{:age 45, :name "paul"}
user=> mapv2
{:age 45, :name "paul", :sex :male}
```

Persistent data structures *behave as though* a complete copy is made each time they're modified. If that were how they were actually implemented, they would be very inefficient and therefore of limited use (like CopyOnWriteArrayList, which we saw in *Copy on Write*, on page 34). Happily, the implementation is much more clever than that and makes use of *structure sharing*.

The easiest persistent data structure to understand is the list. Here's a simple list:

```
user=> (def listv1 (list 1 2 3))
#'user/listv1
user=> listv1
(1 2 3)
```

And here's a diagram of what it looks like in memory:

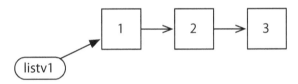

Now let's create a modified version with cons, which returns a copy of the list with an item added to the front:

```
user=> (def listv2 (cons 4 listv1))
#'user/listv2
user=> listv2
(4 1 2 3)
```

The new list can share all of the previous list—no copying necessary:

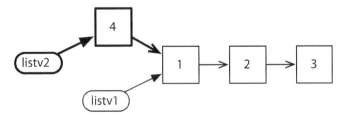

Finally, let's create another modified version:

```
user=> (def listv3 (cons 5 (rest listv1)))
#'user/listv3
user=> listv3
(5 2 3)
```

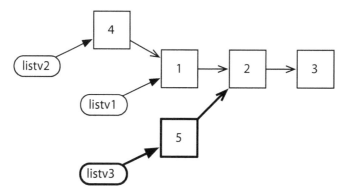

In this instance, the new list only makes use of part of the original, but copying is still not necessary.

We can't always avoid copying. Lists handle only common tails well—if we want to have two lists with different tails, we have no choice but to copy. Here's an example:

```
user=> (def listv1 (list 1 2 3 4))
#'user/listv1
user=> (def listv2 (take 2 listv1))
#'user/listv2
user=> listv2
(1 2)
```

This leads to the following in memory:

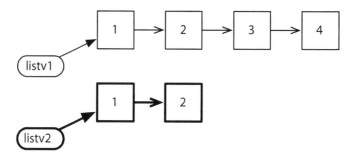

All of Clojure's collections are persistent. Persistent vectors, maps, and sets are more complex to implement than lists, but for our purposes all we need to know is that they share structure and that they provide similar performance bounds to their nonpersistent equivalents in languages like Ruby and Java.

> \|/   **Joe asks:**
> ᠄ᶠ   **Can Non-functional Data Structures Be Persistent?**
>
> It is possible to create a persistent data structure in a non-functional language. We've already seen one in Java (CopyOnWriteArrayList), and Clojure's core data structures are mostly written in Java because Clojure didn't exist when they were written, so it can certainly be done.
>
> Having said that, implementing a persistent data structure in a non-functional language is difficult—difficult to get right and difficult to do efficiently—because the language gives you no help: it's entirely up to you to enforce the persistence contract.
>
> Functional data structures, by contrast, are automatically persistent.

Identity or State?

Persistent data structures are invaluable for concurrent programming because once a thread has a reference to a data structure, it will see no changes made by any other thread. Persistent data structures separate identity from state.

What is the fuel level in your car? Right now, it might be half-full. Sometime later it'll be close to empty, and a few minutes after that (after you stop to fill up) it'll be full. The *identity* "fuel level in your car" is one thing, the *state* of which is constantly changing. "Fuel level in your car" is really a sequence of different values—at 2012-02-23 12:03 it was 0.53; at 2012-02-23 14:30 it was 0.12; and at 2012-02-23 14:31 it was 1.00.

A variable in an imperative language *complects* (interweaves, interconnects) identity and state—a single identity can only ever have a single value, making it easy to lose sight of the fact that the state is really a sequence of values over time. Persistent data structures separate identity from state—if we retrieve the current state associated with an identity, that state is immutable and unchanging, no matter what happens to the identity from which we retrieved it in the future.

Heraclitus put it this way:

> You could not step twice into the same river; for other waters are ever flowing onto you.

Most languages cling to the fallacy that the river is a single consistent entity; Clojure recognizes that it's constantly changing.

Retries

Because Clojure is functional, atoms can be lockless—internally they make use of the compareAndSet() method in java.util.concurrent.AtomicReference. That means that they're very fast and don't block (so there's no danger of deadlock). But it also means that swap! needs to handle the case where the value of the atom has been changed by another thread in between it calling the function to generate a new value and it trying to change that value.

If that happens, swap! will retry. It will discard the value returned by the function and call it again with the atom's new value. We saw something very similar to this already when using ConcurrentHashMap in the code on page 40. This means that it's essential that the function passed to swap! has no side effects—if it did, then those side effects might happen more than once.

Happily, this is where Clojure's functional nature pays off—functional code is naturally side effect–free.

Validators

Imagine that we want to have an atom that never has a negative value. We can guarantee that by providing a *validator* function when we create the atom:

```
user=> (def non-negative (atom 0 :validator #(>= % 0)))
#'user/non-negative
user=> (reset! non-negative 42)
42
user=> (reset! non-negative -1)
IllegalStateException Invalid reference state
```

A validator is a function that's called whenever an attempt is made to change the value of the atom. If it returns true the attempt can succeed, but if it returns false the attempt will be abandoned.

The validator is called *before* the value of the atom has been changed and, just like the function that's passed to swap!, it might be called more than once if swap! retries. Therefore, validators also must not have any side effects.

Watchers

Atoms can also have *watchers* associated with them:

```
user=> (def a (atom 0))
#'user/a
user=> (add-watch a :print #(println "Changed from " %3 " to " %4))
#<Atom@542ab4b1: 0>
user=> (swap! a + 2)
Changed from  0  to  2
2
```

A watcher is added by providing both a key and a watch function. The key is used to identify the watcher (so, for example, if there are multiple watchers, we can remove a specific one by providing the relevant key). The watch function is called whenever the value of the atom changes. It is given four arguments—the key that was given to add-watch, a reference to the atom, the previous value, and the new value.

In the preceding code, we're using the #(...) reader macro again to define an anonymous function that prints out the old (%3) and new (%4) values of the atom.

Unlike validators, watch functions are called after the value has changed and will only be called once, no matter how often swap! retries. A watch function can, therefore, have side effects. Note, however, that by the time the watch function is called, the value of the atom may already have changed again, so watch functions should always use the values passed as arguments and never dereference the atom.

A Hybrid Web Service

In *A Functional Web Service*, on page 75, we created a purely functional web service in Clojure. Although it worked fine, it had a couple of significant limitations—it could only handle a single transcript, and its memory consumption would grow forever. In this section we'll see how to address both of these issues while preserving the functional flavor of the original.

Session Management

We're going to allow our web service to handle multiple transcripts by introducing the concept of a *session*. Each session has a unique numerical identifier, which is generated as follows:

Clojure/TranscriptHandler/src/server/session.clj
```
(def last-session-id (atom 0))
(defn next-session-id []
  (swap! last-session-id inc))
```

This uses an atom, last-session-id, that is incremented each time we want a new session ID. As a result, each time next-session-id is called, it returns a number that is one higher than the last:

```
server.core=> (in-ns 'server.session)
#<Namespace server.session>
server.session=> (next-session-id)
1
server.session=> (next-session-id)
2
server.session=> (next-session-id)
3
```

We're going to keep track of active sessions with another atom called sessions that contains a map from session IDs to session values:

```
(def sessions (atom {}))

(defn new-session [initial]
  (let [session-id (next-session-id)]
    (swap! sessions assoc session-id initial)
    session-id))

(defn get-session [id]
  (@sessions id))
```

We create a new session by passing an initial value to new-session, which gets a new session ID and adds it to sessions by calling swap!. Retrieving a session in get-session is a simple matter of looking it up by its ID.

Session Expiration

If we're not going to continually increase the amount of memory we use, we're going to need some way to delete sessions when they're no longer in use. We could do this explicitly (with a delete-session function, perhaps), but given that we're writing a web service where we can't necessarily rely on clients cleaning up after themselves properly, we're going to implement session expiration (expiry) instead. This requires a small change to the preceding code:

Clojure/TranscriptHandler/src/server/session.clj
```
(def sessions (atom {}))

➤ (defn now []
➤   (System/currentTimeMillis))

(defn new-session [initial]
  (let [session-id (next-session-id)
➤        session (assoc initial :last-referenced (atom (now)))]
    (swap! sessions assoc session-id session)
    session-id))

(defn get-session [id]
  (let [session (@sessions id)]
➤    (reset! (:last-referenced session) (now))
    session))
```

We've added a utility function called now that returns the current time. When new-session creates a session, it adds a :last-referenced entry to the session, another atom containing the current time. This is updated with reset! whenever get-session accesses the session.

Now that every session has a :last-referenced entry, we can expire sessions by periodically checking to see whether any haven't been referenced for more than a certain amount of time:

Clojure/TranscriptHandler/src/server/session.clj
```
(defn session-expiry-time []
  (- (now) (* 10 60 1000)))
(defn expired? [session]
  (< @(:last-referenced session) (session-expiry-time)))

(defn sweep-sessions []
  (swap! sessions #(remove-vals % expired?)))
(def session-sweeper
  (schedule {:min (range 0 60 5)} sweep-sessions))
```

This uses the Schejulure library to create session-sweeper, which schedules sweep-sessions to run once every five minutes.[1] Whenever it runs, it removes (using the remove-vals function provided by the Useful library[2]) any sessions for which expired? returns true, meaning that they were last accessed before session-expiry-time (ten minutes ago).

Putting It All Together

We can now modify our web service to use sessions. First, we need a function that will create a new session:

Clojure/TranscriptHandler/src/server/core.clj
```
(defn create-session []
  (let [snippets (repeatedly promise)
        translations (delay (map translate
                                 (strings->sentences (map deref snippets))))]
    (new-session {:snippets snippets :translations translations})))
```

We're still using an infinite lazy sequence of promises to represent incoming snippets and a map over that sequence to represent translations, but these are now both stored in a session.

Next, we need to modify accept-snippet and get-translation to look up :snippets or :translations within a session:

Clojure/TranscriptHandler/src/server/core.clj
```
(defn accept-snippet [session n text]
  (deliver (nth (:snippets session) n) text))

(defn get-translation [session n]
  @(nth @(:translations session) n))
```

---

1. https://github.com/AdamClements/schejulure
2. https://github.com/flatland/useful

Finally, we define the routes that tie these functions to URIs:

Clojure/TranscriptHandler/src/server/core.clj
```
(defroutes app-routes
  (POST "/session/create" []
    (response (str (create-session))))

  (context "/session/:session-id" [session-id]
    (let [session (get-session (edn/read-string session-id))]
      (routes
        (PUT "/snippet/:n" [n :as {:keys [body]}]
          (accept-snippet session (edn/read-string n) (slurp body))
          (response "OK"))

        (GET "/translation/:n" [n]
          (response (get-translation session (edn/read-string n))))))))
```

This gives us a web service that makes judicious use of mutable data but still feels primarily functional.

Day 1 Wrap-Up

That brings us to the end of day 1. In day 2 we'll look at agents and refs, Clojure's other types of mutable variables.

What We Learned in Day 1

Clojure is an impure functional language, providing a number of types of mutable variables. Today we looked at the simplest of these, the atom.

- The difference between an imperative language and an impure functional language is one of emphasis.

  - In an imperative language, variables are mutable by default, and idiomatic code writes to variables frequently.

  - In a functional language, variables are immutable by default, and idiomatic code writes to them only when absolutely necessary.

- Because functional data structures are persistent, changes made by one thread will not affect a second thread that already has a reference to that data structure.

- This allows us to separate identity from state, recognizing the fact that the state associated with an identity is really a sequence of values over time.

Day 1 Self-Study

Find

- Karl Krukow's blog post "Understanding Clojure's PersistentVector Implementation" for an explanation of how a more complex persistent data structure than a linked list is implemented

- The follow-up to that blog post that describes the implementation of Persistent-HashMap using a "Hash Array Mapped Trie"

Do

- Extend the TournamentServer example from *A Multithreaded Web Service with Mutable State*, on page 87, to allow players to be removed from as well as added to the list.

- Extend the TranscriptServer example from *A Hybrid Web Service*, on page 93, to recover if a snippet doesn't arrive after more than ten seconds.

Day 2: Agents and Software Transactional Memory

Yesterday we looked at atoms. Today we'll look at the other types of mutable variables provided by Clojure: agents and refs. Like atoms, agents and refs are both concurrency aware and work in concert with persistent data structures to maintain the separation of identity and state. When talking about refs, we'll see how Clojure supports software transactional memory, allowing variables to be modified concurrently without locks and yet still retaining consistency.

Agents

An *agent* is similar to an atom in that it encapsulates a reference to a single value, which can be retrieved with deref or @:

```
user=> (def my-agent (agent 0))
#'user/my-agent
user=> @my-agent
0
```

The value of an agent is modified by calling send:

```
user=> (send my-agent inc)
#<Agent@2cadd45e: 1>
user=> @my-agent
1
user=> (send my-agent + 2)
#<Agent@2cadd45e: 1>
user=> @my-agent
3
```

Like swap!, send takes a function together with some optional arguments and calls that function with the current value of the agent. The new value of the agent becomes the return value of the function.

The difference is that send returns immediately (before the value of the agent has been changed)—the function passed to send is called sometime afterward. If multiple threads call send concurrently, execution of the functions passed to send is serialized: only one will execute at a time. This means that they will not be retried and can therefore contain side effects.

Joe asks:
Is an Agent an Actor?

There are some surface similarities between Clojure's agents and actors (which we'll look at in Chapter 5, *Actors*, on page 115). They're different enough that the analogy is likely to be more misleading than helpful, however:

- An agent has a value that can be retrieved directly with deref. An actor encapsulates state but provides no direct means to access it.

- An actor encapsulates behavior; an agent does not—the function that implements an action is provided by the sender.

- Actors provide sophisticated support for error detection and recovery. Agents' error reporting is much more primitive.

- Actors can be remote; agents provide no support for distribution.

- Composing actors can deadlock; composing agents cannot.

Waiting for Agent Actions to Complete

If you look at the preceding REPL session, you can see that the return value of send is a reference to the agent. And when the REPL displays that reference, it also includes the value of the agent—in this case, 1:

```
user=> (send my-agent inc)
#<Agent@2cadd45e: 1>
```

The next time, however, instead of displaying 3, it displays 1 again:

```
user=> (send my-agent + 2)
#<Agent@2cadd45e: 1>
```

This is because the function passed to send is run asynchronously, and it may or may not finish before the REPL queries the agent for its value. With a quick-running task like this, by the time the REPL retrieves the value, there's a good chance that it will have already finished; but if we provide a long-running task with Thread/sleep, you can see that this isn't normally true:

```
user=> (def my-agent (agent 0))
#'user/my-agent
user=> (send my-agent #((Thread/sleep 2000) (inc %)))
#<Agent@224e59d9: 0>
user=> @my-agent
0
user=> @my-agent
1
```

Clojure provides the await function, which blocks until all actions dispatched from the current thread to the given agent(s) have completed (there's also await-for, which allows you to specify a timeout):

```
user=> (def my-agent (agent 0))
#'user/my-agent
user=> (send my-agent #((Thread/sleep 2000) (inc %)))
#<Agent@7f5ff9d0: 0>
user=> (await my-agent)
nil
user=> @my-agent
1
```

Joe asks:
What About Send-Off and Send-Via?

As well as send, agents also support send-off and send-via. The only difference is that send executes the function it's given in a common thread pool, whereas send-off creates a new thread and send-via takes an executor as an argument.

You should use send-off or send-via if the function you pass might block (and therefore tie up the thread that it's executing on) or take a long time to execute. Other than that, the three functions are identical.

Asynchronous updates have obvious benefits over synchronous ones, especially for long-running or blocking operations. They also have added complexity, including dealing with errors. We'll see the tools that Clojure provides to help with this next.

Error Handling

Like atoms, agents also support both validators and watchers. For example, here's an agent that has a validator that ensures that the agent's value never goes negative:

```
user=> (def non-negative (agent 1 :validator (fn [new-val] (>= new-val 0))))
#'user/non-negative
```

Here's what happens if we try to decrement the agent's value until it goes negative:

```
user=> (send non-negative dec)
#<Agent@6257d812: 0>
user=> @non-negative
0
user=> (send non-negative dec)
#<Agent@6257d812: 0>
user=> @non-negative
0
```

As we hoped, the value won't go negative. But what happens if we try to use an agent after it's experienced an error?

```
user=> (send non-negative inc)
IllegalStateException Invalid reference state  clojure.lang.ARef.validate…

user=> @non-negative
0
```

Once an agent experiences an error, it enters a *failed* state by default, and attempts to dispatch new actions fail. We can find out if an agent is failed (and if it is, why) with agent-error, and we can restart it with restart-agent:

```
user=> (agent-error non-negative)
#<IllegalStateException java.lang.IllegalStateException: Invalid reference state>
user=> (restart-agent non-negative 0)
0
user=> (agent-error non-negative)
nil
user=> (send non-negative inc)
#<Agent@6257d812: 1>
user=> @non-negative
1
```

By default, agents are created with the :fail error mode. Alternatively, you can set the error mode to :continue, in which case you don't need to call restart-agent to allow an agent to process new actions after an error. The :continue error mode is the default if you set an *error handler*—a function that's automatically called whenever the agent experiences an error.

Next, we'll see a more realistic example of using an agent.

An In-Memory Log

Something I've often found helpful when working with concurrent programs is an in-memory log—traditional logging can be too heavyweight to be helpful when debugging concurrency issues, involving as it does several context-switches and IO operations for each log operation. Implementing such an in-memory log with threads and locks can be tricky, but an agent-based implementation is almost trivial:

Clojure/Logger/src/logger/core.clj
```
(def log-entries (agent []))

(defn log [entry]
  (send log-entries conj [(now) entry]))
```

Our log is an agent called log-entries initialized to an empty array. The log function uses conj to append a new entry to this array, which consists of a two-element array—the first element is a timestamp (which will be the time that send is called, not the time that conj is called by the agent—potentially sometime later), and the second element is the log message.

Here's a REPL session that shows it in action:

```
logger.core=> (log "Something happened")
#<Agent@bd99597: [[1366822537794 "Something happened"]]>
logger.core=> (log "Something else happened")
#<Agent@bd99597: [[1366822538932 "Something happened"]]>
logger.core=> @log-entries
[[1366822537794 "Something happened"] [1366822538932 "Something else happened"]]
```

In the next section we'll look at the remaining type of shared mutable variable supported by Clojure, the ref.

Software Transactional Memory

Refs are more sophisticated than atoms and agents, providing software transactional memory (STM). Unlike atoms and agents, which only support modifications of a single variable at a time, STM allows us to make concurrent, coordinated changes to multiple variables, much like a database transaction allows concurrent, coordinated changes to multiple records.

Like both atoms and agents, a ref encapsulates a reference to single value, which can be retrieved with deref or @:

```
user=> (def my-ref (ref 0))
#'user/my-ref
user=> @my-ref
0
```

The value of a ref can be set with ref-set, and the equivalent of swap! or send is alter. However, using them isn't as simple as just calling them:

```
user=> (ref-set my-ref 42)
IllegalStateException No transaction running

user=> (alter my-ref inc)
IllegalStateException No transaction running
```

Modifying the value of a ref is possible only inside a transaction.

Transactions

STM transactions are *atomic*, *consistent*, and *isolated*:

Atomic:

From the point of view of code running in another transaction, either all of the side effects of a transaction take place, or none of them do.

Consistent:

Transactions guarantee preservation of invariants specified through validators (like those we've already seen for atoms and agents). If any of the changes attempted by a transaction fail to validate, none of the changes will be made.

Isolated:

Although multiple transactions can execute concurrently, the effect of concurrent transactions will be indistinguishable from those transactions running sequentially.

You may recognize these as the first three of the ACID properties supported by many databases. The missing property is *durability*—STM data will not survive power loss or crashes. If you need durability, you need to use a database.

A transaction is created with dosync:

```
user=> (dosync (ref-set my-ref 42))
42
user=> @my-ref
42
user=> (dosync (alter my-ref inc))
43
user=> @my-ref
43
```

Everything within the body of dosync constitutes a single transaction.

> ### Joe asks:
> ## Are Transactions Really Isolated?
>
> Completely isolated transactions are the right choice for most situations, but isolation can be an excessively strong constraint for some use cases. Clojure does allow you to relax it when appropriate by using commute instead of alter.
>
> Although commute can be a useful optimization, understanding when it's appropriate can be subtle, and we won't cover it further in this book.

Multiple Refs

Most interesting transactions involve more than one ref (otherwise, we might just as well use an atom or agent). The classic example of a transaction is transferring money between accounts—we never want to see an occasion where money has been debited from one account and not credited to the other. Here's a function where both the debit and credit will occur, or neither will:

Clojure/Transfer/src/transfer/core.clj
```
(defn transfer [from to amount]
  (dosync
    (alter from - amount)
    (alter to + amount)))
```

Here's an example of it in use:

```
user=> (def checking (ref 1000))
#'user/checking
user=> (def savings (ref 2000))
#'user/savings
user=> (transfer savings checking 100)
1100
user=> @checking
1100
user=> @savings
1900
```

If the STM runtime detects that concurrent transactions are trying to make conflicting changes, one or more of the transactions will be retried. This means that, as when modifying an atom, transactions should not have side effects.

Retrying Transactions

In the spirit of "show, don't tell," let's see if we can catch a transaction being retried by stress-testing our transfer function. We're going to start by instrumenting it as follows:

Clojure/Transfer/src/transfer/core.clj
```
(def attempts (atom 0))
(def transfers (agent 0))

(defn transfer [from to amount]
  (dosync
    (swap! attempts inc) // Side-effect in transaction - DON'T DO THIS
    (send transfers inc)
    (alter from - amount)
    (alter to + amount)))
```

We're deliberately breaking the "no side effects" rule by modifying an atom within a transaction. In this case, it's OK because we're doing it to illustrate that transactions are being retried, but please don't write code like this in production.

As well as keeping a count in an atom, we're keeping a count in an agent. We'll see why very shortly.

Here's a main method that stress-tests this instrumented transfer function:

Clojure/Transfer/src/transfer/core.clj
```
(def checking (ref 10000))
(def savings (ref 20000))

(defn stress-thread [from to iterations amount]
  (Thread. #(dotimes [_ iterations] (transfer from to amount))))

(defn -main [& args]
  (println "Before: Checking =" @checking " Savings =" @savings)
  (let [t1 (stress-thread checking savings 100 100)
        t2 (stress-thread savings checking 200 100)]
    (.start t1)
    (.start t2)
    (.join t1)
    (.join t2))
  (await transfers)
  (println "Attempts: " @attempts)
  (println "Transfers: " @transfers)
  (println "After: Checking =" @checking " Savings =" @savings))
```

It creates two threads. One thread transfers $100 from the checking account to the savings account 100 times, and the other transfers $100 from the savings account to the checking account 200 times. Here's what I see when I run this:

```
Before: Checking = 10000  Savings = 20000
Attempts:  638
Transfers:  300
After: Checking = 20000  Savings = 10000
```

This is excellent news—the final result is exactly what we would expect, so the STM runtime has successfully ensured that our concurrent transactions have given us the right result. The cost is that it had to perform a number of retries (338 on this occasion) to do so, but the payoff is no locking and no danger of deadlock.

Of course, this isn't a realistic example—two threads both accessing the same refs in a tight loop are guaranteed to conflict with each other. In practice, retries will be much rarer than this in a well-designed system.

Safe Side Effects in Transactions

You may have noticed that although the count maintained by our atom was much larger, the count maintained by our agent was exactly equal to the number of transactions. There is a good reason for this—agents are transaction aware.

If you use send to modify an agent within a transaction, that send will take place only if the transaction succeeds. Therefore, if you want to achieve some side effect when a transaction succeeds, using send is an excellent way to do so.

Joe asks:
What's with the Exclamation Marks?

You may have noticed that some functions have names ending in an exclamation mark—what does this naming convention convey?

Clojure uses an exclamation mark to indicate that functions like swap! and reset! are not transaction-safe. By contrast, we know that we can safely update an agent within a transaction because the function that updates an agent's value is send instead of send!.

Shared Mutable State in Clojure

We've now seen all three of the mechanisms that Clojure provides to support shared mutable state. Each has its own use cases.

An atom allows you to make synchronous changes to a single value—synchronous because when swap! returns, the update has taken place. Updates to one atom are not coordinated with other updates.

An agent allows you to make asynchronous changes to a single value—asynchronous because the update takes place after send returns. Updates to one agent are not coordinated with other updates.

Refs allow you to make synchronous, coordinated changes to multiple values.

Day 2 Wrap-Up

That brings us to the end of day 2. In day 3 we'll see some more extended examples of using mutable variables in Clojure together with some guidance on when to use the different types.

What We Learned in Day 2

In addition to atoms, Clojure also provides agents and refs:

- Atoms enable *independent, synchronous* changes to *single* values.
- Agents enable *independent, asynchronous* changes to *single* values.
- Refs enable *coordinated, synchronous* changes to *multiple* values.

Day 2 Self-Study

Find

- Rich Hickey's presentation "Persistent Data Structures and Managed References: Clojure's Approach to Identity and State"

- Rich Hickey's presentation "Simple Made Easy"

Do

- Extend the TournamentServer from *A Multithreaded Web Service with Mutable State*, on page 87, by using refs and transactions to implement a server that runs a tic-tac-toe tournament.

- Implement a persistent binary search tree using lists to represent nodes. What's the worst-case amount of copying you need to perform? What about the average case?

- Look up *finger trees* and implement your binary search tree using a finger tree. What effect does that have on the average performance and worst-case performance?

Day 3: In Depth

We've now seen all of the ingredients of the "Clojure Way." Today we'll look at some more involved examples of those ingredients in use and gain some insights into how to choose between atoms and STM when faced with a particular concurrency problem.

Dining Philosophers with STM

To start off, we'll revisit the "dining philosophers" problem we examined in Chapter 2, *Threads and Locks*, on page 9, and construct a solution using Clojure's software transactional memory. Our solution will be very similar to (but, as you'll soon see, much simpler than) the condition-variable-based solution from *Condition Variables*, on page 28.

We're going to represent a philosopher as a ref, the value of which contains the philosopher's current state (either :thinking or :eating). Those refs are stored in a vector called philosophers:

Clojure/DiningPhilosphersSTM/src/philosophers/core.clj
```
(def philosophers (into [] (repeatedly 5 #(ref :thinking))))
```

Each philosopher has an associated thread:

Clojure/DiningPhilosphersSTM/src/philosophers/core.clj
```
Line 1  (defn think []
          (Thread/sleep (rand 1000)))

        (defn eat []
     5    (Thread/sleep (rand 1000)))

        (defn philosopher-thread [n]
          (Thread.
            #(let [philosopher (philosophers n)
    10             left (philosophers (mod (- n 1) 5))
                   right (philosophers (mod (+ n 1) 5))]
               (while true
                 (think)
                 (when (claim-chopsticks philosopher left right)
    15             (eat)
                   (release-chopsticks philosopher))))))

        (defn -main [& args]
          (let [threads (map philosopher-thread (range 5))]
    20      (doseq [thread threads] (.start thread))
            (doseq [thread threads] (.join thread))))
```

As with the Java solution, each thread loops forever (line 12), alternating between thinking and attempting to eat. If claim-chopsticks succeeds (line 14), the when control structure first calls eat and then calls release-chopsticks.

The implementation of release-chopsticks is straightforward:

Clojure/DiningPhilosphersSTM/src/philosophers/core.clj
```
(defn release-chopsticks [philosopher]
  (dosync (ref-set philosopher :thinking)))
```

We simply create a transaction with dosync and set our state to :thinking with ref-set.

A First Attempt

The interesting function is claim-chopsticks—here's a first attempt at an implementation:

```
(defn claim-chopsticks [philosopher left right]
  (dosync
    (when (and (= @left :thinking) (= @right :thinking))
      (ref-set philosopher :eating))))
```

As with release-chopsticks, we start by creating a transaction. Within that transaction we check the state of the philosophers to our left and right—if they're both :thinking, we set our status to :eating with ref-set. Because when returns nil if the condition it's given is false, claim-chopsticks will also return nil if we're unable to claim both chopsticks and start eating.

If you try running with this implementation, at first glance it will appear to work. Occasionally, however, you'll see adjacent philosophers eating, which should be impossible, as they share a chopstick. So what's going on?

The problem is that we're accessing the values of left and right with @. Clojure's STM guarantees that no two transactions will make inconsistent modifications to the same ref, but we're not modifying left or right, just examining their values. Some other transaction could modify them, invalidating the condition that adjacent philosophers can't eat simultaneously.

Ensuring That a Value Does Not Change

The solution is to examine left and right with ensure instead of @:

Clojure/DiningPhilosphersSTM/src/philosophers/core.clj
```
(defn claim-chopsticks [philosopher left right]
  (dosync
    (when (and (= (ensure left) :thinking) (= (ensure right) :thinking))
      (ref-set philosopher :eating))))
```

As its name suggests, ensure ensures that the value of the ref it returns won't be changed by another transaction. It's worth comparing this solution to our earlier lock-based solutions. Not only is it significantly simpler, but because it's lockless, it's impossible for it to deadlock.

In the next section we'll look at an alternative implementation that uses a single atom instead of multiple refs and transactions.

Dining Philosophers Without STM

An STM-based approach isn't the only possible solution to dining philosophers in Clojure. Instead of representing each philosopher as a ref and using transactions to ensure that updates to those refs are coordinated, we can use a single atom to represent the state of all the philosophers:

Clojure/DiningPhilosphersAtom/src/philosophers/core.clj
```
(def philosophers (atom (into [] (repeat 5 :thinking))))
```

Its value is a vector of states. If philosophers 0 and 3 are eating, for example, it would be this:

```
[:eating :thinking :thinking :eating :thinking]
```

We need to make a small change to philosopher-thread, as we'll now be referring to a particular philosopher by its index in the array:

Clojure/DiningPhilosphersAtom/src/philosophers/core.clj
```
(defn philosopher-thread [philosopher]
  (Thread.
    #(let [left (mod (- philosopher 1) 5)
           right (mod (+ philosopher 1) 5)]
      (while true
        (think)
        (when (claim-chopsticks! philosopher left right)
          (eat)
          (release-chopsticks! philosopher))))))
```

Implementing release-chopsticks! is just a question of using swap! to set the relevant position in the vector to :thinking:

Clojure/DiningPhilosphersAtom/src/philosophers/core.clj
```
(defn release-chopsticks! [philosopher]
  (swap! philosophers assoc philosopher :thinking))
```

This code makes use of assoc, which we've previously seen used only with a map, but it behaves exactly as you might imagine:

```
user=> (assoc [:a :a :a :a] 2 :b)
[:a :a :b :a]
```

Finally, as before, the most interesting function to implement is claim-chopsticks!:

Clojure/DiningPhilosphersAtom/src/philosophers/core.clj
```
(defn claim-chopsticks! [philosopher left right]
  (swap! philosophers
    (fn [ps]
      (if (and (= (ps left) :thinking) (= (ps right) :thinking))
        (assoc ps philosopher :eating)
        ps)))
  (= (@philosophers philosopher) :eating))
```

The anonymous function passed to swap! takes the current value of the philosophers vector and checks the state of the adjacent philosophers. If they're both thinking, it uses assoc to modify the state of the current philosopher to :eating; otherwise it returns the current value of the vector unmodified.

The last line of claim-chopsticks! checks the new value of philosophers to see whether the swap! successfully modified the state of the current philosopher to :eating.

So we've now seen two "dining philosophers" implementations, one that uses STM and one that doesn't. Is there any reason to prefer one over the other?

Atoms or STM?

As we saw in *Shared Mutable State in Clojure*, on page 105, atoms enable independent changes to single values, whereas refs enable coordinated changes to multiple values. These are quite different sets of capabilities, but as we've seen in this section, it's relatively easy to take an STM-based solution that uses multiple refs and turn it into a solution that uses a single atom instead.

It turns out that this isn't unusual—whenever we need to coordinate modifications of multiple values we can either use multiple refs and coordinate access to them with transactions or collect those values together into a compound data structure stored in a single atom.

So how do you choose?

In many ways it's a question of style and personal preference—both approaches work, so go with whichever seems clearest to you. There will also be differences in relative performance that will depend on the details of your problem and its access patterns, so you should also let the stopwatch (together with your load-test suite) be your guide.

Having said that, although STM gets the headlines, experienced Clojure programmers tend to find that atoms suffice for most problems, as the language's functional nature leads to minimal use of mutable data. As always, the simplest approach that will work is your friend.

Custom Concurrency

Our atom-based "dining philosophers" code works, but the implementation of claim-chopsticks! (see the code on page 109) isn't particularly elegant. Surely it should be possible to avoid the check after calling swap! to see if we were able to claim the chopsticks? Ideally, we'd like a version of swap! that takes a predicate and only swaps the value if the predicate is true. That would enable us to rewrite claim-chopsticks! like this:

Clojure/DiningPhilosphersAtom2/src/philosophers/core.clj
```
(defn claim-chopsticks! [philosopher left right]
  (swap-when! philosophers
    #(and (= (%1 left) :thinking) (= (%1 right) :thinking))
    assoc philosopher :eating))
```

Although Clojure provides no such function, there's no reason we shouldn't write one ourselves:

Clojure/DiningPhilosphersAtom2/src/philosophers/util.clj
```
Line 1 (defn swap-when!
    "If (pred current-value-of-atom) is true, atomically swaps the value
    of the atom to become (apply f current-value-of-atom args). Note that
    both pred and f may be called multiple times and thus should be free
  5 of side effects. Returns the value that was swapped in if the
    predicate was true, nil otherwise."
    [a pred f & args]
    (loop []
      (let [old @a]
  10     (if (pred old)
          (let [new (apply f old args)]
            (if (compare-and-set! a old new)
              new
              (recur)))
  15       nil))))
```

This introduces quite a bit of new stuff. Firstly, the function has a *doc-string*—a string in between the defn and the parameter list—that describes its behavior. This is good practice for any function, but particularly so for utility functions like this that are designed for reuse. As well as forming documentation within the code, doc-strings can be accessed from within the REPL:

```
philosophers.core=> (require '[philosophers.util :refer :all])
nil
philosophers.core=> (clojure.repl/doc swap-when!)
-------------------------
philosophers.util/swap-when!
([atom pred f & args])
  If (pred current-value-of-atom) is true, atomically swaps the value
  of the atom to become (apply f current-value-of-atom args). Note that
  both pred and f may be called multiple times and thus should be free
  of side effects. Returns the value that was swapped in if the
  predicate was true, nil otherwise.
```

The ampersand (&) in the argument list says that swap-when! can take a variable number of arguments (similar to an ellipsis in Java or asterisk in Ruby). Any additional arguments will be captured as an array and bound to args. We use apply, which unpacks its last argument, to pass these additional arguments to f (line 11)—for example, the following are equivalent ways to invoke +:

```
user=> (apply + 1 2 [3 4 5])
15
user=> (+ 1 2 3 4 5)
15
```

Instead of using swap!, the implementation makes use of the low-level compare-and-set! function (line 12). This takes an atom together with old and new values —it atomically sets the value of the atom to the new value if and only if its current value is equal to the old one.

If compare-and-set! succeeds, we return the new value. If it doesn't, we use recur (line 14) to loop back to line 8.

Joe asks:
What Is Loop/Recur?

Unlike many functional languages, Clojure does not provide tail-call elimination, so idiomatic Clojure makes very little use of recursion. Instead, Clojure provides loop/recur.

The loop macro defines a target that recur can jump to (reminiscent of setjmp() and longjmp() in C/C++). For more detail on how this works, see the Clojure documentation.

Day 3 Wrap-Up

This brings us to the end of day 3 and our discussion of how Clojure combines functional programming with concurrency-aware mutable variables.

What We Learned in Day 3

Clojure's functional nature leads to code with few mutable variables. Typically this means that simple atom-based concurrency is sufficient:

• STM-based code in which multiple refs are coordinated through transactions can be transformed into an agent-based solution with those refs consolidated into a single compound data structure accessed via an agent.

• The choice between an STM and an agent-based solution is largely one of style and performance characteristics.

• Custom concurrency constructs can make code simpler and clearer.

Day 3 Self-Study

Find

- Rich Hickey's presentation "The Database as a Value"—note how Datomic effectively treats the entire database as a single value.[3]

Do

- Modify the extended TournamentServer from the exercises at the end of day 2 to use atoms instead of refs and transactions. Which solution is simpler? Which is easier to read? Which provides better performance?

Wrap-Up

Clojure takes a pragmatic approach to concurrency (very appropriate for this Pragmatic Bookshelf title). Recognizing that most of the difficulties with concurrent programming arise from shared mutable state, Clojure is a functional language that facilitates referentially transparent code that is free from side effects. But recognizing that most interesting problems necessarily involve the maintenance of *some* mutable state, it supports a number of concurrency-safe types of mutable variables.

Strengths

For obvious reasons, the strengths of the "Clojure Way" build upon those for functional programming that we saw in the previous chapter. Clojure allows you to solve problems functionally when that's the natural approach, but step outside of pure functional programming when appropriate.

By contrast with variables in traditional imperative languages, which complect identity and state, Clojure's persistent data structures allow its mutable variables to keep identity and state separate. This eliminates a wide range of common problems with lock-based programs. Experienced Clojure programmers find that the idiomatic solution to a concurrent problem often "just works."

Weaknesses

The primary weakness of the "Clojure Way" is that it provides no support for distributed (geographically or otherwise) programming. Related to this, it has no direct support for fault tolerance.

---

3.   http://www.datomic.com

Of course, because it runs on the JVM, there are various third-party libraries available that can be used from Clojure to provide such support (one of these is Akka,[4] which, among other things, supports the actor model that we'll be looking at in the next chapter), but use of such libraries steps outside of idiomatic Clojure.

Other Languages

Although its pure functional nature means that it has a somewhat different "feel," concurrent Haskell provides very similar functionality to what we've seen in this chapter. In particular, it provides a full STM implementation, an excellent introduction to which can be found in Simon Peyton Jones's *Beautiful Concurrency*.[5]

In addition, there are STM implementations available for most mainstream languages, not the least of which is GCC.[6] Having said that, there is evidence that STM provides a less compelling solution when coupled with an imperative language.[7]

Final Thoughts

Clojure has found a good balance between functional programming and mutable state, allowing programmers with experience in imperative languages to get started more easily than they might in a pure functional language. And yet it does so while retaining most of functional programming's benefits, in particular its excellent support for concurrency.

In large part, Clojure accomplishes this by retaining shared mutable state, but with carefully thought-out concurrency-aware semantics. In the next section we'll look at actors, which do away with shared mutable state altogether.

---

4. http://blog.darevay.com/2011/06/clojure-and-akka-a-match-made-in/
5. http://research.microsoft.com/pubs/74063/beautiful.pdf
6. http://gcc.gnu.org/wiki/TransactionalMemory
7. http://www.infoq.com/news/2010/05/STM-Dropped

CHAPTER 5

Actors

An actor is like a rental car—quick and easy to get a hold of when you want one, and if it breaks down you don't bother trying to fix it; you just call the rental company and another one is delivered to you.

The actor model is a general-purpose concurrent programming model with particularly wide applicability. It targets both shared- and distributed-memory architectures, facilitates geographical distribution, and provides especially strong support for fault tolerance and resilience.

More Object-Oriented than Objects

Functional programming avoids the problems associated with shared mutable state by avoiding mutable state. Actor programming, by contrast, retains mutable state but avoids sharing it.

An actor is like an object in an object-oriented (OO) program—it encapsulates state and communicates with other actors by exchanging messages. The difference is that actors run concurrently with each other and, unlike OO-style message passing (which is really just calling a method), actors *really* communicate by sending messages to each other.

Although the actor model is a general approach to concurrency that can be used with almost any language, it's most commonly associated with Erlang.[1] We're going to cover actors in Elixir,[2] a relatively new language that runs on the Erlang virtual machine (BEAM).

Like Clojure (and Erlang), Elixir is an impure, dynamically typed functional language. If you're familiar with Java or Ruby, you should find it easy enough

---

1.   http://www.erlang.org/
2.   http://elixir-lang.org/

to read. This isn't going to be an Elixir tutorial (this is a book about concurrency, after all, not programming languages), but I'll introduce the important language features we're using as we go along. There may be things you just have to take on faith if you're not already familiar with the language—I recommend *Programming Elixir [Tho14]* if you want to go deeper.

In day 1 we'll see the basics of the actor model—creating actors and sending and receiving messages. In day 2 we'll see how failure detection, coupled with the "let it crash" philosophy, allows actor programs to be fault-tolerant. Finally, in day 3 we'll see how actors' support for distributed programming allows us to both scale beyond a single machine and recover from failure of one or more of those machines.

Day 1: Messages and Mailboxes

Today we'll see how to create and stop processes, send and receive messages, and detect when a process has terminated.

 Joe asks:
Actor or Process?

In Erlang, and therefore Elixir, an actor is called a *process*. In most environments a process is a heavyweight entity that consumes lots of resources and is expensive to create. An Elixir process, by contrast, is very lightweight—lighter weight even than most systems' threads, both in terms of resource consumption and startup cost. Elixir programs typically create thousands of processes without problems and don't normally need to resort to the equivalent of thread pools (see *Thread-Creation Redux*, on page 33).

Our First Actor

Let's dive straight in with an example of creating a simple actor and sending it some messages. We're going to construct a "talker" actor that knows how to say a few simple phrases in response to messages.

The messages we'll be sending are *tuples*—sequences of values. In Elixir, a tuple is written using curly brackets, like this:

```
{:foo, "this", 42}
```

This is a 3-tuple (or *triple*), where the first element is a keyword (Elixir's keywords are very similar to Clojure's, even down to the initial colon syntax), the second a string, and the third an integer.

Here's the code for our actor:

Actors/hello_actors/hello_actors.exs
```
defmodule Talker do
  def loop do
    receive do
      {:greet, name} -> IO.puts("Hello #{name}")
      {:praise, name} -> IO.puts("#{name}, you're amazing")
      {:celebrate, name, age} -> IO.puts("Here's to another #{age} years, #{name}")
    end
    loop
  end
end
```

We'll pick through this code in more detail soon, but we're defining an actor that knows how to receive three different kinds of messages and prints an appropriate string when it receives each of them.

Here's code that creates an instance of our actor and sends it a few messages:

Actors/hello_actors/hello_actors.exs
```
pid = spawn(&Talker.loop/0)
send(pid, {:greet, "Huey"})
send(pid, {:praise, "Dewey"})
send(pid, {:celebrate, "Louie", 16})
sleep(1000)
```

First, we *spawn* an instance of our actor, receiving a *process identifier* that we bind to the variable pid. A process simply executes a function, in this case the loop() function within the Talker module, which takes zero arguments.

Next, we send three messages to our newly created actor and finally sleep for a while to give it time to process those messages (using sleep() isn't the best approach—we'll see how to do this better soon).

Here's what you should see when you run it:

```
Hello Huey
Dewey, you're amazing
Here's to another 16 years, Louie
```

Now that we've seen how to create an actor and send messages to it, let's see what's going on under the hood.

Mailboxes Are Queues

One of the most important features of actor programming is that messages are sent *asynchronously*. Instead of being sent directly to an actor, they are placed in a *mailbox*:

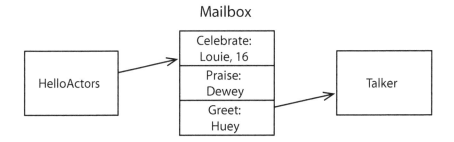

This means that actors are *decoupled*—actors run at their own speed and don't block when sending messages.

An actor runs concurrently with other actors but handles messages sequentially, in the order they were added to the mailbox, moving on to the next message only when it's finished processing the current message. We only have to worry about concurrency when sending messages.

Receiving Messages

An actor typically sits in an infinite loop, waiting for a message to arrive with receive and then processing it. Here's Talker's loop again:

Actors/hello_actors/hello_actors.exs
```
def loop do
  receive do
    {:greet, name} -> IO.puts("Hello #{name}")
    {:praise, name} -> IO.puts("#{name}, you're amazing")
    {:celebrate, name, age} -> IO.puts("Here's to another #{age} years, #{name}")
  end
  loop
end
```

This function implements an infinite loop by calling itself recursively. The receive block waits for a message and then uses pattern matching to work out how to handle it. Incoming messages are compared against each pattern in turn—if a message matches, the variables in the pattern (name and age) are bound to the values in the message and the code to the right of the arrow (->) is executed. That code prints a message constructed using *string interpolation*—the code within each #{...} is evaluated and the resulting value inserted into the string.

The code on page 117 sleeps for a second to allow messages to be processed before exiting. This is an unsatisfactory solution—we can do better.

\\//
〜ᵕ〜   **Joe asks:**

Won't Infinite Recursion Blow Up the Stack?

You might be worried that a function like Talker's loop(), which recurses infinitely, would result in the stack growing forever. Happily, there's no need to worry—in common with many functional languages (Clojure being a prominent exception—see *What Is Loop/Recur?*, on page 112), Elixir implements *tail-call elimination*. Tail-call elimination, as its name suggests, replaces a recursive call with a simple jump if the last thing the function does is call itself.

Linking Processes

We need two things to be able to shut down cleanly. First we need a way to tell our actor to stop when it's finished processing all the messages in its queue. And second, we need some way to know that it has done so.

We can achieve the first of these by having our actor handle an explicit shutdown message (similar to the poison pill we saw in the code on page 38):

Actors/hello_actors/hello_actors2.exs

```elixir
defmodule Talker do
  def loop do
    receive do
      {:greet, name} -> IO.puts("Hello #{name}")
      {:praise, name} -> IO.puts("#{name}, you're amazing")
      {:celebrate, name, age} -> IO.puts("Here's to another #{age} years, #{name}")
      {:shutdown} -> exit(:normal)
    end
    loop
  end
end
```

And second, we need a way to tell that it has exited, which we can do by setting :trap_exit to true and *linking* to it by using spawn_link() instead of spawn():

Actors/hello_actors/hello_actors2.exs

```elixir
Process.flag(:trap_exit, true)
pid = spawn_link(&Talker.loop/0)
```

This means that we'll be notified (with a system-generated message) when the spawned process terminates. The message that's sent is a triple of this form:

```elixir
{:EXIT, pid, reason}
```

All that remains is to send the shutdown message and listen for the exit message:

Actors/hello_actors/hello_actors2.exs
```
send(pid, {:greet, "Huey"})
send(pid, {:praise, "Dewey"})
send(pid, {:celebrate, "Louie", 16})
send(pid, {:shutdown})

receive do
  {:EXIT, ^pid, reason} -> IO.puts("Talker has exited (#{reason})")
end
```

The ^ (caret) in the receive pattern indicates that instead of binding the second element of the tuple to pid, we want to match a message where the second element has the value that's already bound to pid.

Here's what you should see if you run this new version:

```
Hello Huey
Dewey, you're amazing
Here's to another 16 years, Louie
Talker has exited (normal)
```

We'll talk about linking in much more detail tomorrow.

Stateful Actors

Our Talker actor is stateless. It's tempting to think that you would need mutable variables to create a stateful actor, but in fact all we need is recursion. Here, for example, is an actor that maintains a count that increments each time it receives a message:

Actors/counter/counter.ex
```
defmodule Counter do
  def loop(count) do
    receive do
      {:next} ->
        IO.puts("Current count: #{count}")
        loop(count + 1)
    end
  end
end
```

Let's see this in action in Interactive Elixir, iex (the Elixir REPL):

```
iex(1)> counter = spawn(Counter, :loop, [1])
#PID<0.47.0>
iex(2)> send(counter, {:next})
Current count: 1
{:next}
iex(3)> send(counter, {:next})
{:next}
Current count: 2
```

```
iex(4)> send(counter, {:next})
{:next}
Current count: 3
```

We start by using the three-argument form of spawn(), which takes a module name, the name of a function within that module, and a list of arguments, so that we can pass an initial count to Counter.loop(). Then, as we expect, it prints a different number each time we send it a {:next} message—a stateful actor with not a mutable variable in sight. And furthermore, this is an actor that can safely access that state without any concurrency bugs, because messages are handled sequentially.

Hiding Messages Behind an API

Our Counter actor works, but it's not very convenient to use. We need to remember which arguments to pass to spawn() and exactly which message(s) it understands (is it {:next}, :next, or {:increment}?). With that in mind, instead of calling spawn() and sending messages directly to an actor, it's common practice to provide a set of API functions:

Actors/counter/counter.ex
```
defmodule Counter do
➤   def start(count) do
➤     spawn(__MODULE__, :loop, [count])
➤   end
➤   def next(counter) do
➤     send(counter, {:next})
➤   end
    def loop(count) do
      receive do
        {:next} ->
          IO.puts("Current count: #{count}")
          loop(count + 1)
      end
    end
end
```

The implementation of start() makes use of the *pseudo-variable* __MODULE__, which evaluates to the name of the current module. These make using our actor much neater and less error prone:

```
iex(1)> counter = Counter.start(42)
#PID<0.44.0>
iex(2)> Counter.next(counter)
Current count: 42
{:next}
iex(3)> Counter.next(counter)
{:next}
Current count: 43
```

An actor that simply prints its state isn't very useful. Next we'll see how to implement bidirectional communication so that one actor can query another.

Bidirectional Communication

As we've already seen, messages between actors are sent asynchronously—the sender doesn't block. But what happens if we want to receive a reply? What if, for example, we want our Counter actor to return the next number rather than just printing it?

The actor model doesn't provide direct support for replies, but it's something we can build for ourselves very easily by including the identifier of the sending process in the message, which allows the recipient to send a reply:

```
Actors/counter/counter2.ex
defmodule Counter do
  def start(count) do
    spawn(__MODULE__, :loop, [count])
  end
  def next(counter) do
    ref = make_ref()
    send(counter, {:next, self(), ref})
    receive do
      {:ok, ^ref, count} -> count
    end
  end
  def loop(count) do
    receive do
      {:next, sender, ref} ->
        send(sender, {:ok, ref, count})
        loop(count + 1)
    end
  end
end
```

Instead of printing the count, this version sends it back to the sender of the original message as a triple of the following form:

```
{:ok, ref, count}
```

Here ref is a unique reference generated by the sender with make_ref().

Let's prove that it works:

```
iex(1)> counter = Counter.start(42)
#PID<0.47.0>
iex(2)> Counter.next(counter)
42
iex(3)> Counter.next(counter)
43
```

> \\\// **Joe asks:**
> ≚ **Why Reply with a Tuple?**
>
> Our new version of Counter could have simply replied with the count instead of a tuple:
>
> ```
> {:next, sender} ->
>   send(sender, count)
> ```
>
> Although this would certainly work, idiomatic Elixir typically uses tuples as messages, where the first element indicates success or failure. In this instance, we also include a unique reference generated by the client, which ensures that the reply will be correctly identified in the event that there are multiple messages waiting in the client's mailbox.

We'll make one further improvement to Counter before we move on—giving it a name to make it discoverable.

Naming Processes

A message is sent to a process, which means that you need to know its identifier. If it's a process that you created, this is easy, but how do you send a message to a process that you didn't create?

There are various ways to address this, but one of the most convenient is to register a name for the process:

```
iex(1)> pid = Counter.start(42)
#PID<0.47.0>
iex(2)> Process.register(pid, :counter)
true
iex(3)> counter = Process.whereis(:counter)
#PID<0.47.0>
iex(4)> Counter.next(counter)
42
```

We associate a process identifier with a name with Process.register() and retrieve it with Process.whereis(). We can see all registered processes with Process.registered():

```
iex(5)> Process.registered
[:kernel_sup, :init, :code_server, :user, :standard_error_sup,
 :global_name_server, :application_controller, :file_server_2, :user_drv,
 :kernel_safe_sup, :standard_error, :global_group, :error_logger,
 :elixir_counter, :counter, :elixir_code_server, :erl_prim_loader, :elixir_sup,
 :rex, :inet_db]
```

As you can see, the virtual machine automatically registers a number of standard processes at startup. Finally, as a convenience, send() can take a process name instead of a process identifier directly:

```
iex(6)> send(:counter, {:next, self(), make_ref()})
{:next, #PID<0.45.0>, #Reference<0.0.0.107>}
iex(7)> receive do msg -> msg end
{:ok, #Reference<0.0.0.107>, 43}
```

We can use this to modify Counter's API so that it doesn't require a process identifier each time we call it:

Actors/counter/counter3.ex
```
def start(count) do
  pid = spawn(__MODULE__, :loop, [count])
  Process.register(pid, :counter)
  pid
end
def next do
  ref = make_ref()
  send(:counter, {:next, self(), ref})
  receive do
    {:ok, ^ref, count} -> count
  end
end
```

Here it is in use:

```
iex(1)> Counter.start(42)
#PID<0.47.0>
iex(2)> Counter.next
42
iex(3)> Counter.next
43
```

The last thing we'll do today is use what we've seen to create a parallel map function similar to Clojure's pmap. But first a brief interlude.

Interlude—First-Class Functions

Like all functional languages, functions in Elixir are first class—we can bind them to variables, pass them as arguments, and generally treat them as data. Here, for example, is an iex session that shows how we can pass an anonymous function to Enum.map to double every element in an array:

```
iex(1)> Enum.map([1, 2, 3, 4], fn(x) -> x * 2 end)
[2, 4, 6, 8]
```

Elixir also provides a shorthand &(...) syntax for defining anonymous functions that's similar to Clojure's #(...) reader macro:

```
iex(2)> Enum.map([1, 2, 3, 4], &(&1 * 2))
[2, 4, 6, 8]
iex(3)> Enum.reduce([1, 2, 3, 4], 0, &(&1 + &2))
10
```

Given a variable that's been bound to a function, we can call that function with the . (apply) operator:

```
iex(4)> double = &(&1 * 2)
#Function<erl_eval.6.80484245>
iex(5)> double.(3)
6
```

And finally, we can create functions that return functions:

```
iex(6)> twice = fn(fun) -> fn(x) -> fun.(fun.(x)) end end
#Function<erl_eval.6.80484245>
iex(7)> twice.(double).(3)
12
```

We now have all the tools we need to construct our parallel map().

Parallel Map

As we saw earlier, Elixir provides a map() function that can be used to map a function over a collection, but it does so sequentially. Here's an alternative that maps each element of the collection in parallel:

```
Actors/parallel/parallel.ex
defmodule Parallel do
  def map(collection, fun) do
    parent = self()

    processes = Enum.map(collection, fn(e) ->
        spawn_link(fn() ->
            send(parent, {self(), fun.(e)})
          end)
      end)

    Enum.map(processes, fn(pid) ->
        receive do
          {^pid, result} -> result
        end
      end)
  end
end
```

This executes in two phases. In the first, it creates one process for each element of the collection (if the collection has 1,000 elements, it will create 1,000 processes). Each of these applies fun to the relevant element and sends the result back to the parent process. In the second phase, the parent waits for each result.

Let's prove that it works:

```
iex(1)> slow_double = fn(x) -> :timer.sleep(1000); x * 2 end
#Function<6.80484245 in :erl_eval.expr/5>
iex(2)> :timer.tc(fn() -> Enum.map([1, 2, 3, 4], slow_double) end)
{4003414, [2, 4, 6, 8]}
iex(3)> :timer.tc(fn() -> Parallel.map([1, 2, 3, 4], slow_double) end)
{1001131, [2, 4, 6, 8]}
```

This uses :timer.tc(), which times the execution of a function and returns a pair containing the time taken together with the return value. You can see that the sequential version takes a little over four seconds, and the parallel version one second.

Day 1 Wrap-Up

This brings us to the end of day 1. In day 2 we'll see how the actor model helps with error handling and resilience.

What We Learned in Day 1

Actors (processes) run concurrently, do not share state, and communicate by asynchronously sending messages to mailboxes. We covered how to do the following:

- Create a new process with spawn()

- Send a message to a process with send()

- Use pattern matching to handle messages

- Create a link between two processes and receive notification when one terminates

- Implement bidirectional, synchronous messaging on top of the standard asynchronous messaging

- Register a name for a process

Day 1 Self-Study

Find
- The Elixir library documentation

- The video of Erik Meijer and Clemens Szyperski talking to Carl Hewitt about the actor model at Lang.NEXT 2012

Do

- Measure the cost of creating a process on the Erlang virtual machine. How does it compare with the cost of creating a thread on the Java virtual machine?

- Measure the cost of the parallel map function we created compared to a sequential map. When would it make sense to use a parallel map, and when a sequential map?

- Write a parallel reduce function along the lines of the parallel map function we just created.

Day 2: Error Handling and Resilience

As we saw in *Resilient Software for an Unpredictable World*, on page 6, one of the key benefits of concurrency is that it enables us to write fault-tolerant code. Today we'll look at the tools that actors provide that enable us to do so.

First, though, let's use the lessons from yesterday to create a slightly more complicated and realistic example, which we'll use as the basis for today's discussion.

A Caching Actor

We're going to create a simple cache for webpages. A client can add a page to the cache by providing a URL together with the text of the page, query the cache for the page associated with a URL, and query the cache to see how many bytes it contains.

We're going to use a dictionary to store the mapping from URL to page. Like a Clojure map, an Elixir dictionary is a persistent, associative data structure:

```
iex(1)> d = HashDict.new
#HashDict<[]>
iex(2)> d1 = Dict.put(d, :a, "A value for a")
#HashDict<[a: "A value for a"]>
iex(3)> d2 = Dict.put(d1, :b, "A value for b")
#HashDict<[a: "A value for a", b: "A value for b"]>
iex(4)> d2[:a]
"A value for a"
```

We create a new dictionary with HashDict.new, add entries to it with Dict.put(dict, key, value), and look up entries with dict[key].

Here's an implementation of our cache that makes use of the preceding:

Actors/cache/cache.ex
```
defmodule Cache do
  def loop(pages, size) do
    receive do
      {:put, url, page} ->
        new_pages = Dict.put(pages, url, page)
        new_size = size + byte_size(page)
        loop(new_pages, new_size)
      {:get, sender, ref, url} ->
        send(sender, {:ok, ref, pages[url]})
        loop(pages, size)
      {:size, sender, ref} ->
        send(sender, {:ok, ref, size})
        loop(pages, size)
      {:terminate} -> # Terminate request - don't recurse
    end
  end
end
```

It maintains two items of state, pages and size. The first is a dictionary that maps URLs to pages; the second is an integer count of the number of bytes currently stored in the cache (updated with the byte_size() function on line 6).

As before, rather than expecting clients to remember the details of how to start and send messages to this actor, we provide an API they can use. First up is start_link():

Actors/cache/cache.ex
```
def start_link do
  pid = spawn_link(__MODULE__, :loop, [HashDict.new, 0])
  Process.register(pid, :cache)
  pid
end
```

This passes an empty dictionary and zero size to loop() as its initial state, and it registers the resulting process with the name :cache. Finally we have put(), get(), size(), and terminate() functions:

Actors/cache/cache.ex
```
def put(url, page) do
  send(:cache, {:put, url, page})
end

def get(url) do
  ref = make_ref()
  send(:cache, {:get, self(), ref, url})
  receive do
    {:ok, ^ref, page} -> page
  end
end
```

```
def size do
  ref = make_ref()
  send(:cache, {:size, self(), ref})
  receive do
    {:ok, ^ref, s} -> s
  end
end

def terminate do
  send(:cache, {:terminate})
end
```

The put() and terminate() functions simply take their arguments, package them up as a tuple, and send them as a message. The get() and size() methods are slightly more complicated, since they both have to wait for a reply. In this case, they are sending a unique reference using the pattern we saw yesterday.

Here's our actor in use:

```
iex(1)> Cache.start_link
#PID<0.47.0>
iex(2)> Cache.put("google.com", "Welcome to Google ...")
{:put, "google.com", "Welcome to Google ..."}
iex(3)> Cache.get("google.com")
"Welcome to Google ..."
iex(4)> Cache.size()
21
```

So far, so good—we can put an entry into our cache, get it back again, and see how large the cache is.

What happens if we call our actor with invalid parameters by trying to add a nil page, for example?

```
iex(5)> Cache.put("paulbutcher.com", nil)
{:put, "paulbutcher.com", nil}
iex(6)>
=ERROR REPORT==== 22-Aug-2013::16:18:41 ===
Error in process <0.47.0> with exit value: {badarg,[{erlang,byte_size,[nil],[]} …

** (EXIT from #PID<0.47.0>) {:badarg, [{:erlang, :byte_size, [nil], []}, …
```

Unsurprisingly, given that we didn't write any code to check the arguments, this fails. In most languages, the only way to address this would be to add code that anticipates what kinds of bad arguments might be sent and to report an error when they are. Elixir gives us another option—separating error handling out into a separate *supervisor* process. This apparently simple step is transformative, allowing profound improvements in code clarity, maintainability, and reliability.

To see how to write such a supervisor, we need to understand links between processes in more detail.

Fault Detection

In *Linking Processes*, on page 119, we used spawn_link() to create a link between two processes so that we could detect when one of them terminated. Links are one of the most important concepts in Elixir programming—let's investigate them in more depth.

Links Propagate Abnormal Termination

We can establish a link between two processes at any time with Process.link(). Here's a small actor that we can use to investigate how links behave:

```
Actors/links/links.ex
defmodule LinkTest do
  def loop do
    receive do
      {:exit_because, reason} -> exit(reason)
      {:link_to, pid} -> Process.link(pid)
      {:EXIT, pid, reason} -> IO.puts("#{inspect(pid)} exited because #{reason}")
    end
    loop
  end
end
```

Let's create a couple of instances of this actor, link them, and see what happens when one of them fails:

```
iex(1)> pid1 = spawn(&LinkTest.loop/0)
#PID<0.47.0>
iex(2)> pid2 = spawn(&LinkTest.loop/0)
#PID<0.49.0>
iex(3)> send(pid1, {:link_to, pid2})
{:link_to, #PID<0.49.0>}
iex(4)> send(pid2, {:exit_because, :bad_thing_happened})
{:exit_because, :bad_thing_happened}
```

We start by creating two instances of our actor and bind their process identifiers to pid1 and pid2. Then we create a link from pid1 to pid2. Finally, we tell pid2 to exit abnormally.

Immediately, we notice that there's no message printed by pid1 describing why pid2 exited. This is because we haven't set :trap_exit. Linking the processes has still had an effect, however, as we can see if we use Process.info() to query the status of our two processes:

```
iex(5)> Process.info(pid2, :status)
nil
iex(6)> Process.info(pid1, :status)
nil
```

So *both* our processes have terminated, not just pid2. We'll see how to fix this soon, but first let's do another experiment.

Links Are Bidirectional

If we try the same experiment again but this time ask pid1 to exit, we see the same behavior—both our processes terminate:

```
iex(1)> pid1 = spawn(&LinkTest.loop/0)
#PID<0.47.0>
iex(2)> pid2 = spawn(&LinkTest.loop/0)
#PID<0.49.0>
iex(3)> send(pid1, {:link_to, pid2})
{:link_to, #PID<0.49.0>}
iex(4)> send(pid1, {:exit_because, :another_bad_thing_happened})
{:exit_because, :another_bad_thing_happened}
iex(5)> Process.info(pid1, :status)
nil
iex(6)> Process.info(pid2, :status)
nil
```

This is because links are *bidirectional*. Creating a link from pid1 to pid2 also creates a link in the other direction—if one of them fails, both of them do.

Normal Termination

Finally, let's see what happens when one of our linked processes terminates normally (indicated by the special reason :normal):

```
iex(1)> pid1 = spawn(&LinkTest.loop/0)
#PID<0.47.0>
iex(2)> pid2 = spawn(&LinkTest.loop/0)
#PID<0.49.0>
iex(3)> send(pid1, {:link_to, pid2})
{:link_to, #PID<0.49.0>}
iex(4)> send(pid2, {:exit_because, :normal})
{:exit_because, :normal}
iex(5)> Process.info(pid2, :status)
nil
iex(6)> Process.info(pid1, :status)
{:status, :waiting}
```

So normal termination does not result in linked processes terminating.

System Processes

We can allow a process to trap another's exit by setting its :trap_exit flag. This is known in the jargon as making it into a *system process*:

Actors/links/links.ex
```elixir
def loop_system do
  Process.flag(:trap_exit, true)
  loop
end
```

Here it is in action:

```elixir
iex(1)> pid1 = spawn(&LinkTest.loop_system/0)
#PID<0.47.0>
iex(2)> pid2 = spawn(&LinkTest.loop/0)
#PID<0.49.0>
iex(3)> send(pid1, {:link_to, pid2})
{:link_to, #PID<0.49.0>}
iex(4)> send(pid2, {:exit_because, :yet_another_bad_thing_happened})
{:exit_because, :yet_another_bad_thing_happened}
#PID<0.49.0> exited because yet_another_bad_thing_happened
iex(5)> Process.info(pid2, :status)
nil
iex(6)> Process.info(pid1, :status)
{:status, :waiting}
```

This time, we use loop_system() to start pid1. Not only does this mean that it's notified when pid2 has exited (and prints a message to that effect), but it also continues to execute.

Supervising a Process

We now have enough tools at our fingertips to implement a *supervisor*, a system process that monitors one or more worker processes and takes appropriate action if they fail.

Here's a supervisor for the cache actor we created earlier that simply restarts its supervisee, the cache actor, if (when) it fails:

Actors/cache/cache.ex
```elixir
defmodule CacheSupervisor do
  def start do
    spawn(__MODULE__, :loop_system, [])
  end
  def loop do
    pid = Cache.start_link
    receive do
      {:EXIT, ^pid, :normal} ->
        IO.puts("Cache exited normally")
        :ok
```

```
        {:EXIT, ^pid, reason} ->
          IO.puts("Cache failed with reason #{inspect reason} - restarting it")
          loop
      end
    end
    def loop_system do
      Process.flag(:trap_exit, true)
      loop
    end
  end
end
```

This actor starts by marking itself as a system process and then enters loop(), which spawns Cache.loop() and then blocks until that process exits. If it exits normally, then so does the supervisor (by returning :ok), but if it exits for any other reason, loop() recurses and respawns the cache.

Instead of starting an instance of Cache ourselves, we now start CacheSupervisor instead, which creates an instance of Cache on our behalf:

```
iex(1)> CacheSupervisor.start
#PID<0.47.0>
iex(2)> Cache.put("google.com", "Welcome to Google ...")
{:put, "google.com", "Welcome to Google ..."}
iex(3)> Cache.size
21
```

If Cache crashes, it's automatically restarted:

```
iex(4)> Cache.put("paulbutcher.com", nil)
{:put, "paulbutcher.com", nil}
Cache failed with reason {:badarg, [{:erlang, :byte_size, [nil], []}, …
iex(5)>
=ERROR REPORT==== 22-Aug-2013::17:49:24 ===
Error in process <0.48.0> with exit value: {badarg,[{erlang,byte_size,[nil],[]}, …

iex(5)> Cache.size
0
iex(6)> Cache.put("google.com", "Welcome to Google ...")
{:put, "google.com", "Welcome to Google ..."}
iex(7)> Cache.get("google.com")
"Welcome to Google ..."
```

We lose whatever was in the cache when it crashed, of course, but at least there's still a cache for us to use subsequently.

Timeouts

Automatically restarting the cache is great, but it's not a panacea. If two processes both send messages to the cache at around the same time, for example, we might see the following sequence:

1. Process 1 sends a :put message to the cache.
2. Process 2 sends a :get message to the cache.
3. The cache crashes while processing process 1's message.
4. The supervisor restarts the cache, but process 2's message is lost.
5. Process 2 is now deadlocked in a receive, waiting for a reply that will never arrive.

We can handle this by ensuring that our receive times out after a while by adding an after clause. Here's a modified version of get() (we'll need to make the same change to size() as well):

Actors/cache/cache2.ex
```
def get(url) do
  ref = make_ref()
  send(:cache, {:get, self(), ref, url})
  receive do
    {:ok, ^ref, page} -> page
    after 1000 -> nil
  end
end
```

\\//
ĭf   **Joe asks:**
Is Message Delivery Guaranteed?

The problem we just looked at, of a client's message being lost when our cache is restarted, is just one example of a more general problem—what guarantees about message delivery does Elixir provide?

There are two basic guarantees:

- Message delivery is guaranteed if nothing breaks.
- If something does break, you'll know about it (assuming you've linked to, or monitored, the process in question).

It's this second guarantee that forms the bedrock of Elixir's support for writing fault-tolerant code.

The Error-Kernel Pattern

Tony Hoare famously said the following:[3]

> There are two ways of constructing a software design: One way is to make it so simple that there are obviously no deficiencies and the other way is to make it so complicated that there are no obvious deficiencies.

---

3.   http://zoo.cs.yale.edu/classes/cs422/2011/bib/hoare81emperor.pdf

Actor programming naturally supports an approach to writing fault-tolerant code that leverages this observation: the error-kernel pattern.

A software system's *error kernel* is the part that must be correct if the system is to function correctly. Well-written programs make this error kernel as small and as simple as possible—so small and simple that there are obviously no deficiencies.

An actor program's error kernel is its top-level supervisors. These supervise their children—starting, stopping, and restarting them as necessary.

Each module of a program has its own error kernel in turn—the part of the module that must be correct for it to function correctly. Submodules also have error kernels, and so on. This leads to a hierarchy of error kernels in which risky operations are pushed down toward the lower-level actors, as shown in Figure 8, *A hierarchy of error kernels*.

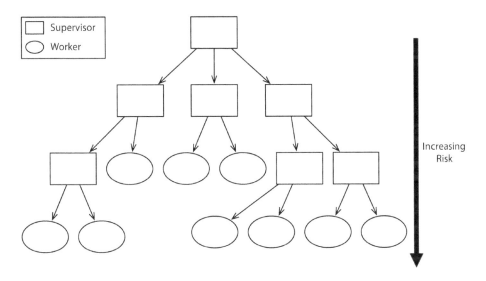

Figure 8—A hierarchy of error kernels

Closely related to the error-kernel pattern is the thorny subject of defensive programming.

Let It Crash!

Defensive programming is an approach to achieving fault tolerance by trying to anticipate possible bugs. Imagine, for example, that we're writing a method that takes a string and returns true if it's all uppercase and false otherwise. Here's one possible implementation:

```
def all_upper?(s) do
  String.upcase(s) == s
end
```

This is a perfectly reasonable method, but if for some reason we pass nil to it, it will crash. With that in mind, some developers would change it to read like this:

```
defmodule Upper do
  def all_upper?(s) do
    cond do
      nil?(s) -> false
      true -> String.upcase(s) == s
    end
  end
end
```

So now the code won't crash if it's given nil, but what if we pass something else that doesn't make sense (a keyword, for example)? And in any case, what does it *mean* to call this function with nil? There's an excellent chance that any code that does so contains a bug—a bug that we've now masked, meaning that we're likely to remain unaware of it until it bites us at some time in the future.

Actor programs tend to avoid defensive programming and subscribe to the "let it crash" philosophy, allowing an actor's supervisor to address the problem instead. This has multiple benefits, including these:

- Our code is simpler and easier to understand, with a clear separation between "happy path" and fault-tolerant code.

- Actors are separate from one another and don't share state, so there's little danger that a failure in one actor will adversely affect another. In particular, a failed actor's supervisor cannot crash because the actor it's supervising crashes.

- As well as fixing the error, a supervisor can log it so that instead of sweeping problems under the carpet, we become aware of them and can take remedial action.

Although it can seem alien at first acquaintance, the "let it crash" philosophy has, together with the error-kernel pattern, repeatedly been proven in production. Some systems have reported availability as high as 99.9999999% (that's nine nines—see *Programming Erlang: Software for a Concurrent World [Arm13]*).

Day 2 Wrap-Up

Day 1 introduced the basics of the actor model, and in day 2, we saw how it facilitates fault tolerance. In day 3 we'll see how the actor model helps with distributed programming.

What We Learned in Day 2

Elixir provides fault detection by allowing processes to be linked, which can be used to create supervisors:

- Links are bidirectional—if process a is linked to process b, then b is also linked to a.

- Links propagate errors—if two processes are linked and one of them terminates abnormally, so will the other.

- If a process is marked as a system process, instead of exiting when a linked process terminates abnormally, it's notified with an :EXIT message.

Day 2 Self-Study

Find

- The documentation for Process.monitor()—how does monitoring a process differ from linking? When might you use monitors and when links?

- How do exceptions work in Elixir? When might you choose to use exception handling instead of supervision and the "let it crash" pattern?

Do

- Messages that don't match a pattern in a receive block remain in a process's mailbox. Use this fact, together with timeouts, to implement a *priority mailbox*, in which high-priority messages are handled ahead of any low-priority messages that might have been sent earlier.

- Create a version of the cache we created in *A Caching Actor*, on page 127, that distributes cache entries across multiple actors according to a hash function. Create a supervisor that starts multiple cache actors and routes incoming messages to the appropriate cache worker. What action should this supervisor take if one of the cache workers fails?

Day 3: Distribution

Everything we've done so far has been on a single computer, but one of the actor model's primary benefits compared to the models we've seen so far is that it supports distribution—sending a message to an actor on another machine is just as easy as sending it to one running locally.

Before talking about distribution, however, we'll take a quick look at one of the most powerful reasons for using Elixir—the OTP library.

OTP

Over the previous two days, we built everything by hand in "raw" Elixir. This is a great way to understand what's going on under the hood, but it would be both tedious and error prone if we had to write every worker and every supervisor from scratch every time. You won't be surprised to hear that a library can automate much of this for us—that library is called OTP.

 Joe asks:
What Does OTP Stand For?

Acronyms often take on a life of their own. IBM might theoretically stand for "International Business Machines," but to most people IBM is just IBM: the acronym has become the name. Similarly BBC no longer really stands for "British Broadcasting Corporation," and OTP no longer really stands for "Open Telecom Platform."

Erlang (and therefore Elixir) originally started out in telecommunications, and many proven Erlang best practices have been codified in OTP. But very little of it is telecom-specific, so OTP is just OTP.

Before we see an example of OTP, we'll take a brief interlude to examine how functions and pattern matching interact in Elixir.

Functions and Pattern Matching

So far we've only talked about pattern matching within receive, but it's used throughout Elixir. In particular, every time you call a function, you're performing a pattern match. Here's a simple function that demonstrates this:

Actors/patterns/patterns.ex
```
defmodule Patterns do
  def foo({x, y}) do
    IO.puts("Got a pair, first element #{x}, second #{y}")
  end
end
```

We're defining a function that takes a single argument and matches that argument against the pattern {x, y}. If we call it with a matching pair, the first element is bound to x and the second to y:

```
iex(1)> Patterns.foo({:a, 42})
Got a pair, first element a, second 42
:ok
```

If we call it with an argument that doesn't match, we get an error:

```
iex(2)> Patterns.foo("something else")
** (FunctionClauseError) no function clause matching in Patterns.foo/1
    patterns.ex:3: Patterns.foo("something else")
    erl_eval.erl:569: :erl_eval.do_apply/6
    src/elixir.erl:147: :elixir.eval_forms/3
```

We can add as many different definitions (or *clauses*) for a function as we need:

Actors/patterns/patterns.ex
```
def foo({x, y, z}) do
  IO.puts("Got a triple: #{x}, #{y}, #{z}")
end
```

When the function is called, the matching clause is executed:

```
iex(2)> Patterns.foo({:a, 42, "yahoo"})
Got a triple: a, 42, yahoo
:ok
iex(3)> Patterns.foo({:x, :y})
Got a pair, first element x, second y
:ok
```

Now let's see how this is used when implementing a server in OTP.

Reimplementing Cache with GenServer

The first aspect of OTP we'll look at is GenServer, a *behaviour* that allows us to automate the details of creating a stateful actor. We'll use it to reimplement the cache we created yesterday.

If the spelling of *behaviour* looks slightly odd to you, that's because behaviours are inherited from Erlang, and Erlang uses the British spelling. Because that's how Elixir spells it, that's how we'll spell it here too.

A behaviour is very similar to an interface in Java—it defines a set of functions. A module specifies that it implements a behaviour with use:

Actors/cache/cache3.ex
```
defmodule Cache do
  use GenServer.Behaviour
  def handle_cast({:put, url, page}, {pages, size}) do
    new_pages = Dict.put(pages, url, page)
    new_size = size + byte_size(page)
    {:noreply, {new_pages, new_size}}
  end
```

```
  def handle_call({:get, url}, _from, {pages, size}) do
    {:reply, pages[url], {pages, size}}
  end

  def handle_call({:size}, _from, {pages, size}) do
    {:reply, size, {pages, size}}
  end
end
```

This version of Cache specifies that it implements GenServer.Behaviour and provides custom implementations of two functions, handle_cast() and handle_call().

The first of these, handle_cast(), handles messages that do not require a reply. It takes two arguments: the first is the message and the second is the current actor state. The return value is a pair of the form {:noreply, new_state}. In our case, we provide one handle_cast() clause that handles :put messages.

The second, handle_call(), handles messages that require a reply. It takes three arguments, the message, the sender, and the current state. The return value is a triple of the form {:reply, reply_value, new_state}. In our case, we provide two handle_call() clauses, one that handles :get messages and one that handles :size messages. Note that like Clojure, Elixir uses variable names that start with an underscore ("_") to indicate that they're unused—hence _from.

As with our previous implementation, we provide an API that clients can use without having to remember the details of how to initialize and send messages:

Actors/cache/cache3.ex
```
def start_link do
  :gen_server.start_link({:local, :cache}, __MODULE__, {HashDict.new, 0}, [])
end

def put(url, page) do
  :gen_server.cast(:cache, {:put, url, page})
end

def get(url) do
  :gen_server.call(:cache, {:get, url})
end

def size do
  :gen_server.call(:cache, {:size})
end
```

Instead of using spawn_link(), we use :gen_server.start_link(). We send messages that don't require a reply with :gen_server.cast() and those that do with :gen_server.call().

We'll see this in action soon, but first we'll see how to create a supervisor with OTP.

An OTP Supervisor

Here's a cache supervisor implemented with OTP's supervisor behaviour:

Actors/cache/cache3.ex
```
defmodule CacheSupervisor do
  def init(_args) do
    workers = [worker(Cache, [])]
    supervise(workers, strategy: :one_for_one)
  end
end
```

As its name suggests, the init() function is called during startup. It takes a single argument (unused in this case) and simply creates a number of workers and sets them up to be supervised. In our case, we're creating a single Cache worker and supervising it using a one-for-one restart strategy.

> ### Joe asks:
> ### What Is a Restart Strategy?
>
> The OTP supervisor behaviour supports a number of different restart strategies, the two most common being *one-for-one* and *one-for-all*.
>
> These strategies govern how a supervisor with multiple workers restarts failed workers. If a single worker fails, a supervisor using the one-for-all strategy will stop and restart all its workers (even those that didn't fail). A supervisor using a one-for-one strategy, by contrast, will only restart the failed worker.
>
> Other restart strategies are possible, but one of these two will suffice in the majority of cases.

As usual, we also provide an API for clients:

Actors/cache/cache3.ex
```
def start_link do
  :supervisor.start_link(__MODULE__, [])
end
```

Take a moment to prove to yourself that this works in a very similar way to the cache and supervisor we implemented from scratch yesterday (I won't show the transcript here, since it's very similar to what we've already seen).

Nodes

Whenever we create an instance of the Erlang virtual machine, we create a *node*. So far, we've only created a single node. Now we'll see how to create and connect multiple nodes.

Joe asks:
What Else Does OTP Do?

As we can see from the preceding code, OTP saves us from writing some boilerplate code, but there's much more to it than just that. It's not obvious from what we've already seen, but servers and supervisors implemented with OTP provide much more functionality than the simple versions we created before. Among other things, they provide the following:

Better restart logic: The simple supervisor we wrote for ourselves has a very dumb approach to restarting its worker—if it terminates abnormally, it's restarted. If the worker process crashed immediately on startup, this supervisor would simply restart it over and over again forever. An OTP supervisor, by contrast, has a maximum restart frequency which, if exceeded, results in the supervisor itself terminating abnormally.

Debugging and logging: An OTP server can be started with various options to enable logging and debugging, which can be very helpful during development.

Hot code swapping: An OTP server can be upgraded dynamically without taking the whole system down.

Lots, lots more: Release management, failover, automated scaling ...

We won't talk further about these features here, but they're powerful reasons to prefer OTP over handwritten code in most circumstances.

Connecting Nodes

For one node to connect to another, they both need to be named. We name a node by starting the Erlang virtual machine with the --name or --sname options. My MacBook Pro happens to have the IP address 10.99.1.50. If I run iex --sname node1@10.99.1.50 --cookie yumyum (the --cookie argument is explained in *How Do I Manage My Cluster?*, on page 144) on my MacBook Pro, for example, I see the name reflected in the prompt:

```
iex(node1@10.99.1.50)1> Node.self
:"node1@10.99.1.50"
iex(node1@10.99.1.50)2> Node.list
[]
```

A node can query its name with Node.self() and list the other nodes it knows about with Node.list(). Right now that list is empty—let's see how to populate it. If I start another Erlang virtual machine on another machine that has the IP address 10.99.1.92 with iex --sname node2@10.99.1.92 --cookie yumyum, I can connect to it from my MacBook Pro with Node.connect():

```
iex(node1@10.99.1.50)3> Node.connect(:"node2@10.99.1.92")
true
iex(node1@10.99.1.50)4> Node.list
[:"node2@10.99.1.92"]
```

Connections are bidirectional—my other machine now also knows about my MacBook Pro:

```
iex(node2@10.99.1.92)1> Node.list
[:"node1@10.99.1.50"]
```

Joe asks:
What If I Only Have One Computer?

If you only have one computer at hand and still want to experiment with clustering, you have a few options:

- Use virtual machines.
- Fire up Amazon EC2 or similar cloud instances.
- Run multiple nodes on a single computer. Although clearly this isn't the most realistic situation, it is by far the easiest, and it allows you to sidestep firewall and network configuration issues if you're having problems getting multiple nodes to work across machines.

Remote Execution

Now that we have two connected nodes, one can execute code on the other:

```
iex(node1@10.99.1.50)5> whoami = fn() -> IO.puts(Node.self) end
#Function<20.80484245 in :erl_eval.expr/5>
iex(node1@10.99.1.50)6> Node.spawn(:"node2@10.99.1.92", whoami)
#PID<8242.50.0>
node2@10.99.1.92
```

These deceptively simple lines of code demonstrate something amazingly powerful—not only has one node executed code on another, but the output appeared on the first node. This is because a process inherits its *group leader* from the process that spawned it, and (among other things) that specifies where output from IO.puts() appears. That's an awful lot going on under the hood!

Remote Messaging

As you would expect, an actor running on one node can send messages to an actor running on another. To demonstrate, let's spawn an instance of the Counter actor we created earlier (see the code on page 120) on one node:

> ### Joe asks:
> # How Do I Manage My Cluster?
>
> A system that allows one machine to execute arbitrary code on another is extremely powerful. Like any powerful tool, it can also be dangerous. In particular, you need to pay careful attention to security when thinking about cluster management. That's where the --cookie argument we gave to iex comes in—an Erlang node will accept connection requests only from nodes that have the same cookie. There are other approaches to securing an Erlang cluster, such as tunneling internode connections over SSL.
>
> Security is not the only question you need to think about. In the preceding example, I chose to specify the IP address in the node name because that's guaranteed to work on most network configurations (and I don't know how your network is configured). But it may not (probably will not) be the best choice for production use.
>
> Cluster design trade-offs are subtle and beyond the scope of this book. Please make sure that you read the documentation about these questions before rolling out a production cluster.

```
iex(node2@10.99.1.92)1> pid = spawn(Counter, :loop, [42])
#PID<0.51.0>
iex(node2@10.99.1.92)2> :global.register_name(:counter, pid)
:yes
```

After spawning it, we register it using :global.register_name(), which is similar to Process.register(), except that the name is cluster-global.

We can then use :global.whereis_name() on another node to retrieve the process identifier and send it messages:

```
iex(node1@10.99.1.50)1> Node.connect(:"node2@10.99.1.92")
true
iex(node1@10.99.1.50)2> pid = :global.whereis_name(:counter)
#PID<7856.51.0>
iex(node1@10.99.1.50)3> send(pid, {:next})
{:next}
iex(node1@10.99.1.50)4> send(pid, {:next})
{:next}
```

Sure enough, we see this on the first node:

```
Current count: 42
Current count: 43
```

Note that again the output appears on the node upon which the actor generating it was spawned.

Distributed Word Count

We're going to finish off our discussion of actors and Elixir by creating a distributed version of the Wikipedia word-count example we've seen in previous chapters. Like the solutions we've already seen, this will be able to leverage multiple cores. Unlike those we've already seen, it will also be able to scale beyond a single machine and recover from failures.

Here's a diagram of the architecture we're aiming for:

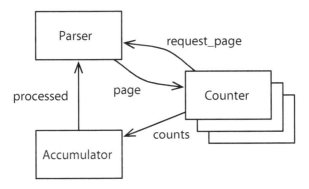

Our solution is divided into three types of actors: one Parser, multiple Counters, and one Accumulator. The Parser is responsible for parsing a Wikipedia dump into pages, Counters count words within pages, and the Accumulator keeps track of total word counts across pages.

Processing is kicked off by a Counter requesting a page from the Parser. When the Counter receives the page, it counts the words contained within and sends them to the Accumulator. Finally, the Accumulator lets the Parser know that the page has been processed.

We'll discuss why we chose this particular arrangement soon, but first let's see how it's implemented, starting with Counter.

Counting Words

Our Counter module implements a simple stateless actor that receives pages from the Parser and delivers the resulting word counts to the Accumulator. Here it is in full:

Actors/word_count/lib/counter.ex
```
defmodule Counter do
  use GenServer.Behaviour
  def start_link do
    :gen_server.start_link(__MODULE__, nil, [])
  end
```

```
    def deliver_page(pid, ref, page) do
      :gen_server.cast(pid, {:deliver_page, ref, page})
    end

10  def init(_args) do
      Parser.request_page(self())
      {:ok, nil}
    end

15  def handle_cast({:deliver_page, ref, page}, state) do
      Parser.request_page(self())

      words = String.split(page)
      counts = Enum.reduce(words, HashDict.new, fn(word, counts) ->
20        Dict.update(counts, word, 1, &(&1 + 1))
        end)
      Accumulator.deliver_counts(ref, counts)
      {:noreply, state}
    end
25 end
```

This follows the normal pattern for an OTP server—a public API (in this case start_link() and deliver_page()) followed by initialization (init()) and message handlers (handle_cast()).

Each Counter kicks things off by calling Parser.request_page() during initialization (line 11).

Each time it receives a page, a Counter starts by requesting another page (line 16—we do this first to minimize latency). It then counts the words contained within the page, building a dictionary called counts (lines 18-21). Finally, those counts are sent to the Accumulator along with the reference (ref) that was sent with the page.

Next, CounterSupervisor allows us to create and supervise multiple Counters:

Actors/word_count/lib/counter.ex
```
defmodule CounterSupervisor do
  use Supervisor.Behaviour
  def start_link(num_counters) do
    :supervisor.start_link(__MODULE__, num_counters)
  end
  def init(num_counters) do
    workers = Enum.map(1..num_counters, fn(n) ->
      worker(Counter, [], id: "counter#{n}")
    end)
    supervise(workers, strategy: :one_for_one)
  end
end
```

CounterSupervisor.init() takes the number of counters we want to create, which we use to create a workers list of that length. Note that each worker needs to have a distinct id, which we achieve by mapping over the range 1..num_counters.

Keeping Track of Totals

The Accumulator actor maintains two elements of state: totals, a dictionary containing accumulated counts, and processed_pages, a set containing the references of all the pages that it's processed.

Actors/word_count/lib/accumulator.ex
```
defmodule Accumulator do
  use GenServer.Behaviour

  def start_link do
    :gen_server.start_link({:global, :wc_accumulator}, __MODULE__,
      {HashDict.new, HashSet.new}, [])
  end

  def deliver_counts(ref, counts) do
    :gen_server.cast({:global, :wc_accumulator}, {:deliver_counts, ref, counts})
  end

  def handle_cast({:deliver_counts, ref, counts}, {totals, processed_pages}) do
    if Set.member?(processed_pages, ref) do
      {:noreply, {totals, processed_pages}}
    else
      new_totals = Dict.merge(totals, counts, fn(_k, v1, v2) -> v1 + v2 end)
      new_processed_pages = Set.put(processed_pages, ref)
      Parser.processed(ref)
      {:noreply, {new_totals, new_processed_pages}}
    end
  end
end
```

We create a global name for our accumulator by passing {:global, wc_accumulator} to :gen_server.start_link() (line 5). We can use this directly when sending messages with :gen_server.cast() (line 10).

When a set of counts is delivered to the accumulator, it first checks to see if it's already processed counts for this page (we'll soon see why this is important and why it might receive counts twice). If it hasn't, it merges the counts into totals with Dict.merge(), the page reference into processed_pages with Set.put(), and notifies the parser that the page has been processed.

Parsing and Fault Tolerance

Parser is the most complex of our three types of actor, so we'll break it down into chunks. First, here's its public API:

Actors/word_count/lib/parser.ex
```
defmodule Parser do
  use GenServer.Behaviour

  def start_link(filename) do
    :gen_server.start_link({:global, :wc_parser}, __MODULE__, filename, [])
  end

  def request_page(pid) do
    :gen_server.cast({:global, :wc_parser}, {:request_page, pid})
  end

  def processed(ref) do
    :gen_server.cast({:global, :wc_parser}, {:processed, ref})
  end
end
```

As with Accumulator, Parser registers itself with a global name during startup. It supports two operations—request_page(), which is called by a Counter to request a page, and processed(), which is called by the Accumulator to indicate that a page has been successfully processed.

Here's the implementation of the message handlers for these two operations:

Actors/word_count/lib/parser.ex
```
def init(filename) do
  xml_parser = Pages.start_link(filename)
  {:ok, {ListDict.new, xml_parser}}
end

def handle_cast({:request_page, pid}, {pending, xml_parser}) do
  new_pending = deliver_page(pid, pending, Pages.next(xml_parser))
  {:noreply, {new_pending, xml_parser}}
end

def handle_cast({:processed, ref}, {pending, xml_parser}) do
  new_pending = Dict.delete(pending, ref)
  {:noreply, {new_pending, xml_parser}}
end
```

Parser maintains two items of state: pending, which is a ListDict of references for pages that have been sent to a Counter but not yet processed, and xml_parser, which is an actor that uses the Erlang xmerl library to parse a Wikipedia dump (we won't show its implementation here—see the code that accompanies this book if you're interested).[4]

---

4. http://www.erlang.org/doc/apps/xmerl/

Handling a :processed message simply requires deleting the processed page from pending. Handling a :request_page message involves retrieving the next available page from the XML parser and passing it to deliver_page():

Actors/word_count/lib/parser.ex
```
defp deliver_page(pid, pending, page) when nil?(page) do
  if Enum.empty?(pending) do
    pending # Nothing to do
  else
    {ref, prev_page} = List.last(pending)
    Counter.deliver_page(pid, ref, prev_page)
    Dict.put(Dict.delete(pending, ref), ref, prev_page)
  end
end

defp deliver_page(pid, pending, page) do
  ref = make_ref()
  Counter.deliver_page(pid, ref, page)
  Dict.put(pending, ref, page)
end
```

The implementation of deliver_page() uses an Elixir feature we've not seen before—a *guard clause* specified by the when in the first deliver_page() clause. A guard clause is a Boolean expression—the function clause matches only if the guard is true.

Let's consider the case when page is non-nil first. In this case, we create a new unique reference with make_ref(), deliver the page to the counter that requested it, and add the page to our pending dictionary.

If page is nil, that indicates that the XML parser has finished parsing the Wikipedia dump. In that case, we remove the oldest entry from pending and send it, and remove and re-add it to pending so that it's now the youngest entry.

Why this second case? Surely every pending batch will eventually be processed. What do we gain by sending it to another Counter?

The Big Win

What we gain is fault tolerance. If a Counter exits or the network goes down or the machine it's running on dies, we'll just end up sending the page it was processing to another Counter. Because each page has a reference associated with it, we know which pages have been processed and won't double-count.

To convince yourself, try starting a cluster. On one machine, start a Parser and an Accumulator. On one or more other machines, start a number of Counters. If you pull the network cable out the back of a machine running counters, or kill the virtual machine they're running in, the remaining counters will continue to process pages, including those that were in progress on that machine.

This is a great example of the benefits of concurrent, distributed development. This program will hardly miss a beat when faced with a hardware failure that would kill a normal sequential or multithreaded program.

Day 3 Wrap-Up

That brings us to the end of day 3 and our discussion of actors.

What We Learned in Day 3

Elixir allows us to create clusters of nodes. An actor on one node can send messages to an actor running on another in exactly the same way as it can to one running locally. As well as allowing us to create systems that leverage multiple distributed computers, it allows us to recover from the failure of one of those computers.

Day 3 Self-Study

Find

- Joe Armstrong's Lambda Jam presentation, "Systems That Run Forever Self-Heal and Scale."

- What is an OTP application? Why might one be more accurately described as a component?

- So far, the state of every actor we've created has been lost if that actor dies. What support does Elixir provide for persistent state?

Do

- The fault-tolerant word-count program we developed can handle failure of a counter or the machine that it's running on, but not the parser or accumulator. Create a version that can handle failure of any actor or node.

Wrap-Up

Alan Kay, the designer of Smalltalk and father of object-oriented programming, had this to say on the essence of object orientation:[5]

> I'm sorry that I long ago coined the term "objects" for this topic because it gets many people to focus on the lesser idea.

---

5.   http://c2.com/cgi/wiki?AlanKayOnMessaging

> The big idea is "messaging" ... The Japanese have a small word—ma—for "that which is in-between"—perhaps the nearest English equivalent is "interstitial." The key in making great and growable systems is much more to design how its modules communicate rather than what their internal properties and behaviors should be.

This captures the essence of actor programming very well—we can think of actors as the logical extension of object-oriented programming to the concurrent world. Indeed, you can think of actors as more object-oriented than objects, with stricter message passing and encapsulation.

Strengths

Actors have a number of features that make them ideal for solving a wide range of concurrent problems.

Messaging and Encapsulation

Actors do not share state and, although they run concurrently with each other, within a single actor everything is sequential. This means that we need only worry about concurrency when considering message flows between actors.

This is a huge boon to the developer. An actor can be tested in isolation and, as long as our tests accurately represent the types of messages that might be delivered and in what order, we can have high confidence that it behaves as it should. And if we do find ourselves faced with a concurrency-related bug, we know where to look—the message flows between actors.

Fault Tolerance

Fault tolerance is built into actor programs from the outset. This enables not only more resilient programs but also simpler and clearer code (through the "let it crash" philosophy).

Distributed Programming

Actors' support for both shared and distributed-memory architectures brings a number of significant advantages:

Firstly, it allows an actor program to scale to solve problems of almost any size. We are not limited to problems that fit on a single system.

Secondly, it allows us to address problems where geographical distribution is an intrinsic consideration. Actors are an excellent choice for programs where different elements of the software need to reside in different geographical locations.

Finally, distribution is a key enabler for resilient and fault-tolerant systems.

Weaknesses

Although a program constructed with actors is easier to debug than one constructed with threads and locks, actors are still susceptible to problems like deadlock plus a few failure modes unique to actors (such as overflowing an actor's mailbox).

As with threads and locks, actors provide no direct support for parallelism. Parallel solutions need to be built from concurrent building blocks, raising the specter of nondeterminism. And because actors do not share state and can only communicate through message passing, they are not a suitable choice if you need fine-grained parallelism.

Other Languages

As with most good ideas, the actor model is not new—it was first described in the 1970s, most notably by Carl Hewitt. The language that has done most to popularize actor programming, however, is unquestionably Erlang. For example, Erlang's creator, Joe Armstrong, is the originator of the "let it crash" philosophy.

Most popular programming languages now have an actor library available; in particular the Akka toolkit can be used to add actor support to Java or any other JVM-based language.[6] If you're interested in learning more about Akka, see the online bonus chapter,[7] which describes actor programming in Scala.

Final Thoughts

Actor programming is one of the most widely applicable programming models out there—not only does it provide support for concurrency, but it also provides distribution, error detection, and fault tolerance. As such, it's a good fit for the kinds of programming problems we find ourselves faced with in today's increasingly distributed world.

In the next chapter we'll look at communicating sequential processes. Although CSP has surface similarities with actors, its emphasis on the channels used for communication, rather than the entities between which communication takes place, leads to it having a very different flavor.

---

6.   http://akka.io
7.   http://media.pragprog.com/titles/pb7con/Bonus_Chapter.pdf

CHAPTER 6

Communicating Sequential Processes

If you're a car nut like me, it's easy to focus on the vehicle and forget about the roads it travels on. It's fascinating to debate the relative merits of turbo-charging versus natural aspiration or a mid- versus a front-engine layout, forgetting that the most important aspect of a car has nothing to do with any of these things. Where you can go and how fast you can get there is primarily defined by the road network, not the car.

Similarly, the features and capabilities of a message-passing system are not primarily defined by the code between which messages are exchanged or their content, but by the transport over which they travel.

In this chapter we'll look at a model that has surface similarities with actors but a very different feel—thanks to a difference in focus.

Communication Is Everything

As we saw in the last chapter, an actor program consists of independent, concurrently executing entities (called actors, or processes in Elixir) that communicate by sending each other messages. Each actor has a mailbox that stores messages until they're handled.

A program using the communicating sequential processes model similarly consists of independent, concurrently executing entities that communicate by sending each other messages. The difference is one of emphasis—instead of focusing on the entities sending the messages, CSP focuses on the *channels* over which they are sent. Channels are first class—instead of each process being tightly coupled to a single mailbox, channels can be independently created, written to, read from, and passed between processes.

Like functional programming and actors, CSP is an old idea that's experiencing a renaissance. CSP's recent popularity is largely due to the Go language.[1] We're going to cover CSP by examining the core.async library,[2] which brings Go's concurrency model to Clojure.

In day 1 we'll introduce the twin pillars upon which core.async is built: channels and go blocks. In day 2 we'll construct a realistic example program with them. Finally, in day 3 we'll see how core.async can be used within ClojureScript to make client-side programming easier.

Day 1: Channels and Go Blocks

The core.async library provides two primary facilities—channels and go blocks. Go blocks allow multiple concurrent tasks to be efficiently multiplexed across a limited pool of threads. But first, let's look at channels.

Using core.async

The core.async library is a relatively recent addition to Clojure and is still in prerelease (so be aware that things may change). To use it, you need to make the library a dependency of your project and then import it. This is slightly complicated by the fact that it defines a few functions with names that clash with core Clojure library functions. To make it easier to experiment with, you can use the channels project in the book's sample code, which imports core.async like this:

```
CSP/channels/src/channels/core.clj
(ns channels.core
  (:require [clojure.core.async :as async :refer :all
            :exclude [map into reduce merge partition partition-by take]])))
```

The :refer :all allows most core.async functions to be used directly, but a few (those with names that clash with core library functions) have to be given the async/ prefix.

You can start a REPL with these definitions loaded by changing the directory to the channels project and typing lein repl.

Channels

A channel is a thread-safe queue—any task with a reference to a channel can add messages to one end, and any task with a reference to it can remove messages from the other. Unlike actors, where messages are sent to and from specific actors, senders don't have to know about receivers, or vice versa.

---

1. http://golang.org
2. http://clojure.com/blog/2013/06/28/clojure-core-async-channels.html

A new channel is created with chan:

```
channels.core=> (def c (chan))
#'channels.core/c
```

We can write to a channel with >!! and read from it with <!!:

```
channels.core=> (thread (println "Read:" (<!! c) "from c"))
#<ManyToManyChannel clojure.core.async.impl.channels.ManyToManyChannel@78fcc563>
channels.core=> (>!! c "Hello thread")
Read: Hello thread from c
nil
```

We're using the handy thread utility macro provided by core.async, which, as its name suggests, runs its code on a separate thread. That thread prints a message containing whatever it reads from the channel. This blocks until we write to the channel with >!!, at which point we see the message.

Buffering

By default, channels are *synchronous* (or *unbuffered*)—writing to a channel blocks until something reads from it:

```
channels.core=> (thread (>!! c "Hello") (println "Write completed"))
#<ManyToManyChannel clojure.core.async.impl.channels.ManyToManyChannel@78fcc563>
channels.core=> (<!! c)
Write completed
"Hello"
```

We can create a *buffered* channel by passing a buffer size to chan:

```
channels.core=> (def bc (chan 5))
#'channels.core/bc
channels.core=> (>!! bc 0)
nil
channels.core=> (>!! bc 1)
nil
channels.core=> (close! bc)
nil
channels.core=> (<!! bc)
0
channels.core=> (<!! bc)
1
channels.core=> (<!! bc)
nil
```

This creates a channel with a buffer large enough to contain five messages. As long as there's space available, writing to a buffered channel completes immediately.

Closing Channels

The previous example demonstrated another feature of channels—they can be closed with close!. Reading from an empty closed channel returns nil, and writing to a closed channel silently discards the message. As you might expect, writing nil to a channel is an error:

```
channels.core=> (>!! (chan) nil)
IllegalArgumentException Can't put nil on channel «...»
```

Here's a function that uses what we've seen so far to read from a channel until it's closed and to return everything read as a vector:

CSP/channels/src/channels/core.clj
```
(defn readall!! [ch]
  (loop [coll []]
    (if-let [x (<!! ch)]
      (recur (conj coll x))
      coll)))
```

This loops with coll initially bound to the empty vector []. Each iteration reads a value from ch and, if the value is not nil, it's added to coll. If the value is nil (the channel has been closed), coll is returned.

And here's writeall!!, which takes a channel and a sequence and writes the entirety of the sequence to the channel, closing it when the sequence is exhausted:

CSP/channels/src/channels/core.clj
```
(defn writeall!! [ch coll]
  (doseq [x coll]
    (>!! ch x))
  (close! ch))
```

Let's see these functions in action:

```
channels.core=> (def ch (chan 10))
#'channels.core/ch
channels.core=> (writeall!! ch (range 0 10))
nil
channels.core=> (readall!! ch)
[0 1 2 3 4 5 6 7 8 9]
```

You won't be surprised to hear that core.async provides utilities that perform similar tasks, saving us the trouble of writing our own:

```
channels.core=> (def ch (chan 10))
#'channels.core/ch
channels.core=> (onto-chan ch (range 0 10))
#<ManyToManyChannel clojure.core.async.impl.channels.ManyToManyChannel@6b16d3cf>
channels.core=> (<!! (async/into [] ch))
[0 1 2 3 4 5 6 7 8 9]
```

The onto-chan function writes the entire contents of a collection onto a channel, closing it when the collection's exhausted. And async/into takes an initial collection (the empty vector in the preceding example) and a channel and returns a channel. That channel will have a single collection written to it—the result of conjoining everything read from the channel with the initial collection.

Next we'll use these utilities to investigate buffered channels in more depth.

Full Buffer Strategies

By default, writing to a full channel blocks, but we can choose an alternative strategy by passing a buffer to chan:

```
channels.core=> (def dc (chan (dropping-buffer 5)))
#'channels.core/dc
channels.core=> (onto-chan dc (range 0 10))
#<ManyToManyChannel clojure.core.async.impl.channels.ManyToManyChannel@147c0def>
channels.core=> (<!! (async/into [] dc))
[0 1 2 3 4]
```

Here we create a channel with a *dropping buffer* large enough to hold five messages, and then we write the numbers 0 to 9 to it. This doesn't block, even though the channel cannot hold so many messages. When we read its contents, we find that only the first five messages are returned—all subsequent messages have been dropped.

Clojure also provides sliding-buffer:

```
channels.core=> (def sc (chan (sliding-buffer 5)))
#'channels.core/sc
channels.core=> (onto-chan sc (range 0 10))
#<ManyToManyChannel clojure.core.async.impl.channels.ManyToManyChannel@3071908b>
channels.core=> (<!! (async/into [] sc))
[5 6 7 8 9]
```

As before, we create a channel large enough to hold five messages, but this time with a *sliding buffer*. When we read its contents, we find that the five most recent messages are returned—writing to a full channel with a sliding buffer drops the oldest message. We'll look into channels in much more detail later, but before then let's look at core.async's other headline feature—go blocks.

Go Blocks

Threads have both an overhead and a startup cost, which is why most modern programs avoid creating threads directly and use a thread pool instead (see *Thread-Creation Redux*, on page 33). Indeed, the thread macro we used earlier today uses a CachedThreadPool under the hood.

Joe asks:

What—No Automatically Growing Buffer?

We've now seen all three types of buffer provided by core.async as standard—blocking, dropping, and sliding. It would be quite possible to create one that simply grows as it needs to accommodate more messages. So why isn't this provided as standard?

The reason is the age-old lesson that, whenever you have an "inexhaustible" resource, sooner or later you will exhaust it. This might be because over time your program is asked to work on larger problems, or it might be a bug that results in messages piling up because whatever should be handling them doesn't do so.

If you avoid thinking about what to do when it happens, eventually this will lead to a damaging, obscure, and difficult-to-diagnose bug sometime in the future. Indeed, flooding a process's mailbox is one of the few ways to comprehensively crash an Erlang system.[a] Better to think about how you want to handle a full buffer today and nip the problem in the bud.

---

a.   http://prog21.dadgum.com/43.html

Thread pools aren't always very convenient to use, though. In particular, they are problematic if the code we want to run might block.

The Problem with Blocking

Thread pools are a great way to handle CPU-intensive tasks—those that tie a thread up for a brief period and then return it to the pool to be reused. But what if we want to do something that involves communication? Blocking a thread ties it up indefinitely, eliminating much of the value of using a thread pool.

There are ways around this, but they typically involve restructuring code to make it *event-driven*, a style of programming that will be familiar to anyone who's done UI programming or worked with any of the recent breed of *evented* servers.

Although this works, it breaks up the natural flow of control and can make code difficult to read and reason about. Worse, it can lead to an excess of global state, with event handlers saving data for use by later handlers. And as we've seen, state and concurrency really don't mix.

Go blocks provide an alternative that gives us the best of both worlds—the efficiency of event-driven code without having to compromise its structure or readability. They achieve this by transparently rewriting sequential code into event-driven code under the hood.

Inversion of Control

In common with other Lisps, Clojure provides a powerful macro system. If you're used to macros in other languages (C/C++ pre-processor macros, for example), Lisp macros can seem like magic, enabling dramatic code transformations. The go macro is particularly magical.

Code within a go block is transformed into a state machine. Instead of blocking when it reads from or writes to a channel, the state machine *parks*, relinquishing control of the thread it's executing on. When it's next able to run, it performs a state transition and continues execution, potentially on another thread.

This represents an inversion of control, allowing the core.async runtime to efficiently multiplex many go blocks over a limited thread pool. Just how efficiently we'll soon see, but first let's see an example.

Parking

Here's a simple example of go in action:

```
channels.core=> (def ch (chan))
#'channels.core/ch
channels.core=> (go
         #_=>   (let [x (<! ch)
         #_=>         y (<! ch)]
         #_=>     (println "Sum:" (+ x y))))
#<ManyToManyChannel clojure.core.async.impl.channels.ManyToManyChannel@13ac7b98>
channels.core=> (>!! ch 3)
nil
channels.core=> (>!! ch 4)
nil
Sum: 7
```

We start by creating a channel ch, followed by a go block that reads two values from it, then prints their sum. Although it looks like the go block should block when it reads from the channel, something far more interesting is going on.

Instead of using <!! to read from the channel, our go block is using <!. The single exclamation mark indicates that this is the *parking* version of a channel read, not the blocking version. As you might expect, >! is the parking version of the blocking >!!.

The go macro converts this sequential code into a state machine with three states:

1. The initial state immediately parks, waiting for something to be available for reading from ch. When it is, the state machine transitions to state 2.

2. Next the state machine binds the value read from ch to x and then parks, waiting for another value to be available, after which it transitions to state 3.

3. Finally, the state machine binds the value read from ch to y, prints a message, and terminates.

> ### Joe asks:
> ## What Happens If I Block in a Go Block?
>
> If you call a blocking function, such as <!!, in a go block, you will simply block the thread it happens to be running on. Your code will probably execute OK (although if you block enough threads, you might deadlock because no more are available), but doing so defeats the purpose of using go blocks. Nothing will warn you if you make this mistake, however, so it's up to you to be on your guard.
>
> Happily, if you make the opposite mistake, you will be warned:
>
> ```
> channels.core=> (<! ch)
> AssertionError Assert failed: <! used not in (go ...) block
> nil  clojure.core.async/<! (async.clj:83)
> ```

Go Blocks Are Cheap

The point of all the go macro's cleverness is efficiency. Because (unlike threads) go blocks are cheap, we can create many of them without running out of resources. This may seem like a small benefit, but the ability to freely create concurrent tasks without worry is transformative.

You may have noticed that go (and thread, for that matter) returns a channel. This channel will have the result of the go block written to it when it's complete:

```
channels.core=> (<!! (go (+ 3 4)))
7
```

We can use this fact to create a small function that creates a very large number of go blocks, allowing us to see just how inexpensive go blocks are:

```
CSP/channels/src/channels/core.clj
(defn go-add [x y]
  (<!! (nth (iterate #(go (inc (<! %))) (go x)) y)))
```

This contender for the title "world's most inefficient addition function" adds x to y by creating a pipeline of y go blocks, each one of which increments its argument by one.

To see how this works, let's build it up in stages:

1. The anonymous function #(go (inc (<! %))) creates a go block that takes a single channel argument, reads a single value from it, and returns a channel containing that value incremented by one.

2. This function is passed to iterate with an initial value of (go x) (a channel that simply has the value x written to it). Recall that iterate returns a lazy sequence of the form (x (f x) (f (f x)) (f (f (f x))) …).

3. We read the y-th element of this sequence with nth, the value of which will be a channel containing the result of incrementing x y times.

4. Finally, we read the value of that channel with <!!.

Let's see it in action:

```
channels.core=> (time (go-add 10 10))
"Elapsed time: 1.935 msecs"
20
channels.core=> (time (go-add 10 1000))
"Elapsed time: 5.311 msecs"
1010
channels.core=> (time (go-add 10 100000))
"Elapsed time: 734.91 msecs"
100010
```

So that's 100,000 go blocks created and executed in around three-quarters of a second. That means that a go block compares very favorably to an Elixir process—a very impressive result given that Clojure runs on the JVM, whereas Elixir runs on the Erlang virtual machine, which was built with efficient concurrency in mind.

Now that we've seen both channels and go blocks in action, let's look at how they can be combined to build more complex operations over channels.

Operations over Channels

If you're thinking that channels have more than a little in common with sequences, you're not wrong. Like sequences, channels represent ordered sets of values. Like sequences, we should be able to implement higher-level functions that operate over all of a channel's contents—functions like map, filter, and so on. And like sequences, we should be able to chain those functions to create composite operations.

Mapping over a Channel

Here's a channel-oriented version of map:

CSP/channels/src/channels/core.clj
```clojure
(defn map-chan [f from]
  (let [to (chan)]
    (go-loop []
      (when-let [x (<! from)]
        (>! to (f x))
        (recur))
      (close! to))
    to))
```

This takes a function (f) and a source channel (from). It starts by creating a destination channel (to), which is returned at the end of the function. Before then, however, it creates a go block with go-loop, a utility function that's equivalent to (go (loop ...)). The body of the loop uses when-let to read from from and bind the value read to x. If x isn't null, the body of the when-let is executed, (f x) is written to to, and the loop executed again. If x is null, to is closed.

Here it is in action:

```clojure
channels.core=> (def ch (chan 10))
#'channels.core/ch
channels.core=> (def mapped (map-chan (partial * 2) ch))
#'channels.core/mapped
channels.core=> (onto-chan ch (range 0 10))
#<ManyToManyChannel clojure.core.async.impl.channels.ManyToManyChannel@9f3d43e>
channels.core=> (<!! (async/into [] mapped))
[0 2 4 6 8 10 12 14 16 18]
```

As you might expect, core.async provides its own version of map-chan, called map<. There's also a channel-oriented version of filter called filter<, mapcat called mapcat<, and so on. As you would expect, these can be combined to create chains of channels:

```clojure
channels.core=> (def ch (to-chan (range 0 10)))
#'channels.core/ch
channels.core=> (<!! (async/into [] (map< (partial * 2) (filter< even? ch))))
[0 4 8 12 16]
```

The preceding code uses to-chan, another core.async utility function, which creates and returns a channel containing the contents of a sequence, closing it when the sequence is exhausted.

We're almost at the end of day 1, but before we're done, let's have a bit of fun.

A Concurrent Sieve of Eratosthenes

Just because we can, here's a concurrent version of the sieve of Eratosthenes. The get-primes function returns a channel to which all the prime numbers up to limit will subsequently be written:

CSP/Sieve/src/sieve/core.clj
```
(defn factor? [x y]
  (zero? (mod y x)))

(defn get-primes [limit]
  (let [primes (chan)
        numbers (to-chan (range 2 limit))]
    (go-loop [ch numbers]
      (when-let [prime (<! ch)]
        (>! primes prime)
        (recur (remove< (partial factor? prime) ch))))
      (close! primes))
    primes))
```

We'll go through how this works in a minute (although I encourage you to work through it yourself first—you should have everything you need to do so). But first, let's prove that it works as advertised. The following main function calls get-primes and then prints out what's written to the channel it returns:

CSP/Sieve/src/sieve/core.clj
```
(defn -main [limit]
  (let [primes (get-primes (edn/read-string limit))]
    (loop []
      (when-let [prime (<!! primes)]
        (println prime)
        (recur)))))
```

And here's what we get when we run it:

```
$ lein run 100000
2
3
5
7
11
⋮
99971
99989
99991
```

Let's see how get-primes works. It starts by creating a channel called primes, which is returned at the end of the function. It then enters a loop, with ch initially bound to numbers, a channel that will have all the numbers from 2 to limit written to it courtesy of to-chan.

The loop reads the first entry from ch, which we know is a prime number (we'll see why this is true soon), so it's written to primes. We then loop back around, except this time ch is bound to the result of (remove< (partial factor? prime) ch).

The remove< function is similar to filter<, except that it returns a channel to which only values for which the predicate returns false are written. In our case, it will be a channel with all values removed for which the prime we've just identified is a factor.

So, get-primes creates a pipeline of channels; the first contains all numbers from 2 to limit, the second has all numbers that are a multiple of 2 removed, the next has all multiples of 3 removed, and so on, as shown in the following diagram:

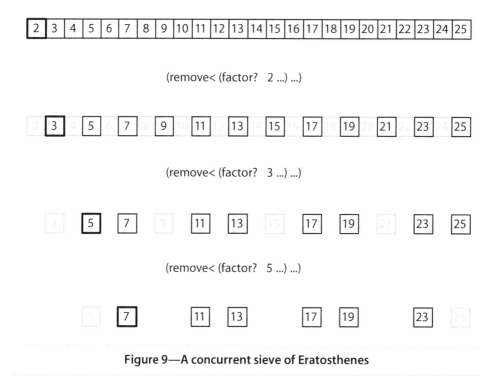

Figure 9—A concurrent sieve of Eratosthenes

I don't want to give you impression that this is an efficient way to implement a parallel prime number sieve—it's too profligate with channels for that to be true. But it's a nice demonstration of how channels can be freely combined to create arbitrary communication patterns.

Day 1 Wrap-Up

This brings us to the end of day 1. In day 2 we'll see how to read from more than one channel and how to construct an IO-intensive program with channels and go blocks.

What We Learned in Day 1

The twin pillars of core.async are channels and go blocks:

- By default, channels are synchronous (unbuffered)—writing to a channel blocks until something reads from it.

- Alternatively, channels can be buffered. Different buffering strategies allow us to decide how to handle a full buffer—we can block, discard the oldest value (sliding buffer), or discard the most recently written value (dropping buffer).

- Go blocks utilize inversion of control to rewrite sequential code as a state machine. Instead of blocking, go blocks are parked, allowing the thread that they're running on to be used by another go block.

- The blocking versions of channel operations end with two exclamation marks (!!), whereas the parking versions end with a single exclamation mark (!).

Day 1 Self-Study

Find

- The core.async documentation

- Either Timothy Baldridge's "Core Async Go Macro Internals" screencasts or Huey Petersen's "The State Machines of core.async" blog post, both of which describe how the go macro implements inversion of control.

Do

- Our implementation of map-chan created and returned a synchronous (unbuffered) channel. What would happen if it used a buffered channel instead? Which is preferable? Under what circumstances (if any) would a buffered channel be an appropriate choice?

- As well as map<, core.async provides map>. How do they differ? Create your own version of map>. When might you use one, and when the other?

- Create a channel-based version of a parallel map (similar to Clojure's existing pmap or the parallel map function we created in Elixir in the previous chapter).

Day 2: Multiple Channels and IO

Today we'll see how core.async makes asynchronous IO both simpler and easier to understand. But before then, we'll look at a feature we've not yet seen—handling multiple channels at a time.

Handling Multiple Channels

So far we've dealt only with a single channel at a time, but there's no reason we have to restrict ourselves to doing so. The alt! function allows us to write code that can deal with more than one channel:

```
channels.core=> (def ch1 (chan))
#'channels.core/ch1
channels.core=> (def ch2 (chan))
#'channels.core/ch2
channels.core=> (go-loop []
        #_=>   (alt!
        #_=>     ch1 ([x] (println "Read" x "from channel 1"))
        #_=>     ch2 ([x] (println "Twice" x "is" (* x 2))))
        #_=>   (recur))
#<ManyToManyChannel clojure.core.async.impl.channels.ManyToManyChannel@d8fd215>
channels.core=> (>!! ch1 "foo")
Read foo from channel 1
nil
channels.core=> (>!! ch2 21)
Twice 21 is 42
nil
```

Here we create two channels, ch1 and ch2, and then we create a go block that loops forever, using alt! to read from both. If there's something available to read from ch1, it's printed. If there's something available to read from ch2, it's doubled and printed.

It should be pretty clear from context what's going on here—the alt! macro takes pairs of arguments, the first of which is a channel and the second of which is code that's executed if there's anything to read from that channel. In our case that code looks similar to an anonymous function—the value read from the channel is bound to x and the subsequent println executed. But it's not an anonymous function—it doesn't start with fn.

This is another example of Clojure's macro system working its magic, allowing alt! to be both more concise and more efficient than it would if it used anonymous functions.

> **Joe asks:**
> # What About Writing to Multiple Channels?
>
> We've only scratched the surface of the alt! macro—as well as reading from multiple channels, it can also be used to write to multiple channels, or even a mix of reads and writes. We're not going to use any of this functionality in this book, but it's worth consulting the documentation if you're interested in exploring alt! further.

Timeouts

The timeout function returns a channel that closes after a certain number of milliseconds:

```
channels.core=> (time (<!! (timeout 10000)))
"Elapsed time: 10001.662 msecs"
nil
```

This can be used in conjunction with alt! to allow other channel operations to time out, as in this example:

```
channels.core=> (def ch (chan))
#'channels.core/ch
channels.core=> (let [t (timeout 10000)]
        #_=>    (go (alt!
        #_=>       ch ([x] (println "Read" x "from channel"))
        #_=>       t (println "Timed out"))))
#<ManyToManyChannel clojure.core.async.impl.channels.ManyToManyChannel@28134be9>
channels.core=>
Timed out
```

Timeouts are nothing new, of course, but this approach in which timeouts are *reified* (represented by a concrete entity) is surprisingly powerful, as we'll see next.

Reified Timeouts

Most systems support timeouts on a per-request basis. Java's URLConnection class, for example, provides the setReadTimeout() method—if the server doesn't respond within the relevant number of milliseconds, read() will throw an IOException.

This is fine if you're making a single request. But what if you want to limit the total time taken by a series of connections? Per-connection timeouts are little help here, but a reified timeout gives you exactly what you need—simply create a single timeout and use it for each connection in the sequence.

To illustrate this in action, let's modify the sieve example we created yesterday so that, instead of taking a numeric limit, it simply generates as many prime numbers as it can in a given number of seconds.

We'll start by modifying get-primes so that it generates primes forever:

CSP/SieveTimeout/src/sieve/core.clj
```
(defn get-primes []
  (let [primes (chan)
        numbers (to-chan (iterate inc 2))]
    (go-loop [ch numbers]
      (when-let [prime (<! ch)]
        (>! primes prime)
        (recur (remove< (partial factor? prime) ch)))
      (close! primes))
    primes))
```

Instead of our initial channel being generated by (range 2 limit), we use the infinite sequence (iterate inc 2).

Here's how we call it:

CSP/SieveTimeout/src/sieve/core.clj
```
(defn -main [seconds]
  (let [primes (get-primes)
        limit (timeout (* (edn/read-string seconds) 1000))]
    (loop []
      (alt!! :priority true
        limit nil
        primes ([prime] (println prime) (recur))))))
```

We're using alt!!, which is, as you would expect, the blocking version of alt!. This blocks until either a new prime is available or limit times out, in which case it simply returns nil. The :priority true option ensures that the clauses passed to alt!! are evaluated in order (by default, if two clauses could execute, one is chosen nondeterministically). This avoids the (admittedly unlikely) event of primes being generated so quickly that there's always one available and the timeout clause never gets evaluated. This is a very natural way to express the problem we're trying to solve—much more natural than anything we could create with per-request timeouts.

In the next section we'll use timeouts, together with Clojure's macro system, to build a convenient utility that addresses a common use case—polling.

Asynchronous Polling

Later today we're going to build an RSS reader. Among other things, it will need to poll the news-feeds it's monitoring to detect new articles. In this section we'll use timeouts, together with Clojure's macro support, to build a utility that makes efficient, asynchronous polling almost trivially easy.

A Polling Function

The timeout function we saw earlier today is exactly what we need to implement polling. Here's a function that takes an interval in seconds, together with a function, and calls that function once every interval:

CSP/Polling/src/polling/core.clj
```
(defn poll-fn [interval action]
  (let [seconds (* interval 1000)]
    (go (while true
          (action)
          (<! (timeout seconds))))))
```

It's simple enough, and it works exactly as you might expect:

```
polling.core=> (poll-fn 10 #(println "Polling at:" (System/currentTimeMillis)))
#<ManyToManyChannel clojure.core.async.impl.channels.ManyToManyChannel@6e624159>
polling.core=>
Polling at: 1388827086165
Polling at: 1388827096166
Polling at: 1388827106168
⋮
```

But there's a problem—you might think that because poll-fn calls the function it's given within a go block, that function should be able to call parking functions. But let's see what happens if we try:

```
polling.core=> (def ch (to-chan (iterate inc 0)))
#'polling.core/ch
polling.core=> (poll-fn 10 #(println "Read:" (<! ch)))
Exception in thread "async-dispatch-1" java.lang.AssertionError:
  Assert failed: <! used not in (go ...) block
nil
```

The problem is that parking calls need to be made *directly* within a go block—Clojure's macro system is unable to perform its magic otherwise.

A Polling Macro

The solution is to write our polling utility as a macro instead of as a function:

CSP/Polling/src/polling/core.clj
```
(defmacro poll [interval & body]
  `(let [seconds# (* ~interval 1000)]
     (go (while true
           (do ~@body)
           (<! (timeout seconds#))))))
```

We can't discuss Clojure macros in detail here, so you'll have to take quite a bit of this on trust. We'll look at poll's expansion soon, but in the meantime here are a few pointers that should help you understand how it works:

- Instead of being directly compiled, a macro returns code that is then compiled in turn.
- The backtick (`) is the syntax quote operator. It takes source code and, instead of executing it, returns a representation of it that can be subsequently compiled.
- Within that code, we can use the ~ (*unquote*) and ~@ (*unquote splice*) operators to refer to arguments passed to the macro.
- The # (*auto-gensym*) suffix indicates that Clojure should automatically generate a unique name (which guarantees that it won't clash with any names used by code passed to the macro).

Let's see it in action:

```
polling.core=> (poll 10
         #_=>   (println "Polling at:" (System/currentTimeMillis))
         #_=>   (println (<! ch)))
#<ManyToManyChannel clojure.core.async.impl.channels.ManyToManyChannel@1bec079e>
polling.core=>
Polling at: 1388829368011
0
Polling at: 1388829378018
1
⋮
```

Because macros are expanded at compile time, the code passed to poll is inlined and therefore directly contained within poll's go block, meaning that we can pass code that contains parking calls. But that's not the only advantage of using a macro—because we're passing a chunk of code rather than a function, the syntax is much more natural—no need to create an anonymous function. In fact, we've created our own control structure.

We can examine the code generated by poll by looking at its macro expansion:

```
polling.core=> (macroexpand-1
          #_=>   '(poll 10
          #_=>       (println "Polling at:" (System/currentTimeMillis))
          #_=>       (println (<! ch))))
(clojure.core/let [seconds__2691__auto__ (clojure.core/* 10 1000)]
  (clojure.core.async/go
    (clojure.core/while true
      (do
        (println "Polling at:" (System/currentTimeMillis))
        (println (<! ch)))
      (clojure.core.async/<! (clojure.core.async/timeout seconds__2691__auto__)))))
```

I've reformatted the output of macroexpand-1 slightly to make it easier to read. You can see how the code that was passed to poll has been pasted (spliced) into the code within the macro itself and how seconds# has been turned into a unique name (to see why this is important, imagine that the code that we passed to poll used seconds to mean something else).

We'll see a practical use of our poll macro in the next section.

Asynchronous IO

IO is one area where asynchronous code comes into its own—instead of the traditional approach of having a thread per connection, asynchronous IO allows us to start a number of operations and receive a notification whenever one of them has data available. Although this is a powerful approach, it can be challenging, with code tending to turn into a mess of callbacks calling callbacks. In this section we'll see how core.async can make it much easier.

In keeping with the word-counting examples from earlier chapters, we're going to build an RSS reader that monitors a set of news feeds and, whenever it sees a new article, counts how many words it contains. We're going to construct this as a pipeline of concurrent go blocks connected by channels:

1. The lowest-level go block monitors a single news feed, polling it once every sixty seconds. After parsing the returned XML, it extracts links to news articles and passes them along the pipeline.

2. The next go block maintains a list of all the articles that have already been retrieved from a particular news feed. Whenever it sees a new article, it passes its URL along the pipeline.

3. The next go block retrieves news articles in turn, counts the words contained within, and passes the resulting counts along the pipeline.

4. The counts from multiple news feeds are merged into a single channel.

5. The highest-level go block monitors this merged channel and prints new counts as they're received.

This structure is shown in Figure 10, *The Structure of the RSS Reader*, on page 172.

Let's start by seeing how to integrate an existing asynchronous IO library into core.async.

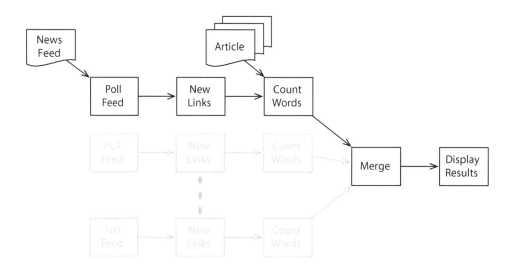

Figure 10—The Structure of the RSS Reader

From Callbacks to Channels

We're going to use the http-kit library.[3] In common with many asynchronous IO libraries, http-kit indicates that an operation has completed by calling a callback function:

```
wordcount.core=> (require '[org.httpkit.client :as http])
nil
wordcount.core=> (defn handle-response [response]
         #_=>    (let [url (get-in response [:opts :url])
         #_=>          status (:status response)]
         #_=>      (println "Fetched:" url "with status:" status)))
#'wordcount.core/handle-response
wordcount.core=> (http/get "http://paulbutcher.com/" handle-response)
#<core$promise$reify__6310@3a9280d0: :pending>
wordcount.core=>
Fetched: http://paulbutcher.com/ with status: 200
```

Our first task is to get http-kit to integrate with core.async by wrapping http/get. We're going to use a function we've not seen before—put! doesn't have to be called within a go block and implements a "fire and forget" write to a channel (and will neither block nor park the task it's called from):

---

3.   http://http-kit.org

CSP/WordCount/src/wordcount/http.clj

```
(defn http-get [url]
  (let [ch (chan)]
    (http/get url (fn [response]
                    (if (= 200 (:status response))
                      (put! ch response)
                      (do (report-error response) (close! ch)))))
    ch))
```

We start by creating a channel, which is returned at the end of the function (a pattern that should be becoming familiar to you by now), and then we call http/get, which returns immediately. At some point in the future, when the GET operation completes, our callback is called. If the status is 200 (success), the callback simply writes the response to the channel, and if the status is anything else, it reports an error and closes the channel.

Next, we'll create a function that polls an RSS feed.

Polling a Feed

As you would hope, now that we've got http-get and poll, polling an RSS feed is simplicity itself:

CSP/WordCount/src/wordcount/feed.clj

```
(def poll-interval 60)

; Simple-minded feed-polling function
; WARNING: Don't use in production (use conditional get instead)

(defn poll-feed [url]
  (let [ch (chan)]
    (poll poll-interval
      (when-let [response (<! (http-get url))]
        (let [feed (parse-feed (:body response))]
          (onto-chan ch (get-links feed) false))))
    ch))
```

The parse-feed and get-links functions use the Rome library to parse the XML returned by the news feed.[4] We won't look at them here, but you can examine the source code if you're interested in the details.

The list of links returned by get-links is written to ch with onto-chan. By default, onto-chan closes the channel when the sequence it's given is exhausted; we disable this behaviour by passing false as the final argument.

Here it is in action:

---

4.   http://rometools.github.io/rome/

```
wordcount.core=> (ns wordcount.feed)
nil
wordcount.feed=> (def feed (poll-feed "http://www.cbsnews.com/feeds/rss/main.rss"))
#'wordcount.feed/feed
wordcount.feed=> (loop []
          #_=>    (when-let [url (<!! feed)]
          #_=>       (println url)
          #_=>       (recur)))
http://www.cbsnews.com/news/three-year-old-dies-after-visit-to-dentist-in-hawaii/
http://www.cbsnews.com/news/obama-unemployment-benefits-expiration-just-plain-cruel/
http://www.cbsnews.com/news/rand-paul-says-hes-suing-over-nsa-surveillance-programs/
⋮
```

Next we'll see how to filter the links returned by poll-feed to remove duplicates.

Don't Try This at Home

Although this simple polling strategy is OK for an example in a book, please don't use it in production. Fetching the entire feed each time you poll places an unnecessarily high load on both your network bandwidth and the server you're polling, a load that can be reduced by using HTTP's conditional get.[a]

_____

a.   http://fishbowl.pastiche.org/2002/10/21/http_conditional_get_for_rss_hackers/

Unique Links

Our poll-feed function simply returns every link it finds every time it polls the news feed, which results in many duplicates. What we really want is a channel that contains just the new links that have appeared on the feed. This is exactly what the following function gives us:

CSP/WordCount/src/wordcount/feed.clj
```
(defn new-links [url]
  (let [in (poll-feed url)
        out (chan)]
    (go-loop [links #{}]
      (let [link (<! in)]
        (if (contains? links link)
          (recur links)
          (do
            (>! out link)
            (recur (conj links link))))))
    out))
```

We start by creating two channels, in and out. The first is the channel returned by poll-feed; the second is where we'll write new links. We then start a loop within a go block that maintains links, a set of all the links we've seen to date, which is initially bound to the empty set #{}. Whenever we read a link from in, we check to see whether it's already in links. If it is, we do nothing; otherwise we write the new link to out and add it to links.

Run this from the REPL, and instead of a new tranche of links being generated every sixty seconds, you should only see new links being returned.

Now that we have a feed of links to new articles, the next step is to fetch each of them in turn and count how many words they contain.

Counting Words

With what we've seen so far, the get-counts function almost writes itself:

CSP/WordCount/src/wordcount/core.clj
```
(defn get-counts [urls]
  (let [counts (chan)]
    (go (while true
          (let [url (<! urls)]
            (when-let [response (<! (http-get url))]
              (let [c (count (get-words (:body response)))]
                (>! counts [url c]))))))
    counts))
```

It takes a channel urls and, for each URL read from it, fetches the article with http-get, counts the words contained within, and writes a two-element array, where the first item is the article's URL and the second is the word count to its output channel.

We're almost done—now we just need to wire everything together.

Putting It All Together

Here's a main function that implements our complete RSS word counter:

CSP/WordCount/src/wordcount/core.clj
```
Line 1 (defn -main [feeds-file]
     2   (with-open [rdr (io/reader feeds-file)]
     3     (let [feed-urls (line-seq rdr)
     4           article-urls (doall (map new-links feed-urls))
     5           article-counts (doall (map get-counts article-urls))
     6           counts (async/merge article-counts)]
     7       (while true
     8         (println (<!! counts)))))))
```

This creates a program that takes a file containing a list of news-feed URLs, one on each line. We create a reader for the file on line 2 (Clojure's with-open function ensures that the file is closed when the reader goes out of scope). And then we convert it into a sequence of URLs with line-seq (line 3). Mapping new-links over this (line 4) turns it into a sequence of channels, each of which will have links to new articles written to it when they're published. And mapping get-counts over that sequence (line 5) gives us a sequence of channels that will have counts written to them whenever an article is published.

Finally, we use async/merge (line 6) to merge this sequence of channels into a single channel that contains anything written to any of its source channels. The code then loops forever, printing anything that's written to that merged channel (line 7). Here it is in action:

```
$ lein run feeds.txt
[http://www.bbc.co.uk/sport/0/football/25611509 10671]
[http://www.wired.co.uk/news/archive/2014-01/04/time-travel 11188]
[http://news.sky.com/story/1190148 3488]
⋮
```

Keep an eye on your CPU usage while running it. Not only is this code very straightforward and easy to read, but it's very efficient, capable of monitoring hundreds of feeds concurrently while barely consuming any CPU resources.

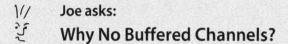

Joe asks:
Why No Buffered Channels?

Take a look at the channels we created today—all of them are unbuffered (synchronous). Newcomers to CSP tend to assume that buffered channels will be used much more frequently than unbuffered, but in fact the opposite is true. Buffered channels do have valid use cases, but think carefully before using one. Make sure that a buffer is necessary.

Day 2 Wrap-Up

That brings us to the end of day 2. In day 3 we'll see how to use core.async client-side via ClojureScript.

What We Learned in Day 2

Channels and go blocks allow us to create efficient asynchronous code that reads naturally, without the complexity that normally results from using callback functions.

- Existing callback-based APIs can be brought into the asynchronous world by providing a minimal callback function that simply writes to a channel.

- The alt! macro allows a task to read from, or write to, multiple channels.

- The timeout function returns a channel that closes after an interval—allowing timeouts to be treated as first-class entities (reified).

- Parking calls need to be directly contained within a go block. Clojure's macros can be used to inline code, allowing larger go blocks to be broken up without falling foul of this limitation.

Day 2 Self-Study

Find

- As well as alt!, core.async also provides alts!. How do they differ? When might you use one and when the other?

- In addition to async/merge, core.async provides a number of ways to combine multiple channels. Find the documentation for pub, sub, mult, tap, mix, and admix. When might they be useful?

Do

- Spend some time working through the order in which things take place in the RSS reader. Notice that because we're using unbuffered channels throughout, the result is very similar to a dataflow program, with earlier go blocks in the pipeline executing as a result of later ones being available to consume data.

  What would happen if you used buffered channels instead? Are there any benefits to doing so? What problems are caused by using buffered channels?

- Implement your own version of async/merge. Remember to handle the case where one or more of the source channels are closed. (Hint: You might find this easier to implement with alts! than with alt!).

- Use Clojure's macro expansion facility to examine the macro expansion of alt!:

  ```
  channels.core=> (macroexpand-1 '(alt! ch1 ([x] (println x)) ch2 ([y] (println y))))
  ```

  You will probably find it easier to understand if you format the code first to get the indentation right and if you remove the clojure.core prefixes. Can you see how alt! achieves the effect of calling an anonymous function without actually doing so?

Day 3: Client-Side CSP

ClojureScript is a version of Clojure that, instead of compiling to Java byte-codes, cross-compiles to JavaScript (see http://clojurescript.com). This means that it's possible to create a web app in which both the server- and client-side code are written in Clojure.

One of the most compelling reasons to do so is that ClojureScript supports core.async, which brings a number of benefits that we'll explore today, not the least of which is a remedy to the bane of the JavaScript developer's life—callback hell.

Concurrency Is a State of Mind

If you've done any significant client-side JavaScript programming, you're probably wondering if I've gone mad—browser-based JavaScript engines are single threaded, so what relevance can core.async possibly have? Don't you need multiple threads for concurrent programming to be useful?

The go macro's inversion of control magic means that ClojureScript can bring the *appearance* of multiple threads to client-side programming even in the absence of true multithreading. This is a form of *cooperative multitasking*—one task won't preemptively interrupt another. As we'll see, this enables dramatic improvements in code structure and clarity.

Joe asks:
What About Web Workers?

Recent browsers support a limited form of truly multithreaded JavaScript via *web workers*.[a] Web workers are intended for background tasks only, however, and don't have access to the DOM.

Web workers can be used in ClojureScript via, for example, the Servant library.[b]

a. http://www.whatwg.org/specs/web-apps/current-work/multipage/workers.html
b. https://github.com/MarcoPolo/servant

Hello, ClojureScript

ClojureScript is very similar to Clojure, but there are a few differences—we'll mention those that will affect us as we run into them.

A typical ClojureScript application has a two-stage compilation process. First, the client-side ClojureScript is compiled to create a JavaScript file, and then the server-side code is compiled and run to create a server that serves pages with that JavaScript included within a <script> tag. Today's examples all make use of the lein-cljsbuild Leiningen plugin to automate this build process.[5] The server-side code resides in src-clj, and the client-side code in src-cljs.

---

5. https://github.com/emezeske/lein-cljsbuild

Let's look at a simple example project, comprising a single page with a single script. Here's the page:

CSP/HelloClojureScript/resources/public/index.html
```
Line 1  <html>
     2    <head>
     3      <title>Hello ClojureScript</title>
     4      <script src="/js/main.js" type="text/javascript"></script>
     5    </head>
     6    <body>
     7      <div id="content">
     8      </div>
     9    </body>
    10  </html>
```

The generated JavaScript is included on line 4. That script will populate the empty <div> on line 7. Here's its source:

CSP/HelloClojureScript/src-cljs/hello_clojurescript/core.cljs
```
Line 1  (ns hello-clojurescript.core
          (:require-macros [cljs.core.async.macros :refer [go]])
          (:require [goog.dom :as dom]
                    [cljs.core.async :refer [<! timeout]]))
     5
        (defn output [elem message]
          (dom/append elem message (dom/createDom "br")))
        (defn start []
          (let [content (dom/getElement "content")]
    10      (go
              (while true
                (<! (timeout 1000))
                (output content "Hello from task 1")))
            (go
    15        (while true
                (<! (timeout 1500))
                (output content "Hello from task 2")))))

        (set! (.-onload js/window) start)
```

One difference between Clojure and ClojureScript is that any macros used by a script need to be referenced separately with :require-macros (line 2). The output function on line 6 uses the Google Closure library (that's closure with an s, not a j) to append a message to a DOM element.[6]

This function is used on lines 13 and 17, each of which is within independently running go blocks. The first prints a message once every second, the other once every second and a half.

---

6. https://developers.google.com/closure/library/

Finally, on line 19, our start function is set to run by associating it with the JavaScript window object's onload attribute. This uses ClojureScript's *dot special form*, which provides JavaScript interoperability, which takes this:

```
(set! (.-onload js/window) start)
```

and translates it into this:

```
window.onload = hello_clojurescript.core.start;
```

We won't look at the code for the server here, since it's very simple (see the accompanying code if you're interested in the details).

Compile the script with lein cljsbuild once, run the server with lein run, and point your browser at http://localhost:3000. You should see something like this:

```
Hello from task 1
Hello from task 2
Hello from task 1
Hello from task 1
Hello from task 2
⋮
```

Who says you need threads to have concurrency?

Independently running concurrent tasks are great as far as they go, but most user interfaces need to interact with the user, which means handling events, the next thing we'll look at.

Handling Events

We'll see how event handling works in ClojureScript by creating a simple animation that reacts to mouse clicks. We're going to create a web page that displays circles that shrink to a point and eventually disappear wherever the user clicks, as shown in Figure 11, *Shrinking circles*, on page 181.

The code for the page is very simple, comprising a single <div> that fills the entire window:

CSP/Animation/resources/public/index.html
```
<html>
  <head>
    <title>Animation</title>
    <script src="/js/main.js" type="text/javascript"></script>
  </head>
  <body>
    <div id="canvas" width="100%" height="100%"></div>
  </body>
</html>
```

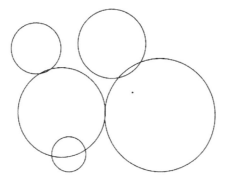

Figure 11—Shrinking circles

To draw on this page, we're going to make use of Google Closure's graphics support, which abstracts away from the details of drawing within different browsers. The create-graphics function takes a DOM element and returns an object that allows us to use it as a graphics surface:

CSP/Animation/src-cljs/animation/core.cljs
```
(defn create-graphics [elem]
  (doto (graphics/createGraphics "100%" "100%")
    (.render elem)))
```

And here's shrinking-circle, which takes such a graphics surface and a position and creates a go block that animates a circle centered on the position:

CSP/Animation/src-cljs/animation/core.cljs
```
Line 1 (def stroke (graphics/Stroke. 1 "#ff0000"))

       (defn shrinking-circle [graphics x y]
         (go
    5      (let [circle (.drawCircle graphics x y 100 stroke nil)]
             (loop [r 100]
               (<! (timeout 25))
               (.setRadius circle r r)
               (when (> r 0)
   10            (recur (dec r))))
             (.dispose circle)))))
```

We start by creating a circle with Google Closure's drawCircle function (line 5) and then enter a loop that uses a 25 ms timeout (line 7) to call setRadius forty times a second. Finally, when the radius has decreased to zero, we delete the circle with dispose (line 11).

Now we need a way to tell when the user clicks the mouse on the page. Google Closure provides the listen function, which allows us to register event listeners.

Like the http/get function we saw yesterday, this takes a callback function that's called whenever an event is available. So as we did yesterday, we're going to translate this into the core.async world by passing a callback that writes events to a channel:

CSP/Animation/src-cljs/animation/core.cljs
```
(defn get-events [elem event-type]
  (let [ch (chan)]
    (events/listen elem event-type
      #(put! ch %))
    ch))
```

We now have all we need to construct our script:

CSP/Animation/src-cljs/animation/core.cljs
```
(defn start []
  (let [canvas (dom/getElement "canvas")
        graphics (create-graphics canvas)
        clicks (get-events canvas "click")]
    (go (while true
          (let [click (<! clicks)
                x (.-offsetX click)
                y (.-offsetY click)]
            (shrinking-circle graphics x y))))))

(set! (.-onload js/window) start)
```

We start by looking up the <div> that we'll be using as our canvas, constructing a graphics object that allows us to draw on it, and getting hold of a channel of mouse-click events. Then we enter a loop that waits for a mouse click, extracts its coordinates with offsetX and offsetY, and creates an animated circle at that position.

This all seems very simple (and it is), but by moving from JavaScript's callback-oriented world to core.async's channel-oriented world, we've achieved something profound—a solution to callback hell.

Taming Callbacks

Callback hell is a term coined to describe the spaghetti code that results from JavaScript's callback-heavy approach—callbacks calling callbacks calling callbacks, with various elements of state stashed away so that one callback can communicate with the next.

Moving to an asynchronous programming model provides us with a way out, as we'll see next.

We're Off to See the Wizard

A *wizard* is a common UI pattern in which the user is taken through a sequence of steps to achieve a goal. The last thing we'll do today is use what we've learned to create a callback-less wizard:

Our wizard comprises a form with a number of fieldsets:

CSP/Wizard/resources/public/index.html
```html
<form id="wizard" action="/wizard" method="post">
  <fieldset class="step" id="step1">
    <legend>Step 1</legend>
    <label>First Name:</label><input type="text" name="firstname" />
    <label>Last Name:</label><input type="text" name="lastname" />
  </fieldset>

  <fieldset class="step" id="step2">
    <legend>Step 2</legend>
    <label>Date of Birth:</label><input type="date" name="dob" />
    <label>Homepage:</label><input type="url" name="url" />
  </fieldset>

  <fieldset class="step" id="step3">
    <legend>Step 3</legend>
    <label>Password:</label><input type="password" name="pass1" />
    <label>Confirm Password:</label><input type="password" name="pass2" />
  </fieldset>
  <input type="button" id="next" value="Next" />
</form>
```

Each <fieldset> represents a single step. We start with all of them hidden:

CSP/Wizard/resources/public/styles.css
```css
label { display:block; width:8em; clear:left; float:left;
    text-align:right; margin-right: 3pt; }
input { display:block; }
.step { display:none; }
```

Our script uses the following utility functions to show and hide the relevant fieldset as necessary:

CSP/Wizard/src-cljs/wizard/core.cljs

```
(defn show [elem]
  (set! (.. elem -style -display) "block"))

(defn hide [elem]
  (set! (.. elem -style -display) "none"))

(defn set-value [elem value]
  (set! (.-value elem) value))
```

These use a variant of the dot special form that allows attribute accesses to be chained, which takes this:

```
(set! (.. elem -style -display) "block")
```

and translates it into this:

```
elem.style.display = "block";
```

Here's the code that implements the wizard control flow:

CSP/Wizard/src-cljs/wizard/core.cljs

```
Line 1 (defn start []
       (go
         (let [wizard (dom/getElement "wizard")
               step1 (dom/getElement "step1")
    5          step2 (dom/getElement "step2")
               step3 (dom/getElement "step3")
               next-button (dom/getElement "next")
               next-clicks (get-events next-button "click")]
           (show step1)
   10      (<! next-clicks)
           (hide step1)
           (show step2)
           (<! next-clicks)
           (set-value next-button "Finish")
   15      (hide step2)
           (show step3)
           (<! next-clicks)
           (.submit wizard)))))

   20 (set! (.-onload js/window) start)
```

We start by getting references to each of the form elements we'll be dealing with and use the get-events function we wrote earlier to get a channel of "Next" button clicks (line 8). Then it's a simple case of showing the first step and waiting for the user to click Next (line 10). When the user clicks, we hide step 1, show step 2, and wait for another click on Next. This continues until every step has been completed, at which point we submit the form (line 18).

What stands out about this code is how unremarkable it is—a wizard is a simple linear sequence of steps, and this code reads like a simple linear sequence of steps. Of course, thanks to the magic of the go macro, we know that it's no such thing—what we've actually created is a state machine that runs when it can and parks when it's waiting for the stimulus that allows it to perform a state transition. But almost all of the time, we can ignore that fact and treat it like the linear code it appears to be.

Day 3 Wrap-Up

This brings us to the end of day 3 and our discussion of core.async's version of communicating sequential processes.

What We Learned in Day 3

ClojureScript is a Clojure variant that cross-compiles to JavaScript, allowing the power of core.async to be brought to bear on client-side development. Not only does this bring a form of cooperative multitasking to single-threaded JavaScript environments, but it also provides a respite from callback hell.

Day 3 Self-Study

Find

- The ClojureScript implementation of core.async supports parking operations like <! and >!, but not their blocking equivalents <!! or >!!. Why not?

- The documentation for take!—how would you use this to convert a channel-based API into a callback-based API? When might this be useful? (Hint: This may be related to the previous question).

Do

- Use core.async to create a simple browser-based game like Snake, Pong, or Breakout.

- Create a native JavaScript version of the wizard we implemented earlier today. How does it compare to the ClojureScript version?

Wrap-Up

On the surface, actor and CSP programs are very similar—both are constructed from independent, concurrently executing tasks that communicate by sending each other messages. But as we've seen in this chapter, their different emphases result in very different flavors.

Strengths

The primary strength of CSP compared to actors is flexibility. In an actor program, the medium of communication is tightly coupled to the unit of execution—each actor has precisely one mailbox. In a CSP program, by contrast, channels are first class and can be independently created, written to, read from, and passed between tasks.

Rich Hickey, creator of the Clojure language, explained his reasons for choosing CSP over actors like this:[7]

> I remain unenthusiastic about actors. They still couple the producer with the consumer. Yes, one can emulate or implement certain kinds of queues with actors (and, notably, people often do), but since any actor mechanism already incorporates a queue, it seems evident that queues are more primitive.

From a more pragmatic point of view, modern implementations of CSP like core.async that use inversion of control to provide asynchronous tasks bring both efficiency and a dramatically improved programming model to application areas that have traditionally been based on callbacks. We've seen two of these—asynchronous IO and UI programming—but there are many others.

Weaknesses

If you compare this chapter with the previous one on actors, two topics are conspicuous by their absence—distribution and fault tolerance. Although there's nothing whatsoever to stop CSP-based languages from supporting both, historically neither has had the same level of focus and support as either has had within actor-based languages—there's no CSP equivalent of OTP.

As with both threads and locks and actors, CSP programs are susceptible to deadlock and have no direct support for parallelism. Parallel solutions need to be built from concurrent building blocks, raising the specter of nondeterminism.

Other Languages

Like actors, CSP has been around since the 1970s, when it was introduced by Tony Hoare. The two models have largely coevolved, each learning from the other over the years.

---

7.   http://clojure.com/blog/2013/06/28/clojure-core-async-channels.html

In the 1980s, CSP formed the basis for the language occam (upon which this author cut his parallel-programming teeth),[8] but without question the language that's done most to popularize the model recently is Go.

The inversion of control–based approach to asynchronous tasks provided by both core.async and Go is becoming widely adopted, with support available in, among others, F#,[9] C#,[10] Nemerle,[11] and Scala.[12]

Final Thoughts

Most of the differences between actors and CSP result from the differing focus of the communities that have developed around them. The actor community has concentrated on fault tolerance and distribution, and the CSP community on efficiency and expressiveness. Choosing between them, therefore, is largely a question of deciding which of these aspects is most important to you.

CSP is the last general-purpose programming model we'll be looking at. In the next chapter we're going to look at our first special-purpose model.

8. http://en.wikipedia.org/wiki/Occam_programming_language
9. http://blogs.msdn.com/b/dsyme/archive/2007/10/11/introducing-f-asynchronous-workflows.aspx
10. http://msdn.microsoft.com/en-us/library/hh191443.aspx
11. https://github.com/rsdn/nemerle/wiki/Computation-Expression-macro#async
12. http://docs.scala-lang.org/sips/pending/async.html

CHAPTER 7

Data Parallelism

Data parallelism is like an eight-lane highway. Even though each vehicle is traveling at a relatively modest speed, the number of cars that pass a particular point is huge because many vehicles can travel side-by-side.

All the approaches we've discussed so far have been applicable to a wide variety of programming problems. Data-parallel programming, by contrast, is relevant only to a much narrower range. As its name suggests, it's a parallel-programming technique, not a concurrency technique (recall that concurrency and parallelism are related but different—see *Concurrent or Parallel?*, on page 1).

The Supercomputer Hidden in Your Laptop

In this chapter we're going to see how to leverage the supercomputer hidden in your laptop—the graphics processing unit or GPU. A modern GPU is a powerful data-parallel processor, capable of eclipsing the CPU when used for number-crunching, a practice that is commonly referred to as *general-purpose computing on the GPU* or GPGPU programming.

Over the years, a number of technologies have emerged to abstract away from the details of GPU implementation. We'll be using the Open Computing Language, or OpenCL, to write GPGPU code.[1]

In day 1 we'll see the basics of constructing an OpenCL kernel, together with the host program that compiles and executes it. In day 2 we'll look at how a kernel is mapped onto hardware in more depth. Finally, in day 3 we'll see how OpenCL can interoperate with graphics code written with the Open Graphics Library, or OpenGL.[2]

---

1. http://www.khronos.org/opencl/
2. http://www.opengl.org

Day 1: GPGPU Programming

Today we'll see how to create a simple GPGPU program that multiplies two arrays in parallel, and then we'll benchmark it to see just how much faster the GPU is than the CPU. First, though, we'll spend a little time examining what makes a GPU so powerful when it comes to number-crunching.

Graphics Processing and Data Parallelism

Computer graphics is all about manipulating data—huge amounts of data. And doing it quickly. A scene in a 3D game is constructed from a myriad of tiny triangles, each of which needs to have its position on the screen calculated in perspective relative to the viewpoint, clipped, lit, and textured twenty-five or more times a second.

The great thing about this is that although the amount of data that needs to be processed is huge, the actual operations on that data are relatively simple vector or matrix operations. This makes them very amenable to *data parallelization*, in which multiple computing units perform the same operations on different items of data in parallel.

Modern GPUs are exceptionally sophisticated, powerful parallel processors capable of rendering *billions* of triangles a second. The good news is that although they were originally designed with graphics alone in mind, their capabilities have evolved to the point that they're useful for a much wider range of applications.

Data parallelism can be implemented in many different ways. We'll look briefly at a couple of them: pipelining and multiple ALUs.

Pipelining

Although we tend to think of multiplying two numbers as a single atomic operation, down at the level of the gates on a chip, it actually takes several steps. These steps are typically arranged as a pipeline:

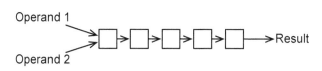

For the five-element pipeline shown here, if it takes a single clock cycle for each step to complete, multiplying a pair of numbers will take five clock cycles. But if we have lots of numbers to multiply, things get much better because (assuming our memory subsystem can supply the data fast enough) we can keep the pipeline full:

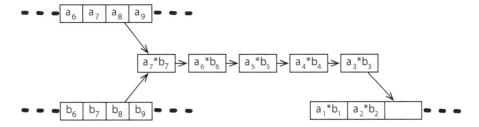

So multiplying a thousand pairs of numbers takes a whisker over a thousand clock cycles, not the five thousand we might expect from the fact that multiplying a single pair takes five clock cycles.

Multiple ALUs

The component within a CPU that performs operations such as multiplication is commonly known as the *arithmetic logic unit*, or ALU:

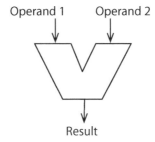

Couple multiple ALUs with a wide memory bus that allows multiple operands to be fetched simultaneously, and operations on large amounts of data can again be parallelized, as shown in Figure 12, *Large Amounts of Data Parallelized with Multiple ALUs*, on page 192.

GPUs typically have a 256-bit or wider memory bus, allowing (for example) eight or more 32-bit floating-point numbers to be fetched at a time.

A Confused Picture

To achieve their performance, real-world GPUs combine pipelining and multiple ALUs with a wide range of other techniques that we'll not cover here. By itself, this would make understanding the details of a single GPU complex. Unfortunately, there's little commonality between different GPUs (even those produced by a single manufacturer). If we had to write code that directly targeted a particular architecture, GPGPU programming would be a nonstarter.

OpenCL targets multiple architectures by defining a C-like language that allows us to express a parallel algorithm abstractly. Each different GPU

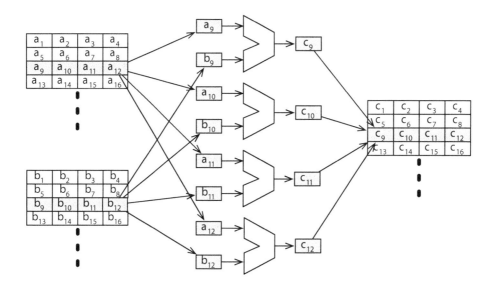

Figure 12—Large Amounts of Data Parallelized with Multiple ALUs

manufacturer then provides its own compilers and drivers that allow that program to be compiled and run on its hardware.

Our First OpenCL Program

To parallelize our array multiplication task with OpenCL, we need to divide it up into work-items that will then be executed in parallel.

Work-Items

If you're used to writing parallel code, you will be used to worrying about the *granularity* of each parallel task. Typically, if each task performs too little work, your code performs badly because thread creation and communication overheads dominate.

OpenCL work-items, by contrast, are typically very small. To multiply two 1,024-element arrays pairwise, for example, we could create 1,024 work-items (see Figure 13, *Work Items for Pairwise Multiplication*, on page 193).

Your task as a programmer is to divide your problem into the smallest work-items you can. The OpenCL compiler and runtime then worry about how best to schedule those work-items on the available hardware so that that hardware is utilized as efficiently as possible.

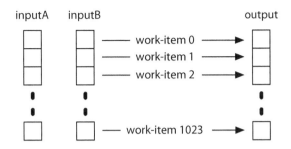

Figure 13—Work Items for Pairwise Multiplication

Optimizing OpenCL

You won't be surprised to hear that the real-world picture isn't quite this simple. Optimizing an OpenCL application often involves thinking carefully about the available resources and providing hints to the compiler and runtime to help them schedule your work-items. Sometimes this includes restricting the available parallelism for efficiency purposes.

As always, however, premature optimization is the root of all programming evil. In the majority of cases, you should aim for maximum parallelism and the smallest possible work-items and worry about optimization only afterward.

Kernels

We specify how each work-item should be processed by writing an OpenCL kernel. Here's a kernel that we could use to implement the preceding:

DataParallelism/MultiplyArrays/multiply_arrays.cl

```
__kernel void multiply_arrays(__global const float* inputA,
                              __global const float* inputB,
                              __global float* output) {

  int i = get_global_id(0);
  output[i] = inputA[i] * inputB[i];
}
```

This kernel takes pointers to two input arrays, inputA and inputB, and an output array, output. It calls get_global_id() to determine which work-item it's handling and then simply writes the result of multiplying the corresponding elements of inputA and inputB to the appropriate element of output.

To create a complete program, we need to embed our kernel in a host program that performs the following steps:

1. Create a context within which the kernel will run together with a command queue.
2. Compile the kernel.
3. Create buffers for input and output data.
4. Enqueue a command that executes the kernel once for each work-item.
5. Retrieve the results.

The OpenCL standard defines both C and C++ bindings. However, unofficial bindings are available for most major languages, so you can write your host program in almost any language you like. We're going to stick to C to start with because that's the language the OpenCL standard uses and because it gives the best picture of what's going on under the hood. In day 3 we'll see a host program written in Java.

In the next few sections, we'll put together a complete OpenCL host program. To make the underlying structure as clear as possible, I'm going to play a bit fast and loose and not include any error handling—don't worry, we'll come back to this later. You'll also notice that there are a lot of NULL arguments to functions—again, don't worry about these too much right now; we'll revisit the API in more detail after we've got a better feeling for the big picture.

Create a Context

An OpenCL context represents an environment within which OpenCL kernels can execute. To create a context, we first need to identify the platform that we want to use and which devices within that platform we want to execute our kernel (we'll talk about platforms and devices in more detail later):

DataParallelism/MultiplyArrays/multiply_arrays.c
```
cl_platform_id platform;
clGetPlatformIDs(1, &platform, NULL);

cl_device_id device;
clGetDeviceIDs(platform, CL_DEVICE_TYPE_GPU, 1, &device, NULL);

cl_context context = clCreateContext(NULL, 1, &device, NULL, NULL, NULL);
```

We want a simple context that only contains a single GPU, so after identifying a platform with clGetPlatformIDs(), we pass CL_DEVICE_TYPE_GPU to clGetDeviceIDs() to get the ID of a GPU. Finally, we create a context by passing that device ID to clCreateContext().

Create a Command Queue

Now that we have a context, we can use it to create a command queue:

DataParallelism/MultiplyArrays/multiply_arrays.c
```
cl_command_queue queue = clCreateCommandQueue(context, device, 0, NULL);
```

The clCreateCommandQueue() method takes a context and a device and returns a queue that enables commands to be sent to that device.

Compile the Kernel

Next we need to compile our kernel into code that will run on the device:

DataParallelism/MultiplyArrays/multiply_arrays.c
```
char* source = read_source("multiply_arrays.cl");
cl_program program = clCreateProgramWithSource(context, 1,
  (const char**)&source, NULL, NULL);
free(source);
clBuildProgram(program, 0, NULL, NULL, NULL, NULL);
cl_kernel kernel = clCreateKernel(program, "multiply_arrays", NULL);
```

We start by reading the source code for the kernel from multiply_arrays.cl into a string (you can see the source of read_source() in the code that accompanies the book) that is then passed to clCreateProgramWithSource(). That's then built with clBuildProgram() and turned into a kernel with clCreateKernel().

Create Buffers

Kernels work on data stored within buffers:

DataParallelism/MultiplyArrays/multiply_arrays.c
```
#define NUM_ELEMENTS 1024

cl_float a[NUM_ELEMENTS], b[NUM_ELEMENTS];
random_fill(a, NUM_ELEMENTS);
random_fill(b, NUM_ELEMENTS);
cl_mem inputA = clCreateBuffer(context, CL_MEM_READ_ONLY | CL_MEM_COPY_HOST_PTR,
  sizeof(cl_float) * NUM_ELEMENTS, a, NULL);
cl_mem inputB = clCreateBuffer(context, CL_MEM_READ_ONLY | CL_MEM_COPY_HOST_PTR,
  sizeof(cl_float) * NUM_ELEMENTS, b, NULL);
cl_mem output = clCreateBuffer(context, CL_MEM_WRITE_ONLY,
  sizeof(cl_float) * NUM_ELEMENTS, NULL, NULL);
```

We start by creating two arrays, a and b, both of which we fill with random values with random_fill():

DataParallelism/MultiplyArrays/multiply_arrays.c
```
void random_fill(cl_float array[], size_t size) {
  for (int i = 0; i < size; ++i)
    array[i] = (cl_float)rand() / RAND_MAX;
}
```

Our two input buffers, inputA and inputB, are both read-only from the point of view of the kernel (CL_MEM_READ_ONLY) and initialized by copying from their respective source arrays (CL_MEM_COPY_HOST_PTR). The output buffer output is write-only (CL_MEM_WRITE_ONLY).

Execute the Work Items

We're now finally in a position to execute the work-items that will perform the array multiplication task:

DataParallelism/MultiplyArrays/multiply_arrays.c
```
clSetKernelArg(kernel, 0, sizeof(cl_mem), &inputA);
clSetKernelArg(kernel, 1, sizeof(cl_mem), &inputB);
clSetKernelArg(kernel, 2, sizeof(cl_mem), &output);

size_t work_units = NUM_ELEMENTS;
clEnqueueNDRangeKernel(queue, kernel, 1, NULL, &work_units, NULL, 0, NULL, NULL);
```

We start by setting the kernel's arguments with clSetKernelArg() and then call clEnqueueNDRangeKernel(), which queues an *N-dimensional range* (NDRange) of work-items. In our case, *N* is 1 (the third argument to clEnqueueNDRangeKernel() —we'll see an example with *N*>1 later), and the number of work-items is 1,024.

Retrieve Results

Once our kernel has finished executing, we need to retrieve the results:

DataParallelism/MultiplyArrays/multiply_arrays.c
```
cl_float results[NUM_ELEMENTS];
clEnqueueReadBuffer(queue, output, CL_TRUE, 0, sizeof(cl_float) * NUM_ELEMENTS,
  results, 0, NULL, NULL);
```

We create the results array and copy from the output buffer with the clEnqueueRead-Buffer() function.

Clean-Up

The final task for our host program is to clean up after itself:

DataParallelism/MultiplyArrays/multiply_arrays.c
```
clReleaseMemObject(inputA);
clReleaseMemObject(inputB);
clReleaseMemObject(output);
clReleaseKernel(kernel);
clReleaseProgram(program);
clReleaseCommandQueue(queue);
clReleaseContext(context);
```

Profiling

Now that we have a working kernel, let's see what kind of performance it's giving us. We can use OpenCL's profiling API to answer that question:

DataParallelism/MultiplyArraysProfiled/multiply_arrays.c

```
cl_event timing_event;
size_t work_units = NUM_ELEMENTS;
clEnqueueNDRangeKernel(queue, kernel, 1, NULL, &work_units,
    NULL, 0, NULL, &timing_event);

cl_float results[NUM_ELEMENTS];
clEnqueueReadBuffer(queue, output, CL_TRUE, 0, sizeof(cl_float) * NUM_ELEMENTS,
    results, 0, NULL, NULL);
cl_ulong starttime;
clGetEventProfilingInfo(timing_event, CL_PROFILING_COMMAND_START,
    sizeof(cl_ulong), &starttime, NULL);
cl_ulong endtime;
clGetEventProfilingInfo(timing_event, CL_PROFILING_COMMAND_END,
    sizeof(cl_ulong), &endtime, NULL);
printf("Elapsed (GPU): %lu ns\n\n", (unsigned long)(endtime - starttime));
clReleaseEvent(timing_event);
```

We start by passing an event, timing_event, to clEnqueueNDRangeKernel() on line 3. Once that command has completed, we can query the event for timing information with clGetEventProfilingInfo() (lines 10 and 13).

If I redefine NUM_ELEMENTS to be 100,000, the GPU in my MacBook Pro runs this in approximately 43,000 nanoseconds. For comparison, let's try the same with a simple loop running on the CPU:

DataParallelism/MultiplyArraysProfiled/multiply_arrays.c

```
for (int i = 0; i < NUM_ELEMENTS; ++i)
  results[i] = a[i] * b[i];
```

This multiplies the same 100,000 elements in around 400,000 nanoseconds, so for this task the GPU is more than nine times faster than a single CPU core.

A Word of Warning

Profiling the command that multiplies the two arrays is slightly misleading. Before we executed it, we copied our input data into the inputA and inputB buffers. And after it ran, we retrieved the results by copying from the output buffer.

These copies are relatively expensive—for a simple task like pairwise multiplication, they are probably too expensive to justify using the GPU in practice. A real-world OpenCL application would either perform more involved operations on its operands or work on data that was already resident on the GPU.

In the interests of clarity, my array multiplication example wasn't very careful with a few aspects of the OpenCL API. Let's rectify that now.

Multiple Return Values

Many OpenCL functions can return multiple return values. For example, a platform might support multiple devices, and clGetDeviceIDs() might therefore return more than one device. Here's its prototype:

```
cl_int clGetDeviceIDs(cl_platform_id platform,
                      cl_device_type device_type,
                      cl_uint        num_entries,
                      cl_device_id*  devices,
                      cl_uint*       num_devices);
```

The devices parameter is a pointer to an array of length num_entries, and num_devices is a pointer to a single integer. One way to call clGetDeviceIDs() would be with a fixed-length array:

```
cl_device_id devices[8];
cl_uint num_devices;
clGetDeviceIDs(platform, CL_DEVICE_TYPE_ALL, 8, devices, &num_devices);
```

After clGetDeviceIDs() returns, num_devices will have been set to the number of available devices, and the first num_devices entries of the devices array will have been filled in.

This works fine, but what if there are more than eight available devices? We could just pass a "large" array, but experience demonstrates that whenever we create code with a fixed limit, sooner or later that limit will be exceeded. Happily, all OpenCL functions that return an array provide us with a way to find out how large that array should be by calling them twice:

```
cl_uint num_devices;
clGetDeviceIDs(platform, CL_DEVICE_TYPE_ALL, 0, NULL, &num_devices);

cl_device_id* devices = (cl_device_id*)malloc(sizeof(cl_device_id) * num_devices);
clGetDeviceIDs(platform, CL_DEVICE_TYPE_ALL, num_devices, devices, NULL);
```

The first time we call clGetDeviceIDs() we pass NULL for its devices argument. After it returns, num_devices is set to the number of available devices. We can then dynamically allocate an array of the right size and then call getDeviceIDs() a second time.

Error Handling

OpenCL functions report errors with error codes. CL_SUCCESS indicates that the function succeeded; any other value indicates that it failed. So calling clGetDeviceIDs() with error handling looks something like this:

```
cl_int status;

cl_uint num_devices;
status = clGetDeviceIDs(platform, CL_DEVICE_TYPE_ALL, 0, NULL, &num_devices);
if (status != CL_SUCCESS) {
  fprintf(stderr, "Error: unable to determine num_devices (%d)\n", status);
  exit(1);
}

cl_device_id* devices = (cl_device_id*)malloc(sizeof(cl_device_id) * num_devices);
status = clGetDeviceIDs(platform, CL_DEVICE_TYPE_ALL, num_devices, devices, NULL);
if (status != CL_SUCCESS) {
  fprintf(stderr, "Error: unable to retrieve devices (%d)\n", status);
  exit(1);
}
```

Unsurprisingly, most OpenCL programs use some kind of utility function or macro to remove this boilerplate, such as seen here:

DataParallelism/MultiplyArraysWithErrorHandling/multiply_arrays.c
```
#define CHECK_STATUS(s) do { \
    cl_int ss = (s); \
    if (ss != CL_SUCCESS) { \
      fprintf(stderr, "Error %d at line %d\n", ss, __LINE__); \
      exit(1); \
    } \
  } while (0)
```

This allows us to write the following:

DataParallelism/MultiplyArraysWithErrorHandling/multiply_arrays.c
```
CHECK_STATUS(clSetKernelArg(kernel, 0, sizeof(cl_mem), &inputA));
```

Instead of returning an error code, some OpenCL functions take an error_ret parameter. For example, clCreateContext() has the following prototype:

```
cl_context clCreateContext(const cl_context_properties* properties,
                           cl_uint num_devices,
                           const cl_device_id* devices,
                           void (CL_CALLBACK* pfn_notify)(const char* errinfo,
                                                          const void* private_info,
                                                          size_t cb,
                                                          void* user_data),
                           void* user_data,
                           cl_int* errcode_ret);
```

Here's how we can call it with error handling:

DataParallelism/MultiplyArraysWithErrorHandling/multiply_arrays.c
```
cl_int status;
cl_context context = clCreateContext(NULL, 1, &device, NULL, NULL, &status);
CHECK_STATUS(status);
```

Various other error-handling styles are common in OpenCL code—you should pick one that works well with your preferred style.

Day 1 Wrap-Up

That brings us to the end of day 1. In day 2 we'll look at the OpenCL platform, execution, and memory models in more detail.

What We Learned in Day 1

OpenCL allows us to leverage the data-parallel capabilities of GPUs for general-purpose programming, realizing dramatic performance gains in the process.

- OpenCL parallelizes a task by dividing it up into work-items.
- We specify how each work-item should be processed by writing a kernel.
- To execute a kernel, a host program does the following:

  1. Creates a context within which the kernel will run, together with a command queue
  2. Compiles the kernel
  3. Creates buffers for input and output data
  4. Enqueues a command that executes the kernel once for each work-item
  5. Retrieves the results

Day 1 Self-Study

Find

- The OpenCL specification
- The OpenCL API reference card
- The language used to define an OpenCL kernel is C-like. How does it differ from C?

Do

- Modify our array multiplication kernel to deal with arrays of different types, and profile the resulting performance. How does it vary with data type? Does the size (in bytes) of the data type have any bearing on performance, both in absolute terms and in comparison to CPU performance?

- We created and initialized our buffers by passing CL_MEM_COPY_HOST_PTR to clCreateBuffer(). Rewrite the host to use CL_MEM_USE_HOST_PTR or CL_MEM_-ALLOC_HOST_PTR (you will need to do more than just change the flag for the code to remain functional), and benchmark the resulting performance. What are the trade-offs between different buffer-allocation strategies?

- Rewrite the host to use clEnqueueMapBuffer() instead of clCreateBuffer() and profile the result. When might this be an appropriate choice? When might it not?

- The OpenCL language provides a number of data types over and above those provided by standard C—in particular, it includes vector types such as float4 or ulong3. Rewrite our kernel to multiply two buffers of vectors. How are these vector types represented on the host?

Day 2: Multiple Dimensions and Work-Groups

Yesterday we saw how to use clEnqueueNDRangeKernel() to execute a set of work-items that processed a unidimensional array. Today we'll see how to extend that to multidimensional arrays and take advantage of OpenCL's work-groups to increase the size of the problems we can tackle.

Multidimensional Work-Item Ranges

When a host calls clEnqueueNDRangeKernel() to execute a kernel, it defines an index space. Each point in this index space is identified by a unique global ID that represents one work-item.

A kernel can find the global ID of the work-item it's executing by calling get_global_id(). In the example we saw yesterday the index space was unidimensional, and therefore the kernel only needed to call get_global_id() once. Today we'll create a kernel that multiplies two-dimensional matrices and therefore calls get_global_id() twice.

Matrix Multiplication

First let's take a quick detour to revisit the linear algebra we learned at school and remind ourselves how matrix multiplication works.

A matrix is a two-dimensional array of numbers. We can multiply a $w{\times}n$ matrix by an $m{\times}w$ matrix (note that the width of the first matrix must equal the height of the second) to get an $m{\times}n$ matrix. For example, multiplying a 2×4 matrix by a 3×2 matrix will give us a 3×4 result.

To calculate the value at (i, j) in the output matrix, we take the sum of multiplying every number in the jth row of the first matrix by the corresponding number in the ith column of the second matrix.

$$\begin{pmatrix} a & b \\ c & d \end{pmatrix}\begin{pmatrix} w & x \\ y & z \end{pmatrix} = \begin{pmatrix} aw + by & ax + bz \\ cw + dy & cx + dz \end{pmatrix}$$

Here's code that implements this sequentially:

```
#define WIDTH_OUTPUT WIDTH_B
#define HEIGHT_OUTPUT HEIGHT_A

float a[HEIGHT_A][WIDTH_A] = «initialize a»;
float b[HEIGHT_B][WIDTH_B] = «initialize b»;
float r[HEIGHT_OUTPUT][WIDTH_OUTPUT];

for (int j = 0; j < HEIGHT_OUTPUT; ++j) {
  for (int i = 0; i < WIDTH_OUTPUT; ++i) {
    float sum = 0.0;
    for (int k = 0; k < WIDTH_A; ++k) {
      sum += a[j][k] * b[k][i];
    }
    r[j][i] = sum;
  }
}
```

As you can see, as the number of elements in our array increases, the work required to multiply them increases dramatically, making large-matrix multiplication a very CPU-intensive task indeed.

Parallel Matrix Multiplication

Here's a kernel that can be used to multiply two-dimensional matrices:

DataParallelism/MatrixMultiplication/matrix_multiplication.cl
```
Line 1  __kernel void matrix_multiplication(uint widthA,
                                            __global const float* inputA,
                                            __global const float* inputB,
                                            __global float* output) {

5       int i = get_global_id(0);
        int j = get_global_id(1);

        int outputWidth = get_global_size(0);
10      int outputHeight = get_global_size(1);
        int widthB = outputWidth;

        float total = 0.0;
        for (int k = 0; k < widthA; ++k) {
15        total += inputA[j * widthA + k] * inputB[k * widthB + i];
        }
        output[j * outputWidth + i] = total;
      }
```

This kernel executes within a two-dimensional index space, each point of which identifies a location in the output array. It retrieves this point by calling get_global_id() twice (lines 6 and 7).

It can find out the range of the index space by calling get_global_size(), which this kernel uses to find the dimensions of the output matrix (lines 9 and 10). This also gives us widthB, which is equal to outputWidth, but we have to pass widthA as a parameter.

The loop on line 14 is just the inner loop from the sequential version we saw earlier—the only difference being that because OpenCL buffers are unidimensional, we can't write the following:

```
output[j][i] = total;
```

Instead, we have to use a little arithmetic to determine the correct offset:

```
output[j * outputWidth + i] = total;
```

The host program required to execute this kernel is very similar to the one we saw yesterday, the only significant difference being the arguments passed to clEnqueueNDRangeKernel():

DataParallelism/MatrixMultiplication/matrix_multiplication.c
```
size_t work_units[] = {WIDTH_OUTPUT, HEIGHT_OUTPUT};
CHECK_STATUS(clEnqueueNDRangeKernel(queue, kernel, 2, NULL, work_units,
  NULL, 0, NULL, NULL));
```

This creates a two-dimensional index space by setting work_dim to 2 (the third argument) and specifies the extent of each dimension by setting global_work_size to a two-element array (the fifth argument).

This kernel shows an even more dramatic performance benefit than the one we saw yesterday. On my MacBook Pro, multiplying a 200×400 matrix by a 300×200 matrix takes approximately 3 ms, compared to 66 ms on the CPU, a speedup of more than 20x.

Because this kernel is performing much more work per data element, we continue to see a significant speedup even if we take the overhead of copying data between the CPU and GPU into account. On my MacBook Pro, those copies take around 2 ms, for a total time of 5 ms, which still gives us a 13x speedup.

All the code we've run so far simply assumes that there's an OpenCL-compatible GPU available. Clearly this may not always be true, so next let's see how we can find out which OpenCL platforms and devices are available to a particular host.

Querying Device Info

OpenCL provides a number of functions that allow us to query the parameters of platforms, devices, and most other API objects. Here, for example, is a function that uses clGetDeviceInfo() to query and print a device parameter with a value of type string:

DataParallelism/FindDevices/find_devices.c
```c
void print_device_param_string(cl_device_id device,
                               cl_device_info param_id,
                               const char* param_name) {
  char value[1024];
  CHECK_STATUS(clGetDeviceInfo(device, param_id, sizeof(value), value, NULL));
  printf("%s: %s\n", param_name, value);
}
```

Different parameters have values of different types (string, integer, array of size_t, and so on). Given a range of functions like the preceding, we can query the parameters of a particular device as follows:

DataParallelism/FindDevices/find_devices.c
```c
void print_device_info(cl_device_id device) {
  print_device_param_string(device, CL_DEVICE_NAME, "Name");
  print_device_param_string(device, CL_DEVICE_VENDOR, "Vendor");
  print_device_param_uint(device, CL_DEVICE_MAX_COMPUTE_UNITS, "Compute Units");
  print_device_param_ulong(device, CL_DEVICE_GLOBAL_MEM_SIZE, "Global Memory");
  print_device_param_ulong(device, CL_DEVICE_LOCAL_MEM_SIZE, "Local Memory");
  print_device_param_sizet(device, CL_DEVICE_MAX_WORK_GROUP_SIZE, "Workgroup size");
}
```

The code that accompanies this book includes a program called find_devices that uses this kind of code to query both the platforms and devices available. If I run it on my MacBook Pro, here's what it prints:

```
Found 1 OpenCL platform(s)

Platform 0
Name: Apple
Vendor: Apple

Found 2 device(s)

Device 0
Name: Intel(R) Core(TM) i7-3720QM CPU @ 2.60GHz
Vendor: Intel
Compute Units: 8
Global Memory: 17179869184
Local Memory: 32768
Workgroup size: 1024
```

```
Device 1
Name: GeForce GT 650M
Vendor: NVIDIA
Compute Units: 2
Global Memory: 1073741824
Local Memory: 49152
Workgroup size: 1024
```

So there is a single platform available, the default Apple OpenCL implementation. Within that platform are two devices, the CPU and GPU.

There are a few interesting things we can see from this:

- OpenCL can target more than just GPUs (in addition to CPUs, it can also target dedicated OpenCL accelerators).

- The GPU in my MacBook Pro provides two compute units (we'll see what a compute unit is soon).

- The GPU has 1 GiB of global memory.

- Each compute unit has 48 KiB of local memory and supports a maximum work-group size of 1024.

In the next sections, we'll look at OpenCL's platform and memory models and the implications they have for our code.

 Joe asks:

Why Does OpenCL Target CPUs?

It comes as a surprise to many, but modern CPUs have long supported data-parallel instructions. Intel processors, for example, support the streaming SIMD extensions (SSE) and more recently the advanced vector extensions (AVX). OpenCL can provide an excellent way to exploit these instruction sets as well as the multiple cores that most CPUs now provide.

Platform Model

An OpenCL platform consists of a host that's connected to one or more devices. Each device has one or more *compute units*, each of which provides a number of processing elements, as shown in Figure 14, *The OpenCL Platform Model*, on page 206.

Work-items execute on processing elements. A collection of work-items executing on a single compute unit is a *work-group*. The work-items in a work-group share local memory, which brings us to OpenCL's memory model.

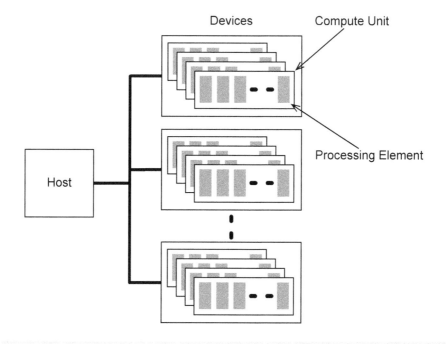

Figure 14—The OpenCL Platform Model

Memory Model

A work-item executing a kernel has access to four different memory regions:

Global memory: Memory available to all work-items executing on a device

Constant memory: A region of global memory that remains constant during execution of a kernel

Local memory: Memory local to a work-group; can be used for communication between work-items executing in that work-group (We'll see an example of this soon.)

Private memory: Memory private to a single work-item

As we've seen in previous chapters, a reduce operation over a collection can be a very effective approach to solving a wide range of problems. In the next section we'll see how to implement a data-parallel reduce.

Data-Parallel Reduce

In this section we'll create a kernel that finds the minimum element of a collection in parallel by reducing over that collection with the min() operator.

> ### Joe asks:
> # Is This How OpenCL Devices Actually Work?
>
> The OpenCL platform and memory models don't prescribe how the underlying hardware has to work. Instead they are abstractions of that hardware—different OpenCL devices have a range of different physical architectures.
>
> For example, one OpenCL device might have local memory that really is local to a compute unit, whereas another might have local memory that in reality is mapped onto a region of global memory. Or one device might have its own distinct global memory, and another might have direct access to the host's memory.
>
> These architectural differences can have significant implications when it comes to optimizing OpenCL code, a subject that's beyond the scope of this chapter.

Implementing this sequentially is straightforward:

DataParallelism/FindMinimumOneWorkGroup/find_minimum.c
```
cl_float acc = FLT_MAX;
for (int i = 0; i < NUM_VALUES; ++i)
  acc = fmin(acc, values[i]);
```

We'll see how to parallelize this in two steps—first with a single work-group and then with multiple work-groups.

A Single Work-Group Reduce

To make things simpler (we'll see why this helps soon), I'm going to assume that the number of elements in the array we want to reduce is a power of two and small enough to be processed by a single work-group. Given that, here's a kernel that will perform our reduce operation:

DataParallelism/FindMinimumOneWorkGroup/find_minimum.cl
```
Line 1  __kernel void find_minimum(__global const float* values,
                                   __global float* result,
                                   __local float* scratch) {
          int i = get_global_id(0);
    5     int n = get_global_size(0);
          scratch[i] = values[i];
          barrier(CLK_LOCAL_MEM_FENCE);
          for (int j = n / 2; j > 0; j /= 2) {
            if (i < j)
    10        scratch[i] = min(scratch[i], scratch[i + j]);
            barrier(CLK_LOCAL_MEM_FENCE);
          }
          if (i == 0)
            *result = scratch[0];
    15  }
```

The algorithm has three distinct phases:

1. It copies the array from global to local (scratch) memory (line 6).
2. It performs the reduce (lines 8–12).
3. It copies the result to global memory (line 14).

The reduce operation proceeds by creating a reduce tree very similar to the one we saw when looking at Clojure's reducers (see *Divide and Conquer*, on page 67):

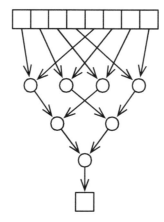

After each loop iteration, half the work-items become inactive—only work-items for which i < j is true perform any work (this is why we're assuming that the number of elements in the array is a power of two—so we can repeatedly halve the array). The loop exits when only a single work-item is left active. Each active work-item performs a min() between its value and the corresponding value in the remaining half of the array. By the time the loop exits, the first item in the scratch array will be the final value of the reduce operation, and the first work-item in the work-group copies this value to result.

The other interesting thing about this kernel is its use of barriers (lines 7 and 11) to synchronize access to local memory.

Barriers

A *barrier* is a synchronization mechanism that allows work-items to coordinate their use of local memory. If one work-item in a work-group executes barrier(), then all work-items in that work-group must execute the same barrier() before any of them can proceed beyond that point (a type of synchronization commonly known as a *rendezvous*). In our reduction kernel, this serves two purposes:

- It ensures that one work-item doesn't start reducing until all work-items have copied their value from global to local memory and that one work-item doesn't move on to loop iteration $n + 1$ until all work-items have finished loop iteration n.

- OpenCL only provides relaxed memory consistency. This is very similar to the Java Memory Model we saw in *Memory Visibility*, on page 15—changes made to local memory by one work-item are not guaranteed visible to other work-items except at specific synchronization points, such as barriers. So executing a barrier at the end of each loop iteration guarantees that the results of iteration n are visible to the work-items executing iteration $n + 1$.

Executing the Kernel

Executing this kernel is very similar to what we've already seen—the only substantive new thing we need to worry about is how to create a local buffer:

DataParallelism/FindMinimumOneWorkGroup/find_minimum.c

```
CHECK_STATUS(clSetKernelArg(kernel, 2, sizeof(cl_float) * NUM_VALUES, NULL));
```

We allocate a local buffer by calling clSetKernelArg() with arg_size set to the size of the buffer we want to create and arg_value set to NULL.

A reduce that runs within a single work-group is great, but as we've seen, work-groups are restricted in size (no more than 1,024 elements on the GPU in my MacBook Pro, for example). Next, we'll see how to parallelize over multiple work-groups.

A Multiple-Work-Group Reduce

Extending our reduce across multiple work-groups is a simple matter of dividing the input array into work-groups and reducing each independently, as shown in Figure 15, *Extending the Reduce across Multiple Work-Groups*, on page 210.

If, for example, each work-group operates on 64 values at a time, this will reduce an array of N items to $N/64$ items. This smaller array can then be reduced in turn, and so on, until only a single result remains.

Achieving this requires a few small changes to our kernel to allow it to operate on a work-group that represents a section of a larger problem. To this end, OpenCL provides work-items with a local ID, which is an ID just for within that work-group, as shown in Figure 16, *The Local ID with a Work-Group*, on page 210.

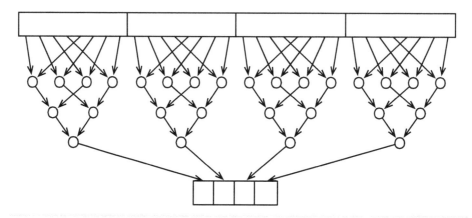

Figure 15—Extending the Reduce across Multiple Work-Groups

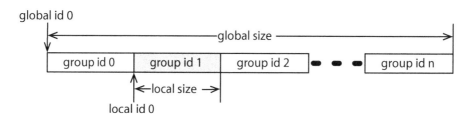

Figure 16—The Local ID with a Work-Group

Here's a kernel that makes use of local IDs:

DataParallelism/FindMinimumMultipleWorkGroups/find_minimum.cl

```
__kernel void find_minimum(__global const float* values,
                           __global float* results,
                           __local float* scratch) {
    int i = get_local_id(0);
    int n = get_local_size(0);
    scratch[i] = values[get_global_id(0)];
    barrier(CLK_LOCAL_MEM_FENCE);
    for (int j = n / 2; j > 0; j /= 2) {
      if (i < j)
        scratch[i] = min(scratch[i], scratch[i + j]);
      barrier(CLK_LOCAL_MEM_FENCE);
    }
    if (i == 0)
      results[get_group_id(0)] = scratch[0];
}
```

In place of get_global_id() and get_global_size(), we're now calling get_local_id() and get_local_size(), which return the ID relative to the start of the work-group and size of the work-group, respectively. We still have to call get_global_id() to copy the right value from global memory to local, and results is now an array indexed by the get_group_id().

The final piece of this puzzle is to change the host program to create work-groups of the appropriate size:

```
DataParallelism/FindMinimumMultipleWorkGroups/find_minimum.c
size_t work_units[] = {NUM_VALUES};
size_t workgroup_size[] = {WORKGROUP_SIZE};
CHECK_STATUS(clEnqueueNDRangeKernel(queue, kernel, 1, NULL, work_units,
  workgroup_size, 0, NULL, NULL));
```

If we set local_work_size to NULL, as we have been doing up to now, the OpenCL platform is free to create work-groups of whatever size it sees fit. By explicitly setting local_work_size, we guarantee that work-groups are the size required by our kernel (up to the maximum size supported by the device, of course—see *Querying Device Info*, on page 204, to determine how to find this).

Day 2 Wrap-Up

This brings us to the end of day 2. In day 3 we'll see an example of an application that implements a physics simulation with OpenCL and integrates with OpenGL to display the results.

What We Learned in Day 2

OpenCL defines platform, execution, and memory models that abstract the details of the underlying hardware.

- Work-items execute on processing elements.
- Processing elements are grouped into compute units.
- A group of work-items executing on a single compute unit is a work-group.
- Work-items in a work-group communicate through local memory using barriers to synchronize and ensure consistency.

Day 2 Self-Study

Find

- By default, a command queue processes commands in order. How do you enable out-of-order execution?

- What is an event wait list? How might you use event wait lists to impose constraints on when commands sent to an unordered command queue are executed?

- What does clEnqueueBarrier() do? When might you use barriers and when might you use wait lists?

Do

- Extend the reduce example to handle any number of elements, not just powers of two.

- Modify the reduce example to target multiple devices. If you have only a single OpenCL-compatible device, you can target the CPU as well, or you can partition your GPU with clCreateSubDevices(). You will need to create a command queue for each device, partition the problem so that some work-items are executed on one device and some on the other, and synchronize between the command queues.

- The reduce algorithm we looked at today is very simple. An Internet search will uncover many approaches to creating a more efficient reduce. How fast can you get it on your particular device? Do the optimizations that work best on your GPU also work effectively on the CPU?

Day 3: OpenCL and OpenGL—Keeping It on the GPU

Today we'll put together a complete OpenCL application that both runs and visualizes a simple physics simulation. In the process, we'll see not only how to create a kernel that executes the simulation in parallel but also how to integrate OpenCL with OpenGL and avoid the overhead of buffer copies by keeping everything on the GPU.

Water Ripples

The simulation we're going to create is of water ripples. It's not going to be a hyperaccurate physical simulation, but it will be good enough to look convincing as a graphical effect in a game—to simulate, for example, the surface of a pond during a rain shower.

LWJGL

We're going to move away from C for this example and instead use Java together with the Lightweight Java Graphics Library (LWJGL),[3] because that makes creating a cross-platform GUI easier.

LWJGL provides Java wrappers for both OpenCL and OpenGL, allowing a Java program to access OpenGL and OpenCL's C APIs. As OpenGL's name suggests,

---

3.   http://www.lwjgl.org

it has close ties with OpenCL. In particular, as we'll see later, it's possible for an OpenCL kernel executing on the GPU to directly operate on OpenGL buffers.

OpenCL code in LWJGL looks very similar to what we've already seen in C. Here, for example, is code to initialize an OpenCL context, queue, and kernel:

DataParallelism/Zoom/src/main/java/com/paulbutcher/Zoom.java
```
CL.create();
CLPlatform platform = CLPlatform.getPlatforms().get(0);
List<CLDevice> devices = platform.getDevices(CL_DEVICE_TYPE_GPU);
CLContext context = CLContext.create(platform, devices, null, drawable, null);
CLCommandQueue queue = clCreateCommandQueue(context, devices.get(0), 0, null);

CLProgram program =
  clCreateProgramWithSource(context, loadSource("zoom.cl"), null);
Util.checkCLError(clBuildProgram(program, devices.get(0), "", null));
CLKernel kernel = clCreateKernel(program, "zoom", null);
```

As you can see, both the method names and arguments are almost identical to the equivalent C code. The few small changes are necessary to handle differences between the languages, such as the absence of pointers in Java, but broadly speaking it's possible to transliterate an OpenGL host program written in C to Java with LWJGL.

Displaying a Mesh in OpenGL

We're not going to spend much time talking about the OpenGL element of this example. But we do need to spend a little time understanding how our example displays the mesh that represents the water surface so that we know the task that faces our OpenCL code.

An OpenGL 3D scene is constructed from triangles. In our case, we're creating a mesh out of triangles arranged like this:

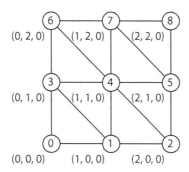

We specify the position of each triangle with two steps—a *vertex buffer* that defines a set of vertices (points in 3D space) and an *index buffer* that defines which of those vertices are used to draw each triangle.

So in the preceding example, vertex 0 is at (0, 0, 0), vertex 1 is at (1, 0, 0), vertex 2 is at (2, 0, 0), and so on. The vertex buffer will therefore contain [0, 0, 0, 1, 0, 0, 2, 0, 0, 0, 1, 0, 1, 1, 0, ...].

As for the index buffer, the first triangle will use vertices 0, 1, and 3; the second 1, 3, and 4; the third 1, 2, and 4; and so on. The index buffer we create defines a *triangle strip* in which, after specifying the first triangle with three vertices, we only need a single additional vertex to define the next triangle:

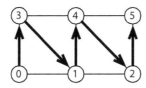

So our index buffer will contain [0, 3, 1, 4, 2, 5, ...].

The code that accompanies this book includes a Mesh class that generates initial values for the vertex and index buffers. Our sample uses this to create a 64×64 mesh with x- and y-coordinates ranging from -1.0 to 1.0:

DataParallelism/Zoom/src/main/java/com/paulbutcher/Zoom.java
```
Mesh mesh = new Mesh(2.0f, 2.0f, 64, 64);
```

The z-coordinates are all initialized to zero—we'll modify them during animation to simulate ripples.

This data is then copied to OpenGL buffers as follows:

DataParallelism/Zoom/src/main/java/com/paulbutcher/Zoom.java
```
int vertexBuffer = glGenBuffers();
glBindBuffer(GL_ARRAY_BUFFER, vertexBuffer);
glBufferData(GL_ARRAY_BUFFER, mesh.vertices, GL_DYNAMIC_DRAW);

int indexBuffer = glGenBuffers();
glBindBuffer(GL_ELEMENT_ARRAY_BUFFER, indexBuffer);
glBufferData(GL_ELEMENT_ARRAY_BUFFER, mesh.indices, GL_STATIC_DRAW);
```

Each buffer has an ID allocated by glGenBuffers(), is bound to a target with glBindBuffer(), and has its initial values set with glBufferData(). The index buffer has the GL_STATIC_DRAW usage hint, indicating that it won't change (is static). The vertex buffer, by contrast, has the GL_DYNAMIC_DRAW hint because it will change between animation frames.

Before we implement the ripple code, we'll start with something easier—a simple kernel that increases the size of the mesh over time.

Accessing an OpenGL Buffer from an OpenCL Kernel

Here's the kernel that implements our zoom animation:

DataParallelism/Zoom/src/main/resources/zoom.cl
```
__kernel void zoom(__global float* vertices) {

  unsigned int id = get_global_id(0);
  vertices[id] *= 1.01;
}
```

It takes the vertex buffer as an argument and multiplies every entry in that buffer by 1.01, increasing the size of the mesh by 1% every time it's called.

Before we can pass the vertex buffer to our kernel, we first need to create an OpenCL buffer that references it:

DataParallelism/Zoom/src/main/java/com/paulbutcher/Zoom.java
```
CLMem vertexBufferCL =
  clCreateFromGLBuffer(context, CL_MEM_READ_WRITE, vertexBuffer, null);
```

This buffer object can then be used in our main rendering loop as follows:

DataParallelism/Zoom/src/main/java/com/paulbutcher/Zoom.java
```
while (!Display.isCloseRequested()) {
  glClear(GL_COLOR_BUFFER_BIT | GL_DEPTH_BUFFER_BIT);
  glLoadIdentity();
  glTranslatef(0.0f, 0.0f, planeDistance);
  glDrawElements(GL_TRIANGLE_STRIP, mesh.indexCount, GL_UNSIGNED_SHORT, 0);

  Display.update();

➤  Util.checkCLError(clEnqueueAcquireGLObjects(queue, vertexBufferCL, null, null));
➤  kernel.setArg(0, vertexBufferCL);
➤  clEnqueueNDRangeKernel(queue, kernel, 1, null, workSize, null, null, null);
➤  Util.checkCLError(clEnqueueReleaseGLObjects(queue, vertexBufferCL, null, null));
➤  clFinish(queue);
}
```

Before an OpenCL kernel can use an OpenGL buffer, we need to acquire it with clEnqueueAcquireGLObjects(). We can then set it as an argument to our kernel and call clEnqueueNDRangeKernel() as normal. Finally, we release the buffer with clEnqueueReleaseGLObjects() and wait for the commands we've dispatched to finish with clFinish().

Run this code, and you should see the mesh start out small and quickly grow to the point that a single triangle fills the screen.

Now that we've got a simple animation working that integrates OpenGL with OpenCL, we'll look at the more sophisticated kernel that implements our water ripples.

Simulating Ripples

We're going to simulate expanding rings of ripples. Each expanding ring is defined by a 2D point on the mesh (the center of the expanding ring) together with a time (the time at which the ring started expanding). As well as taking a pointer to the OpenGL vertex buffer, our kernel takes an array of ripple centers together with a corresponding array of times (where time is measured in milliseconds):

DataParallelism/Ripple/src/main/resources/ripple.cl

```
#define AMPLITUDE 0.1
#define FREQUENCY 10.0
#define SPEED 0.5
#define WAVE_PACKET 50.0
#define DECAY_RATE 2.0
__kernel void ripple(__global float* vertices,
                     __global float* centers,
                     __global long* times,
                     int num_centers,
                     long now) {
  unsigned int id = get_global_id(0);
  unsigned int offset = id * 3;
  float x = vertices[offset];
  float y = vertices[offset + 1];
  float z = 0.0;

  for (int i = 0; i < num_centers; ++i) {
    if (times[i] != 0) {
      float dx = x - centers[i * 2];
      float dy = y - centers[i * 2 + 1];
      float d = sqrt(dx * dx + dy * dy);
      float elapsed = (now - times[i]) / 1000.0;
      float r = elapsed * SPEED;
      float delta = r - d;
      z += AMPLITUDE *
        exp(-DECAY_RATE * r * r) *
        exp(-WAVE_PACKET * delta * delta) *
        cos(FREQUENCY * M_PI_F * delta);
    }
  }
  vertices[offset + 2] = z;
}
```

We start by determining the x- and y-coordinates of the vertex that's being processed by the current work-item (lines 13 and 14). In the loop (lines 17–30) we calculate a new z-coordinate that we write back to the vertex buffer on line 31.

Within the loop, we examine each ripple center with a nonzero start time in turn. For each, we start by determining the distance d between the point we're calculating and the ripple center (line 21). Next, we calculate the radius r of the expanding ripple ring (line 23) and δ, the distance between our point and this ripple ring (line 24):

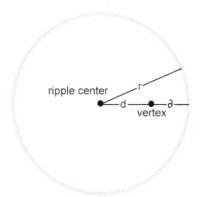

Finally, we can combine δ and r to get z:

$$z = Ae^{-Dr^2}e^{-W\delta^2}\cos(F\pi\delta)$$

Here, A, D, W, and F are constants representing the amplitude of the wave packet, the rate at which it decays as it expands, the width of the wave packet, and the frequency, respectively.

The final piece of the puzzle is to extend our host application to create our ripple centers:

DataParallelism/Ripple/src/main/java/com/paulbutcher/Ripple.java
```
int numCenters = 16;
int currentCenter = 0;
FloatBuffer centers = BufferUtils.createFloatBuffer(numCenters * 2);
centers.put(new float[numCenters * 2]);
centers.flip();
LongBuffer times = BufferUtils.createLongBuffer(numCenters);
times.put(new long[numCenters]);
times.flip();

CLMem centersBuffer =
  clCreateBuffer(context, CL_MEM_READ_ONLY | CL_MEM_COPY_HOST_PTR,centers, null);
CLMem timesBuffer =
  clCreateBuffer(context, CL_MEM_READ_ONLY | CL_MEM_COPY_HOST_PTR, times, null);
```

And start a new ripple whenever the mouse is clicked:

DataParallelism/Ripple/src/main/java/com/paulbutcher/Ripple.java

```
while (Mouse.next()) {
  if (Mouse.getEventButtonState()) {
    float x = ((float)Mouse.getEventX() / Display.getWidth()) * 2 - 1;
    float y = ((float)Mouse.getEventY() / Display.getHeight()) * 2 - 1;

    FloatBuffer center = BufferUtils.createFloatBuffer(2);
    center.put(new float[] {x, y});
    center.flip();
    clEnqueueWriteBuffer(queue, centersBuffer, 0,
      currentCenter * 2 * FLOAT_SIZE, center, null, null);
    LongBuffer time = BufferUtils.createLongBuffer(1);
    time.put(System.currentTimeMillis());
    time.flip();

    clEnqueueWriteBuffer(queue, timesBuffer, 0,
      currentCenter * LONG_SIZE, time, null, null);
    currentCenter = (currentCenter + 1) % numCenters;
  }
}
```

Compile and run this code, click on the mesh a few times, and you should see something like Figure 17, *Ripples*, on page 219.

So there we have it—we've created a physical simulation in which both the calculations to perform the simulation and the 3D visualization of the results are carried out on the GPU in parallel. All the data necessary to perform both the calculation and the visualization resides permanently on the GPU, no copying required.

Day 3 Wrap-Up

That brings us to the end of day 3 and our discussion of data parallelism on the GPU via OpenCL.

What We Learned in Day 3

An OpenCL kernel running on a GPU can directly access buffers used by an OpenGL application running on the same GPU. We covered how to do the following:

- Create an OpenCL view of an OpenGL buffer with clCreateFromGLBuffer()

- Acquire an OpenGL buffer before passing it to a kernel with clEnqueueAcquireGLObjects()

- Release the buffer after the kernel has finished with clEnqueueReleaseGLObjects()

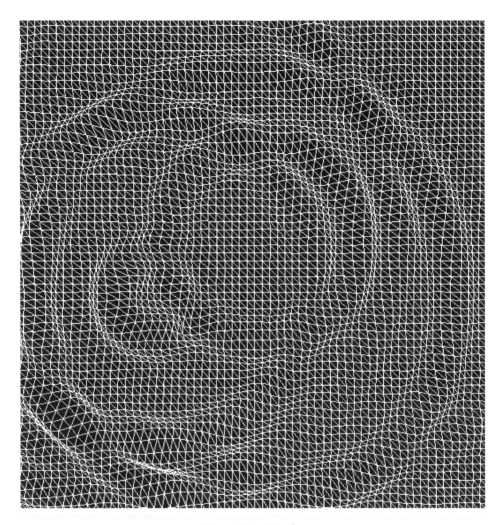

Figure 17—Ripples

Day 3 Self-Study

Find

- What is an image object? How does it differ from an ordinary OpenCL buffer? Do image objects have use cases in kernels that don't interoperate with OpenGL?

- What is a sampler object? What problems can it help solve?

- What are atomic functions? When might you use atomic functions instead of barriers?

Do

- Without using atomic functions, create a kernel that takes a buffer of integers with values between 0 and 32 and implements a histogram by counting how many instances of each value there are in the buffer. Can you extend your solution to do the same for a buffer that contains values between 0 and 1024?

- Write a kernel to perform the same task as above but using atomic functions this time. How do the two solutions compare?

Wrap-Up

For some reason, data parallelism seems to be ignored in many mainstream discussions of parallelism. As you can see, however, it's an extremely powerful way to dramatically improve your code's performance and one that all programmers should have in their repertoire.

Strengths

Data parallelism is ideal whenever you're faced with a problem where large amounts of numerical data needs to be processed. It's particularly appropriate for scientific and engineering computing and for simulation. Examples include fluid dynamics, finite element analysis, n-body simulation, simulated annealing, ant-colony optimization, neural networks, and so on.

GPUs are not only powerful data-parallel processors; they are also extremely efficient in their power consumption, typically returning much better GFLOPS/watt results than a traditional CPU. This is one of the primary reasons why many of the fastest supercomputers in the world make extensive use of either GPUs or dedicated data-parallel coprocessors.[4]

Weaknesses

Within its niche, data-parallel programming in general, and GPGPU programming specifically, is hard to beat. But it's not an approach that lends itself to all problems. In particular, although it is possible to use these techniques to create solutions to nonnumerical problems (natural language processing, for example), doing so is not straightforward—the current toolset is very much focused on number-crunching.

Optimizing an OpenCL kernel can be tricky, and effective optimization often depends on understanding underlying architectural details. This can be a

---

4.   http://www.top500.org/lists/2013/06/

particular issue if you need to write high-performance cross-platform code. For some problems, the need to copy data from the host to the device can dominate execution time, negating or reducing the benefit to be gained from parallelizing the computation.

Other Languages

Other GPGPU frameworks include CUDA,[5] DirectCompute,[6] and RenderScript Computation.[7]

Final Thoughts

GPGPU programming is an example of data parallelism in the small—on a single machine. In the next chapter we'll look at the Lambda Architecture, which allows us to exploit data parallelism in the large—across multiple machines.

---

5. http://www.nvidia.com/object/cuda_home_new.html

6. http://msdn.com/directx

7. http://developer.android.com/guide/topics/renderscript/compute.html

CHAPTER 8

The Lambda Architecture

If you need to ship freight in bulk from one side of the country to the other, nothing can beat a fleet of 18-wheeler trucks. But they're not the right choice for delivering a single package, so an integrated shipping company also maintains a fleet of smaller cargo vans that perform local collections and deliveries.

The Lambda Architecture similarly combines the large-scale batch-processing strengths of MapReduce with the real-time responsiveness of stream processing to allow us to create scalable, responsive, and fault-tolerant solutions to Big Data problems.

Parallelism Enables Big Data

The advent of Big Data has brought about a sea change in data processing over recent years. Big Data differs from traditional data processing through its use of parallelism—only by bringing multiple computing resources to bear can we contemplate processing terabytes of data. The Lambda Architecture is a particular approach to Big Data popularized by Nathan Marz, derived from his time at BackType and subsequently Twitter.

Like last week's topic, GPGPU programming, the Lambda Architecture leverages data parallelism. The difference is that it does so on a huge scale, distributing both data and computation over clusters of tens or hundreds of machines. Not only does this provide enough horsepower to make previously intractable problems tractable, but it also allows us to create systems that are fault tolerant against both hardware failure and human error.

The Lambda Architecture has many facets. In this chapter we're going to concentrate on its parallel and distributed aspects only (for a more complete discussion, see Nathan's book, *Big Data [MW14]*). In particular, we're going to concentrate on its two primary building blocks, the batch layer and the speed layer, as shown in Figure 18, *The batch and speed layers*, on page 224.

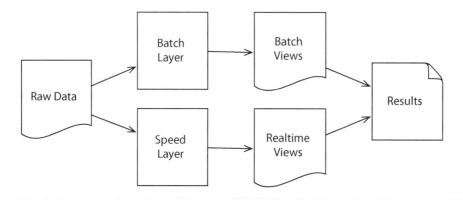

Figure 18—The batch and speed layers

The batch layer uses batch-oriented technologies like MapReduce to precompute batch views from historical data. This is effective, but latency is high, so we add a speed layer that uses low-latency techniques like stream processing to create real-time views from new data as it arrives. The two types of views are then combined to create query results.

The Lambda Architecture is by far the most complicated subject we're going to cover in this book. It builds upon several underlying technologies, the most important of which is MapReduce. In day 1, therefore, we'll concentrate solely upon MapReduce without worrying about how it fits into the wider picture. In day 2 we'll look at the problems of traditional data systems and how MapReduce can solve them when used within the batch layer of the Lambda Architecture. Finally, in day 3 we'll complete our picture of the Lambda Architecture by introducing stream processing and show how it can be used to construct the speed layer.

Day 1: MapReduce

MapReduce is a broad term. Sometimes it's used to describe the common pattern of breaking an algorithm down into two steps: a map over a data structure, followed by a reduce operation. Our functional word count (see the code on page 59) is an example of exactly this (remember that frequencies is implemented using reduce). As we saw in *Day 2: Functional Parallelism*, on page 61, one of the benefits of breaking an algorithm down in this way is that it lends itself to parallelization.

But MapReduce can also be used to mean something more specific—a system that takes an algorithm encoded as a map followed by a reduce and efficiently distributes it across a cluster of computers. Not only does such a system

> **Joe asks:**
> # Why the Name?
>
> There's been a lot of speculation about where the name comes from. I can do no better than quote the father of the Lambda Architecture, Nathan Marz:[a]
>
>> The name is due to the deep similarities between the architecture and functional programming. At the most fundamental level, the Lambda Architecture is a general way to compute functions on all your data at once.
>
> _____
>
> a.   http://www.manning-sandbox.com/message.jspa?messageID=126599

automatically partition both the data and its processing between the machines within the cluster, but it also continues to operate if one or more of those machines fails.

MapReduce in this more specific sense was pioneered by Google.[1] Outside of Google, the most popular MapReduce framework is Hadoop.[2]

Today we'll use Hadoop to create a parallel MapReduce version of the Wikipedia word-count example we've seen in previous chapters. Hadoop supports a wide variety of languages—we're going to use Java.

Practicalities

Running Hadoop locally is very straightforward and is the normal starting point for developing and debugging a MapReduce job. Going beyond that to running on a cluster used to be difficult—not all of us have a pile of spare machines lying around, waiting to be turned into a cluster. And even if we did, installing, configuring, and maintaining a Hadoop cluster is notoriously time-consuming and involved.

Happily, cloud computing has dramatically improved matters by providing access to virtual servers on demand and by the hour. Even better, many providers now offer managed Hadoop clusters, dramatically simplifying configuration and maintenance.

In this chapter we'll be using Amazon Elastic MapReduce, or EMR,[3] to run the examples. The means by which we start and stop clusters, and copy data to and from them, are specific to EMR, but the general principles apply to any Hadoop cluster.

_____

1.   http://research.google.com/archive/mapreduce.html
2.   http://hadoop.apache.org
3.   http://aws.amazon.com/elasticmapreduce/

To run the examples, you will need to have an Amazon AWS account with the AWS and EMR command-line tools installed.[4,5]

Joe asks:

What's the Deal with Hadoop Releases?

Hadoop has a perversely confusing version-numbering scheme, with the 0.20.x, 1.x, 0.22.x, 0.23.x, 2.0.x, 2.1.x, and 2.2.x releases all in active use as I'm writing this. These releases support two different APIs, commonly known as the "old" (in the org.apache.hadoop.mapred package) and the "new" (in org.apache.hadoop.mapreduce), to varying degrees.

On top of this, various Hadoop distributions bundle a particular Hadoop release with a selection of third-party components.[a,b,c]

The examples in this chapter all use the new API and have been tested against Amazon's 3.0.2 AMI, which uses Hadoop 2.2.0.[d]

---

a. http://hortonworks.com
b. http://www.cloudera.com
c. http://www.mapr.com
d. http://docs.aws.amazon.com/ElasticMapReduce/latest/DeveloperGuide/emr-plan-hadoop-version.html

Hadoop Basics

Hadoop is all about processing large amounts of data. Unless your data is measured in gigabytes or more, it's unlikely to be the right tool for the job. Its power comes from the fact that that it splits data into sections, each of which is then processed independently by separate machines.

As you might expect, a MapReduce task is constructed from two primary types of components, mappers and reducers. *Mappers* take some input format (by default, lines of plain text) and map it to a number of key/value pairs. *Reducers* then convert these key/value pairs to the ultimate output format (normally also a set of key/value pairs). Mappers and reducers are distributed across many different physical machines (there's no requirement for there to be the same number of mappers as reducers), as shown in Figure 19, *Hadoop high-level data flow*, on page 227.

The input typically comprises one or more large text files. Hadoop splits these files (the size of each split depends on exactly how its configured, but a typical

---

4. http://aws.amazon.com/cli/
5. http://docs.aws.amazon.com/ElasticMapReduce/latest/DeveloperGuide/emr-cli-reference.html

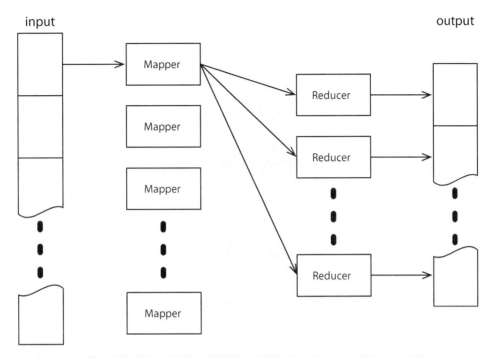

input   output

Figure 19—Hadoop high-level data flow

size would be 64 MB) and sends each split to a single mapper. The mapper outputs a number of key/value pairs, which Hadoop then sends to the reducers.

The key/value pairs from a single mapper are sent to multiple reducers. Which reducer receives a particular key/value pair is determined by the key—Hadoop guarantees that all pairs with the same key will be processed by the same reducer, no matter which mapper generated them. For obvious reasons, this is commonly called the *shuffle* phase.

Hadoop calls the reducer once for each key, with a list of all the values associated with it. The reducer combines these values and generates the final output (which is typically, but not necessarily, also key/value pairs).

So much for the theory—let's see it in action by creating a Hadoop version of the Wikipedia word-count example we've already seen in previous chapters.

Counting Words with Hadoop

We're going to start with a slightly simplified problem—counting the number of words in a collection of plain-text files (we'll see how to extend this to counting the words in a Wikipedia XML dump soon).

Our mapper will process text a line at a time, break each line into words and output a single key/value pair for each word. The key will be the word itself, and the value will be the constant integer 1. Our reducer will take all the key/value pairs for a given word and sum the values, generating a single key/value pair for each word, where the value is a count of the number of times that word occurred in the input:

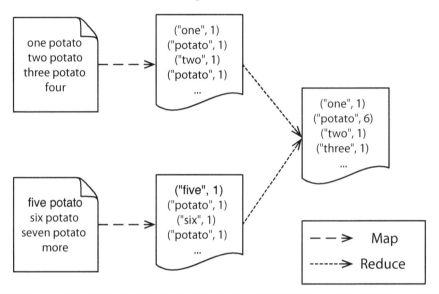

Figure 20—Counting words with Hadoop

The Mapper

Our mapper, `Map`, extends Hadoop's `Mapper` class, which takes four type parameters—the input key type, the input value type, the output key type, and the output value type:

LambdaArchitecture/WordCount/src/main/java/com/paulbutcher/WordCount.java

```
public static class Map extends Mapper<Object, Text, Text, IntWritable> {
  private final static IntWritable one = new IntWritable(1);

  public void map(Object key, Text value, Context context)
    throws IOException, InterruptedException {

    String line = value.toString();
    Iterable<String> words = new Words(line);
    for (String word: words)
      context.write(new Text(word), one);
  }
}
```

Hadoop uses its own types to represent input and output data (we can't use plain Strings and Integers). Our mapper handles plain text data, not key/value pairs, so the input key type is unused (we pass Object) and the input value type is Text. The output key type is also Text, with a value type of IntWritable.

The map() method will be called once for each line of the input split. It starts by converting the line to a plain Java String (line 7) and then splits the String into words (line 8). Finally it iterates over those words, generating a single key/value pair for each of them, where the key is the word and the value the constant integer 1 (line 10).

The Reducer

Our reducer, Reduce, extends Hadoop's Reducer class. Like Mapper, this also takes type parameters indicating the input and output key and value types (in our case, Text for both key types and IntWritable for both value types):

LambdaArchitecture/WordCount/src/main/java/com/paulbutcher/WordCount.java

```java
public static class Reduce extends Reducer<Text, IntWritable, Text, IntWritable> {
  public void reduce(Text key, Iterable<IntWritable> values, Context context)
    throws IOException, InterruptedException {
    int sum = 0;
    for (IntWritable val: values)
      sum += val.get();
    context.write(key, new IntWritable(sum));
  }
}
```

The reduce() method will be called once for each key, with values containing a collection of all the values associated with that key. Our mapper simply sums the values and generates a single key/value pair associating the word with its total occurrences.

Now that we've got both our mapper and our reducer, our final task is to create a *driver*, which tells Hadoop how to run them.

The Driver

Our driver is a Hadoop Tool, which implements a run() method:

LambdaArchitecture/WordCount/src/main/java/com/paulbutcher/WordCount.java

```java
public class WordCount extends Configured implements Tool {

  public int run(String[] args) throws Exception {
    Configuration conf = getConf();
    Job job = Job.getInstance(conf, "wordcount");
    job.setJarByClass(WordCount.class);
    job.setMapperClass(Map.class);
    job.setReducerClass(Reduce.class);
```

```
      job.setOutputKeyClass(Text.class);
10    job.setOutputValueClass(IntWritable.class);
      FileInputFormat.addInputPath(job, new Path(args[0]));
      FileOutputFormat.setOutputPath(job, new Path(args[1]));
      boolean success = job.waitForCompletion(true);
      return success ? 0 : 1;
15  }

    public static void main(String[] args) throws Exception {
      int res = ToolRunner.run(new Configuration(), new WordCount(), args);
      System.exit(res);
20  }
  }
```

This is mostly boilerplate, simply informing Hadoop of what we're doing. We set the mapper and reducer classes on lines 7 and 8, and the output key and value types on lines 9 and 10. We don't need to set the input key and value type, because Hadoop assumes by default that we're processing text files. And we don't need to independently set the mapper output or reducer input key/value types, because Hadoop assumes by default that they're the same as the output key/value types.

Next we tell Hadoop where to find the input data and where to write the output data on lines 11 and 12, and finally, we start the job and wait for it to complete on line 13.

Now that we've got a complete Hadoop job, all that remains is to run it on some data.

Running Locally

We'll start by running locally. This won't give us any of the benefits of parallelism or fault tolerance, but it does give us a way to check that everything's working before the additional effort and expense of running on a full cluster.

First we'll need some text to process. The input directory contains two text files comprising the literary masterpiece we'll be analyzing:

LambdaArchitecture/WordCount/input/file1.txt
```
one potato two potato three potato four
```

LambdaArchitecture/WordCount/input/file2.txt
```
five potato six potato seven potato more
```

Not exactly gigabytes of data, to be sure, but there's enough there to verify that the code works. We can count the text in these files by building with mvn package and then running a local instance of Hadoop with this:

```
$ hadoop jar target/wordcount-1.0-jar-with-dependencies.jar input output
```

After Hadoop's finished running, you should find that you have a new directory called output, which contains two files—_SUCCESS and part-r-00000. The first is an empty file that simply indicates that the job ran successfully. The second should contain the following:

```
five  1
four  1
more  1
one 1
potato  6
seven 1
six 1
three 1
two 1
```

Now that we've demonstrated that we can successfully run our job on a small file locally, we're in a position to run it on a cluster and process much more data.

> ### Joe asks:
> ### Are Results Always Sorted?
>
> You might have noticed that the results are sorted in (alphabetical) key order. Hadoop guarantees that keys will be sorted before being passed to a reducer, a fact that is very helpful for some tasks.
>
> Be careful, however. Although the keys are sorted before they're passed to each reducer, as we'll see, by default there's no ordering between reducers. This is something that can be controlled by setting a partitioner, but this isn't something we'll cover further here.

Running on Amazon EMR

Running a Hadoop job on Amazon Elastic MapReduce requires a number of steps. We won't go into EMR in depth. But I do want to cover the steps in enough detail for you to be able to follow along.

Input and Output

By default, EMR takes its input from and writes its output to Amazon S3.[6] S3 is also the location of the JAR file containing the code to execute and where log files are written.

---

6. http://aws.amazon.com/s3/

So to start, we'll need an S3 bucket containing some plain-text files. A Wikipedia dump won't do, because it's XML, not plain text. The sample code for this chapter includes a project called ExtractWikiText that extracts the text from a Wikipedia dump, after which you can upload it to your S3 bucket. You'll then need to upload the JAR file you built to another S3 bucket.

Uploading Large Files to S3

If, like me, your "broad"-band connection starts to wheeze when asked to upload large files, you might want to consider creating a short-lived Amazon EC2 instance with which to download the Wikipedia dump, extract the text from it, and upload it to S3. Unsurprisingly, Amazon provides excellent bandwidth between EC2 and S3, which can save your broadband's blushes.

Creating a Cluster

You can create an EMR cluster in many different ways—we're going to use the elastic-mapreduce command-line tool:

```
$ elastic-mapreduce --create --name wordcount --num-instances 11 \
--master-instance-type m1.large --slave-instance-type m1.large \
--ami-version 3.0.2 --jar s3://pb7con-lambda/wordcount.jar \
--arg s3://pb7con-wikipedia/text --arg s3://pb7con-wikipedia/counts
Created job flow j-2LSRGPBSR79ZV
```

This creates a cluster called "wordcount" with 11 instances, 1 master and 10 slaves, each of type m1.large running the 3.0.2 machine image (AMI).[7] The final arguments tell EMR where to find the JAR we uploaded to S3, where to find the input data, and where to put the results.

Monitoring Progress

We can use the job flow identifier returned when we created the cluster to establish an SSH connection to the master node:

```
$ elastic-mapreduce --jobflow j-2LSRGPBSR79ZV --ssh
```

Now that we've got a command line on the master, we can monitor the progress of the job by looking at the log files:

```
$ tail -f /mnt/var/log/hadoop/steps/1/syslog
INFO org.apache.hadoop.mapreduce.Job (main):  map 0% reduce 0%
INFO org.apache.hadoop.mapreduce.Job (main):  map 1% reduce 0%
INFO org.apache.hadoop.mapreduce.Job (main):  map 2% reduce 0%
INFO org.apache.hadoop.mapreduce.Job (main):  map 3% reduce 0%
INFO org.apache.hadoop.mapreduce.Job (main):  map 4% reduce 0%
```

---

7.   http://aws.amazon.com/ec2/instance-types/

Examining the Results

In my tests, this configuration takes a little over an hour to count all the words in Wikipedia. Once it's finished, you should find a number of files in the S3 bucket you specified:

```
part-r-00000
part-r-00001
part-r-00002
⋮
part-r-00028
```

These files, taken in aggregate, contain the full set of results. Results are sorted within each result partition, but not across partitions (see *Are Results Always Sorted?*, on page 231).

So we can now count words in plain-text files, but ideally we'd like to process a Wikipedia dump directly. We'll look at how to do so next.

Processing XML

An XML file is, after all, just a text file with a little added structure, so you would be forgiven for thinking that we could process it in much the same way as we saw earlier. Doing so won't work, however, because Hadoop's default splitter divides files at line boundaries, meaning that it's likely to split files in the middle of XML tags.

Although Hadoop doesn't come with an XML-aware splitter as standard, it turns out that another Apache project, Mahout,[8] does provide one—XmlInput-Format.[9] To use it, we need to make a few small changes to our driver:

LambdaArchitecture/WordCountXml/src/main/java/com/paulbutcher/WordCount.java

```
public int run(String[] args) throws Exception {
    Configuration conf = getConf();
    conf.set("xmlinput.start", "<text");
    conf.set("xmlinput.end", "</text>");

    Job job = Job.getInstance(conf, "wordcount");
    job.setJarByClass(WordCount.class);
    job.setInputFormatClass(XmlInputFormat.class);
    job.setMapperClass(Map.class);
    job.setCombinerClass(Reduce.class);
    job.setReducerClass(Reduce.class);
    job.setOutputKeyClass(Text.class);
    job.setOutputValueClass(IntWritable.class);
```

---

8. http://mahout.apache.org
9. https://github.com/apache/mahout/blob/trunk/integration/src/main/java/org/apache/mahout/text/wikipedia/XmlInputFormat.java

```
   FileInputFormat.addInputPath(job, new Path(args[0]));
15 FileOutputFormat.setOutputPath(job, new Path(args[1]));

   boolean success = job.waitForCompletion(true);
   return success ? 0 : 1;
}
```

We're using setInputFormatClass() (line 8) to tell Hadoop to use XmlInputFormat instead of the default splitter and setting the xmlinput.start and xmlinput.end (lines 3 and 4) within the configuration to let the splitter know which tags we're interested in.

If you look closely at the value we're using for xmlinput.start, something might strike you as slightly odd—we're setting it to <text, which isn't a well-formed XML tag. XmlInputFormat doesn't perform a full XML parse; instead it simply looks for start and end patterns. Because the <text> tag takes attributes, we just search for <text instead of <text>.

We also need to tweak our mapper slightly:

LambdaArchitecture/WordCountXml/src/main/java/com/paulbutcher/WordCount.java

```
private final static Pattern textPattern =
  Pattern.compile("^<text.*>(.*)</text>$", Pattern.DOTALL);

public void map(Object key, Text value, Context context)
  throws IOException, InterruptedException {

  String text = value.toString();
  Matcher matcher = textPattern.matcher(text);
  if (matcher.find()) {
    Iterable<String> words = new Words(matcher.group(1));
    for (String word: words)
      context.write(new Text(word), one);
  }
}
```

Each split consists of the text between the xmlinput.start and xmlinput.end patterns, including the matching patterns. So we use a little regular-expression magic to strip the <text></text> tags before counting words (to avoid overcounting the word *text*).

You may have noticed one other thing about our driver—we're setting a *combiner* with setCombinerClass() (line 10). A combiner is an optimization that allows key/value pairs to be combined before they're sent to a reducer (see Figure 21, *Using a combiner*, on page 235. In my tests, this decreases runtime from a little over an hour to around forty-five minutes.

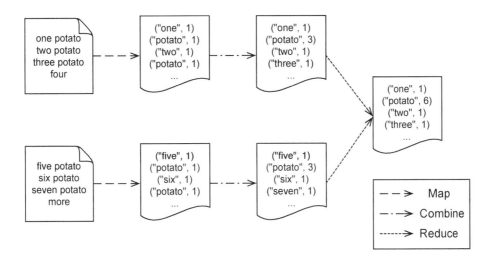

Figure 21—Using a combiner

In our case, our reducer works just as well as a combiner, but some algorithms will require a separate combiner. Hadoop does not guarantee use of a combiner if one is provided, so we need to make sure that our algorithm doesn't depend on whether, or how often, it is used.

Day 1 Wrap-Up

That's it for day 1. In day 2 we'll see how to use Hadoop to construct the batch layer of the Lambda Architecture.

What We Learned in Day 1

Breaking a problem into a map over a data structure followed by a reduce operation makes it easy to parallelize. MapReduce, in the sense we're using the term in this chapter, specifically means a system that efficiently and fault-tolerantly distributes jobs constructed from maps and reduces over multiple machines. Hadoop is a MapReduce system that does the following:

- It splits input between a number of mappers, each of which generates key/value pairs.

- These are then sent to reducers, which generate the final output (typically also a set of key/value pairs).

- Keys are partitioned between reducers such that all pairs with the same key are handled by the same reducer.

Joe asks:
Is It All About Speed?

It's tempting to think that all Hadoop gives us is speed—allowing us to process large bodies of data more quickly than we could on a single machine, and certainly that's a very important benefit. But there's more to it than that:

- When we start talking about clusters of hundreds of machines, failure stops being a risk and becomes a likelihood. Any system that failed when one machine in the cluster failed would rapidly become unworkable. For that reason, Hadoop has been constructed from the ground up to be able to handle and recover from failure.

- Related to the preceding, we need to consider not only how to retry tasks that were in progress on a failed node, but also how to avoid loss of data if one or more discs fails. By default, Hadoop uses the Hadoop distributed file system (HDFS), a fault-tolerant distributed file system that replicates data across multiple nodes.

- Once we start talking about gigabytes or more of data, it becomes unreasonable to expect that we'll be able to fit intermediate data or results in memory. Hadoop stores key/value pairs within HDFS during processing, allowing us to create jobs that process much larger datasets than will fit in memory.

Taken together, these aspects are transformative. It's no coincidence that this chapter is the only one in which we've executed our Wikipedia word-count example on an entire Wikipedia dump—MapReduce is the only technology we're going to cover that realistically allows that quantity of data to be processed.

Day 1 Self-Study

Find

- The documentation for Hadoop's streaming API, which allows MapReduce jobs to be created in languages like Ruby, Python, or Perl

- The documentation for Hadoop's pipes API, which allows MapReduce jobs to be created in C++

- A large number of libraries build on top of the Hadoop Java API to make it easier to construct more complex MapReduce jobs. For example, you might want to take a look at Cascading, Cascalog, or Scalding.

Do

- While a word-count job is running, kill one of the machines in the cluster (not the master—Hadoop is unable to recover if the master fails). Examine the logs while you do so to see how Hadoop retries the work that was assigned to that machine. Verify that the results are the same as for a job that doesn't experience a failure.

- Our word-count program does what it claims, but it's not very helpful if we want to answer the question "What are the top 100 most commonly used words on Wikipedia?" Implement a secondary sort (the Internet has many articles about how to do so) to generate fully sorted output from our word-count job.

- The "top-ten pattern" is an alternative way to solve the "most common words on Wikipedia" problem. Create a version of our word-count program that uses this pattern.

- Not all problems can be solved by a single MapReduce job—often it's necessary to chain multiple jobs, with the output of one forming the input for the next. One example is the PageRank algorithm. Create a Hadoop program that calculates the page rank of each Wikipedia page. How many iterations does it take before the results stabilize?

Day 2: The Batch Layer

Yesterday we saw how we could use Hadoop to parallelize across a cluster of machines. MapReduce can be used to solve a huge range of problems, but today we're going to concentrate on how it fits into the Lambda Architecture.

Before we look at that, however, let's consider the problem that the Lambda Architecture exists to solve—what's wrong with traditional data systems?

Problems with Traditional Data Systems

Data systems are nothing new—we've been using databases to answer questions about the data stored within them for almost as long as computers have existed. Traditional databases work well up to a point, but the volume of data we're trying to handle these days is pushing them beyond the point where they can cope.

Scaling

Some techniques enable a traditional database to scale beyond a single machine (replication, sharding, and so on), but these become harder and harder to apply as the number of machines and the query volume grows. Beyond a certain point, adding machines simply doesn't help.

Maintenance Overhead

Maintaining a database spread over a number of machines is hard. Doing so without downtime is even more so—if you need to reshard your database, for example. Then there's fault tolerance, backup, and ensuring data integrity, all of which become exponentially more difficult as the volume of data and queries increases.

Complexity

Replication and sharding typically require support at the application layer—your application needs to know which replicas to query and which shards to update (which will typically vary from query to query in nonobvious ways). Often many of the facilities that programmers have grown used to, such as transaction support, disappear when a database is sharded, meaning that programmers have to handle failures and retries explicitly. All of this increases the chances of mistakes being made.

Human Error

An often-forgotten aspect of fault tolerance is coping with human error. Most data corruptions don't result from a disk going bad, but rather from a mistake on the part of either an administrator or a developer. If you're lucky, this will be something that you spot quickly and can recover from by restoring from a backup, but not all errors are this obvious. What if you have an error that results in widespread corruption that goes undetected for a couple of weeks? How are you going to repair your database?

Sometimes you can undo the damage by understanding the effects of the bug and then creating a one-off script to fix up the database. Sometimes you can undo it by replaying from log files (assuming your log files capture all the information you need). And sometimes you're simply out of luck. Relying on luck is not a good long-term strategy.

Reporting and Analysis

Traditional databases excel at operational support—the day-to-day running of the business. They're much less effective when it comes to reporting and analysis, both of which require access to historical information.

A typical solution is to have a separate data warehouse that maintains historical data in an alternative structure. Data moves from the operational database to the data warehouse through a process known as *extract, transform, load* (ETL). Not only is this complicated, but it depends upon accurately predicting which information you'll need ahead of time—it's not at all uncommon to find that some report or analysis you would like to perform is impossible because the information you would need to run it has been lost or captured in the wrong structure.

In the next section we'll see how the Lambda Architecture addresses all these issues. Not only does it allow us to handle the vast quantities of data modern applications are faced with, but it also does so simply, recovering from both technical failure and human error and maintaining the complete historical record that will enable us to perform any reporting or analysis we might dream up in the future.

Eternal Truths

We can divide information into two categories—raw data and derived information.

Consider a page on Wikipedia—pages are constantly being updated and improved, so if I view a particular page today, I may well see something different from what I saw yesterday. But pages aren't the raw data from which Wikipedia is constructed—a single page is the result of combining many edits by many different contributors. These edits are the raw data from which pages are derived.

Furthermore, although pages change from day to day, edits don't. Once a contributor has made an edit, that edit never changes. Some subsequent edit might modify or undo its effect, and therefore the derived page, but edits themselves are immutable.

You can make the same distinction in any data system. The balance of your bank account is derived from a sequence of raw debits and credits. Facebook's friend graph is derived from a sequence of raw friend and unfriend events. And like Wikipedia edits, both debits and credits and friend and unfriend events are immutable.

This insight, that raw data is eternally true, is the fundamental basis of the Lambda Architecture. In the next section we'll see how it leverages that insight to address the problems of traditional data systems.

Data Is Better Raw

At this point, your ears should be pricking up. As we've seen in previous chapters, immutability and parallelism are a marriage made in heaven.

> ### Joe asks:
> ### Is All Raw Data Really Immutable?
>
> At first it can be difficult to see how some kinds of raw data could be eternally true. What about a user's home address, for example? What happens if that person moves to a different house?
>
> This is still immutable—we just need to add a timestamp. Instead of recording "Charlotte lives at 22 Acacia Avenue," we record that "On March 1, 1982, Charlotte lived at 22 Acacia Avenue." That will remain true, whatever happens in the future.

An Appealing Fantasy

Let's allow ourselves to fantasize briefly. Imagine that you had an infinitely fast computer that could process terabytes of data in an instant. You would only ever hold on to raw data—there would be no point keeping track of any of the information derived from it, because we could derive it as and when we needed it.

At a stroke, in this fantasy land we've eliminated most of the complexity associated with a traditional database, because when data is immutable, storing it becomes trivial. All our storage medium needs to do is allow us to append new data as and when it becomes available—we don't need elaborate locking mechanisms or transactions, because once it's been stored it will never change.

It gets better. When data is immutable, multiple threads can access it in parallel without any concern of interfering with each other. We can take copies of it and operate on those copies, without worrying about them becoming out-of-date, so distributing the data across a cluster immediately becomes much easier.

Of course, we don't live in this fantasy land, but you might be surprised how close we can get by leveraging the power of MapReduce.

Fantasy (Almost) Becomes Reality

If we know ahead of time which queries we want to run against our raw data, we can precompute a *batch view*, which either directly contains the derived data that will be returned by those queries or contains data that can easily be combined to create it. Computing these batch views is the job of the Lambda Architecture's batch layer.

> \\//
> ꙮ
> **Joe asks:**
> # What About Deleting Data?
>
> Occasionally we have good reasons to delete raw data. This might be because it's outlived its usefulness, or it might be for regulatory or security reasons (data-protection laws may forbid retention of some data beyond a certain period, for example).
>
> This doesn't invalidate anything we've said so far. Data we choose to delete is still eternally true, even if we choose to forget it.

As an example of the first type of batch view, consider building Wikipedia pages from a sequence of edits—the batch view will simply comprise the text of each page, built by combining all the edits of that page.

The second type of batch view is slightly more complex, so that's what we'll concentrate on for the remainder of today. We're going to use Hadoop to build batch views that will allow us to query how many edits a Wikipedia contributor has made over a period of days.

Wikipedia Contributors

The kind of query that we'd ideally like to make is, "How many contributions did Fred Bloggs make between 3:15 p.m. on Tuesday, June 5, 2012, and 10:45 a.m. on Thursday, June 7, 2012?" To do so, however, we'd need to maintain and index a record of the exact time of every contribution. If we really need to make this kind of query, then we'll need to pay the price, but in reality we're unlikely to need to make queries at this fine a granularity—a day-by-day basis is likely to be more than enough.

So our batch view could consist of simple daily totals:

Fred's Contributions	Fred's Counts
2012-02-26 15:04:16	
2012-02-26 16:23:43	
2012-02-26 18:59:03	2012-02-26: 3
2012-02-27 12:56:32	2012-02-27: 1
2012-02-28 17:09:12 $\longrightarrow$	2012-02-28: 2
2012-02-28 18:54:28	2012-03-02: 1
2012-03-02 12:00:36	2012-03-05: 1
2012-03-05 10:34:19	

This would work well enough if we were always interested in periods of a few days, but queries for periods of several months would still require combining many values (potentially, for example, 365 to determine how many contributions a user had made in a year). We can decrease the amount of work required to answer this kind of query by keeping track of periods of both months and days:

Fred's Contributions	Fred's Counts
2012-02-26 15:04:16	2012-02-26: 3
2012-02-26 16:23:43	2012-02-27: 1
2012-02-26 18:59:03	2012-02-28: 2
2012-02-27 12:56:32	2012-02: 6
2012-02-28 17:09:12	2012-03-02: 1
2012-02-28 18:54:28	2012-03-05: 1
2012-03-02 12:00:36	2012-03: 2
2012-03-05 10:34:19	

This would allow us to decrease the amount of work required to count a user's contributions within a year from summing 365 values to 12. And we can handle periods that neither start nor finish at the beginning of a month by summing monthly values and either adding or subtracting daily values:

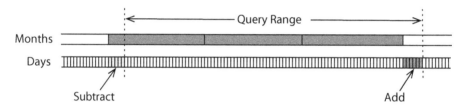

Contributor Logging

Sadly, we don't have access to a live feed of Wikipedia contributors. But if we did, it might look something like this:

```
2012-09-01T14:18:13Z 123456789 1234 Fred Bloggs
2012-09-01T14:18:15Z 123456790 54321 John Doe
2012-09-01T14:18:16Z 123456791 6789 Paul Butcher
⋮
```

The first column is a timestamp, the second is an identifier representing the contribution, the third is an identifier representing the user who made the contribution, and the remainder of the line is the username.

Although Wikipedia doesn't publish such a feed, it does provide periodic XML dumps containing a full history (you're looking for enwiki-latest-stub-meta-history).[10]

---

10. http://dumps.wikimedia.org/enwiki

The sample code for this chapter includes an ExtractWikiContributors project that will take one of these dumps and create a file of the preceding form.

In the next section we'll construct a Hadoop job that takes these log files and generates the data required for our batch view.

Counting Contributions

As always, our Hadoop job consists of a mapper and a reducer. The mapper is very straightforward, simply parsing a line of the contributor log and generating a key/value pair in which the key is the contributor ID and the value is the timestamp of the contribution:

LambdaArchitecture/WikiContributorsBatch/src/main/java/com/paulbutcher/WikipediaContributors.java
```java
public static class Map extends Mapper<Object, Text, IntWritable, LongWritable> {

  public void map(Object key, Text value, Context context)
    throws IOException, InterruptedException {

    Contribution contribution = new Contribution(value.toString());
    context.write(new IntWritable(contribution.contributorId),
      new LongWritable(contribution.timestamp));
  }
}
```

Most of the work is done by the Contribution class:

LambdaArchitecture/WikiContributorsBatch/src/main/java/com/paulbutcher/Contribution.java
```java
class Contribution {
  static final Pattern pattern = Pattern.compile("^([^\\s]*) (\\d*) (\\d*) (.*)$");
  static final DateTimeFormatter isoFormat = ISODateTimeFormat.dateTimeNoMillis();

  public long timestamp;
  public int id;
  public int contributorId;
  public String username;

  public Contribution(String line) {
    Matcher matcher = pattern.matcher(line);
    if(matcher.find()) {
      timestamp = isoFormat.parseDateTime(matcher.group(1)).getMillis();
      id = Integer.parseInt(matcher.group(2));
      contributorId = Integer.parseInt(matcher.group(3));
      username = matcher.group(4);
    }
  }
}
```

We could parse a log file line in various ways—in this case, we're using a regular expression (line 2). If it matches, we use the ISODateTimeFormat class from the Joda-Time library to parse the timestamp and convert it to a long value representing the number of milliseconds since January 1, 1970 (line 13).[11] The contribution and contributor IDs are then just simple integers, and the contributor's username is the remainder of the line.

Our reducer is more involved:

LambdaArchitecture/WikiContributorsBatch/src/main/java/com/paulbutcher/WikipediaContributors.java
```
Line 1  public static class Reduce
          extends Reducer<IntWritable, LongWritable, IntWritable, Text> {
          static DateTimeFormatter dayFormat = ISODateTimeFormat.yearMonthDay();
          static DateTimeFormatter monthFormat = ISODateTimeFormat.yearMonth();

  5       public void reduce(IntWritable key, Iterable<LongWritable> values,
                             Context context) throws IOException, InterruptedException {
          HashMap<DateTime, Integer> days = new HashMap<DateTime, Integer>();
          HashMap<DateTime, Integer> months = new HashMap<DateTime, Integer>();
 10       for (LongWritable value: values) {
            DateTime timestamp = new DateTime(value.get());
            DateTime day = timestamp.withTimeAtStartOfDay();
            DateTime month = day.withDayOfMonth(1);
            incrementCount(days, day);
 15         incrementCount(months, month);
          }
          for (Entry<DateTime, Integer> entry: days.entrySet())
            context.write(key, formatEntry(entry, dayFormat));
          for (Entry<DateTime, Integer> entry: months.entrySet())
 20         context.write(key, formatEntry(entry, monthFormat));
        }
      }
```

For each contributor, we build two HashMaps, days (line 8) and months (line 9). We populate these by iterating over timestamps (remember that values will be a list of timestamps) using the Joda-Time utility methods withTimeAtStartOfDay() and withDayOfMonth() to convert that timestamp to midnight on the day of the contribution and midnight on the first day of the month (lines 12 and 13, respectively). We then increment the relevant count in days and months using a simple utility method:

LambdaArchitecture/WikiContributorsBatch/src/main/java/com/paulbutcher/WikipediaContributors.java
```
private void incrementCount(HashMap<DateTime, Integer> counts, DateTime key) {
  Integer currentCount = counts.get(key);
  if (currentCount == null)
    counts.put(key, 1);
  else
    counts.put(key, currentCount + 1);
}
```

---

11. http://www.joda.org/joda-time/

Finally, once we've finished building our maps, we iterate over each map and generate an output for each day and month in which there was at least one contribution (lines 17 to 20).

This is slightly involved because, as we've seen, the output from a Hadoop job is always a set of key/value pairs, but what we want to output are three values—the contributor ID, a date (either a month or a day), and a count. We could do this by defining a composite value. This way, our key is the contributor ID and the value is a composite value containing the date and the count. But our case is simple enough that we can instead just use a string as the value type and format it appropriately with formatEntry():

LambdaArchitecture/WikiContributorsBatch/src/main/java/com/paulbutcher/WikipediaContributors.java
```
private Text formatEntry(Entry<DateTime, Integer> entry,
                         DateTimeFormatter formatter) {
  return new Text(formatter.print(entry.getKey()) + "\t" + entry.getValue())
}
```

Here's a section of this job's output:

```
463 2001-11-24  1
463 2002-02-14  1
463 2001-11-26  6
463 2001-10-01  1
463 2002-02 1
463 2001-10 1
463 2001-11 7
```

This contains exactly the data that we need, but a collection of text files isn't particularly convenient. In the next section we'll talk about the serving layer, which indexes and combines the output of the batch layer.

 Joe asks:
Can We Generate Batch Views Incrementally?

The batch layer we've described so far recomputes entire batch views from scratch each time it's run. This will certainly work, but it's probably performing more work than necessary—why not update batch views incrementally with the new data that's arrived since the last time the batch view was generated?

The simple answer is that there's nothing to stop you from doing so, and this can be a useful optimization. But you can't rely exclusively on incremental updates—much of the power of the Lambda Architecture derives from the fact that we can always rebuild from scratch if we need to. So feel free to implement an incremental algorithm if the optimization is worth the additional effort, but recognize that this can never be a replacement for recomputation.

Completing the Picture

The batch layer isn't enough on its own to create a complete end-to-end application. That requires the next element of the Lambda Architecture—the serving layer.

The Serving Layer

The batch view we've just generated needs to be indexed so that we can make queries against it, and we need somewhere to put the application logic that decides how to combine elements of the batch view to satisfy a particular query. This is the duty of the serving layer:

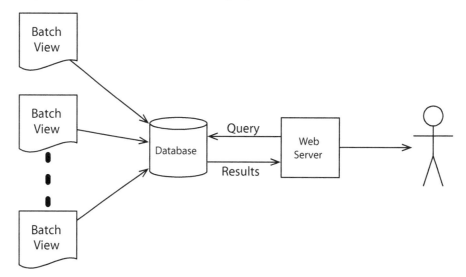

We're going to leave the serving layer as an exercise for the reader, as it has little relevance to the subject matter of this book, but it's worth mentioning one particular aspect of it—the database.

Although you could build the serving layer on top of a traditional database, its access patterns are rather different from a traditional application. In particular, there's no requirement for random writes—the only time the database is updated is when the batch views are updated, which requires a batch update.

Therefore a category emerges of serving-layer databases optimized for this usage pattern, the most well-known of which are ElephantDB and Voldemort.[12,13]

---

12. https://github.com/nathanmarz/elephantdb
13. http://www.project-voldemort.com/voldemort/

Almost Nirvana

Taken together, the batch and serving layers give us a data system that addresses all the problems we identified at the beginning of the day:

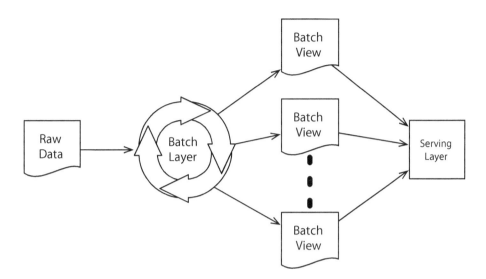

The batch layer runs in an infinite loop, regenerating batch views from our raw data. Each time a batch run completes, the serving layer updates its database.

Because it only ever operates on immutable raw data, the batch layer can easily exploit parallelism. Raw data can be distributed across a cluster of machines, enabling batch views to be recomputed in an acceptable period of time even when dealing with terabytes of input.

The immutability of raw data also means that the system is intrinsically hardened against both technical failure and human error. Not only is it much easier to back up raw data, but if there's a bug, the worst that can happen is that batch views are temporarily incorrect—we can always correct them by fixing the bug and recomputing them.

Finally, because we retain all raw data, we can always generate any report or analysis that might occur to us in the future.

There's an obvious problem, though—latency. If the batch layer takes an hour to run, then our batch views will always be at least an hour out-of-date. This is where tomorrow's subject, the speed layer, comes into play.

Day 2 Wrap-Up

This brings us to the end of day 2. In day 3 we'll complete our picture of the Lambda Architecture by looking at the speed layer.

What We Learned in Day 2

Information can be divided into raw data and derived information. Raw data is eternally true and therefore immutable. The batch layer of the Lambda Architecture leverages this to allow us to create systems that are

- highly parallel, enabling terabytes of data to be processed;

- simple, making them both easier to create and less error prone;

- tolerant of both technical failure and human error; and

- capable of supporting both day-to-day operations and historical reporting and analysis.

The primary drawback of the batch layer is latency, which the Lambda Architecture addresses by running the speed layer alongside.

Day 2 Self-Study

Find

- The approaches we've discussed here are not the only way to tackle building a data system that leverages Hadoop—other options include HBase, Pig, and Hive. All three of these have more in common with a traditional data system than what we've seen today. Pick one and compare it to the Lambda Architecture's batch layer. When might you choose one, and when the other?

Do

- Finish the system we built today by creating a serving layer that takes the output of the batch layer, puts it in a database, and allows queries about the number of edits made by a particular user over a range of days. You can build it either on top of a traditional database or on top of ElephantDB.

- Extend the preceding to build batch views incrementally—to do this, you will need to provide the Hadoop cluster with access to the serving layer's database. How much more efficient is it? Is it worth the additional effort? For which types of application would incremental batch view construction make sense? For which would it not?

Day 3: The Speed Layer

As we saw yesterday, the batch layer of the Lambda Architecture solves all the problems we identified with traditional data systems, but it does so at the expense of latency. The speed layer exists to solve that problem. The following figure shows how the batch and speed layers work together:

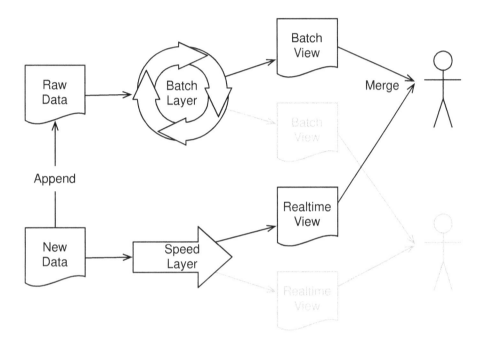

Figure 22—The Lambda Architecture

As new data arrives, we both append it to the raw data that the batch layer works on and send it to the speed layer. The speed layer generates real-time views, which are combined with batch views to create fully up-to-date answers to queries.

Real-time views contain only information derived from the data that arrived since the batch views were last generated and are discarded when the data they were built from is processed by the batch layer.

Today we'll see how to use Storm to create the speed layer.[14]

---

14. http://storm.incubator.apache.org

Designing the Speed Layer

Different applications have different interpretations of real time—some require new data to be available in seconds, some in milliseconds. But whatever your particular application's performance requirements are, it's unlikely that they can be met with a pure batch-oriented approach.

Building the speed layer is therefore intrinsically more difficult than building the batch layer because it's forced to take an incremental approach. This in turn means that it can't restrict itself to only processing raw data and can't rely on the nice properties of raw data we identified yesterday. So we're back to traditional databases that support random writes and all the complexity (locking, transactions, and so forth) that comes with them.

On the plus side, the speed layer only needs to handle that portion of our data that hasn't already been handled by the batch layer (typically a few hours' worth). Once the batch layer catches up, older data can be expired from the speed layer.

Synchronous or Asynchronous?

One obvious way to build the speed layer would be to do so as a traditional synchronous database application. Indeed, you can think of a traditional database application as a degenerate case of the Lambda Architecture in which the batch layer never runs:

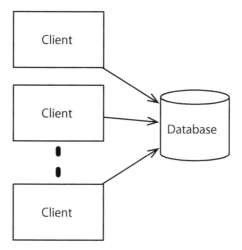

In this approach, clients communicate directly with the database and block while it's processing each update. This is a perfectly reasonable approach, and for some applications it may be the only one that meets their operational requirements. But in many cases, an asynchronous architecture will be better:

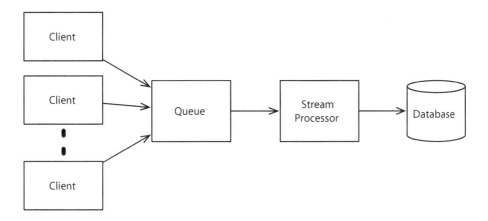

In this approach, clients add updates to a queue (implemented with, for example, Kafka or Kestrel[15,16]) as they arrive and without blocking. A stream processor then handles these updates in turn and performs the database update.

Using a queue decouples clients from database updates, making it more complex to coordinate updates with other actions. For applications in which this is acceptable, the benefits are significant:

- Because clients don't block, fewer clients can handle higher volumes of data, leading to greater throughput.

- Spikes in demand might lead to a synchronous system timing out or dropping updates as clients or the database becoming overloaded. An asynchronous system, by contrast, will simply fall behind, storing unhandled updates in the queue and catching up when demand returns to normal levels.

- As we'll see during the remainder of today, the stream processor can exploit parallelism, distributing processing over multiple computing resources in order to provide both fault tolerance and improved performance.

For these reasons, and because synchronous speed-layer implementations are largely uninteresting as far as parallelism and concurrency are concerned, we're not going to consider them further in this book. Before we look at an asynchronous implementation, however, we should touch on one other subject—expiring data.

---

15. http://kafka.apache.org
16. http://robey.github.io/kestrel/

Expiring Data

If your batch layer takes (say) two hours to run, you would be forgiven for thinking that your speed layer will need to handle two hours' worth of data. In fact, it will need to handle up to twice that amount, as shown in the figure:

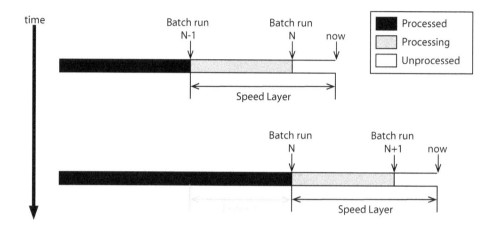

Figure 23—Expiring data in the speed layer

Imagine that batch run *N*-1 has just completed and batch run *N* is just about to start. If each takes two hours to run, that means that our batch views will be two hours out-of-date. The speed layer therefore needs to serve requests for those two hours' worth of data plus any data that arrives before batch run *N* completes, for a total of four hours' worth.

When batch run *N* does complete, we then need to expire the data that represents the oldest two hours but still retain the most recent two hours' worth. It is certainly possible to come up with schemes that allow you to do this, but the easiest solution can be to run two copies of the speed layer in parallel and ping-pong between them, as shown in Figure 24, *Ping-pong speed layers*, on page 253.

Whenever a batch run completes and new data becomes available in the batch views, we switch from the speed layer that's currently serving queries to its counterpart with more recent data. The now-idle speed layer then clears its database and starts building a new set of views from scratch, starting at the point where the new batch run started.

Not only does this approach save us from having to identify which data to delete from the speed layer's database, but it also improves performance and

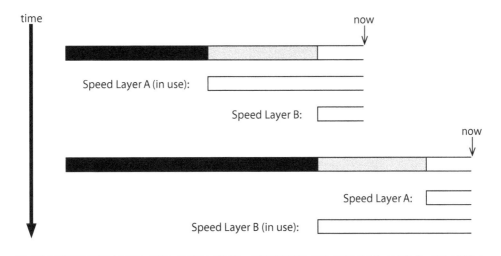

Figure 24—Ping-pong speed layers

reliability by ensuring that each iteration of the speed layer starts from a clean database. The cost, of course, is that we have to maintain two copies of the speed layer's data and twice the computing resources, but this cost is unlikely to be significant in relative terms, given that the speed layer is only handling a very small fraction of the total data.

Storm

We're going to spend the rest of today looking at the outline of an asynchronous speed layer implementation in Storm. Storm is a big subject, so we'll cover it in only enough detail to give a taste—refer to the Storm documentation for more depth.[17]

Storm aims to do for real-time processing what Hadoop has for batch processing—to make it easy to distribute computation across multiple machines in order to improve both performance and fault tolerance.

Spouts, Bolts, and Topologies

A Storm system processes streams of tuples. Storm's tuples are similar to those we saw in Chapter 5, *Actors*, on page 115, the primary difference being that unlike Elixir's tuples, the elements of a Storm tuple are named.

Tuples are created by *spouts* and processed by *bolts*, which can create tuples in turn. Spouts and bolts are connected by streams to form a *topology*. Here's

---

17. http://storm.incubator.apache.org/documentation/Home.html

a simple topology in which a single spout creates tuples that are processed by a pipeline of bolts:

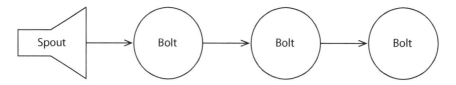

Figure 25—A simple topology

Topologies can be much more complex than this—bolts can consume multiple streams, and a single stream can be consumed by multiple bolts to create a directed acyclic graph, or DAG:

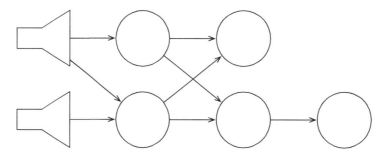

Figure 26—A complex topology

Even our simple pipeline topology is more complex than it appears, however, because spouts and bolts are both parallel and distributed.

Workers

Not only do spouts and bolts run in parallel with each other, but they are also internally parallel—each is implemented as a set of workers. Figure 27, *Spout and bolt workers*, on page 255 shows what our simple pipeline topology might look like if each spout and bolt had three workers.

As our diagram shows, the workers of each node of the pipeline can send tuples to any of the workers in their downstream node. We'll see how to control exactly which worker receives a tuple when we discuss stream grouping later.

Finally, workers are distributed—if we're running on a four-node cluster, for example, then our spout's workers might be on nodes 1, 2, and 3; the first bolt's workers might be on nodes 2 and 4 (two on node 2, one on node 4); and so on.

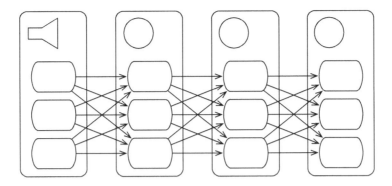

Figure 27—Spout and bolt workers

The beauty of Storm is that we don't need to explicitly worry about this distribution—all we need to do is specify our topology, and the Storm runtime allocates workers to nodes and makes sure that tuples are routed appropriately.

Fault Tolerance

A large part of the reason for distributing a single spout or bolt's workers across multiple machines is fault tolerance. If one of the machines in our cluster fails, our topology can continue to operate by routing tuples to the machines that are still operating.

Storm keeps track of the dependencies between tuples—if a particular tuple's processing isn't completed, Storm fails and retries the spout tuple(s) upon which it depends. This means that, by default, Storm provides an "at least once" processing guarantee. Applications need to be aware of the fact that tuples might be retried and continue to function correctly if they are.

Enough theory—let's see how we can use Storm to create an outline implementation of a speed layer for our Wikipedia contributor application.

 Joe asks:
 What If My Application Can't Handle Retries?

Storm's default "at least once" semantics are adequate for most applications, but some need a stronger "exactly once" processing guarantee.

Storm supports "exactly once" semantics via the Trident API.[a] Trident is not covered in this book.

---

a.   http://storm.incubator.apache.org/documentation/Trident-tutorial.html

Counting Contributions with Storm

Here's a possible topology for our speed layer:

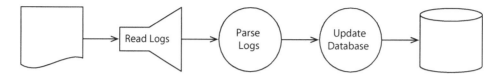

We start with a spout that imports contributor logs and converts them to a stream of tuples. This is consumed by a bolt that parses log entries and outputs a stream of parsed log entries. Finally, this stream is in turn consumed by a bolt that updates a database containing our real-time view.

We're going to build a slightly different topology from this, however, for a couple of reasons. First, we don't have access to a log of Wikipedia contributors; second, the details of updating a database are uninteresting from our point of view (with our focus on parallelism and concurrency). The following figure shows what we're going to build instead.

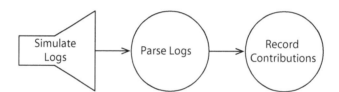

We're going to create a spout that simulates a Wikipedia contributor feed and then a parser, and finally we'll record the real-time views in memory. This wouldn't be a good production approach, but it will serve our purpose of exploring Storm.

Simulating the Contribution Log

Here's the code for our spout, which simulates a contributor feed by generating random log entries:

LambdaArchitecture/WikiContributorsSpeed/src/main/java/com/paulbutcher/RandomContributorSpout.java
```
Line 1  public class RandomContributorSpout extends BaseRichSpout {

          private static final Random rand = new Random();
          private static final DateTimeFormatter isoFormat =
    5       ISODateTimeFormat.dateTimeNoMillis();

          private SpoutOutputCollector collector;
          private int contributionId = 10000;
```

```
10  public void open(Map conf, TopologyContext context,
        SpoutOutputCollector collector) {

      this.collector = collector;
    }
15
    public void declareOutputFields(OutputFieldsDeclarer declarer) {
      declarer.declare(new Fields("line"));
    }

20  public void nextTuple() {
      Utils.sleep(rand.nextInt(100));
      ++contributionId;
      String line = isoFormat.print(DateTime.now()) + " " + contributionId + " " +
        rand.nextInt(10000) + " " + "dummyusername";
25    collector.emit(new Values(line));
    }
  }
```

We indicate that we're creating a spout by deriving from BaseRichSpout (line 1).
Storm calls our open() method (line 10) during initialization—we simply keep
a record of the SpoutOutputCollector, which is where we'll send our output. Storm
also calls our declareOutputFields() method (line 16) during initialization to find
out how the tuples generated by this spout are structured—in this case, the
tuples have a single field called line.

The method that does most of the work is nextTuple() (line 20). We start by
sleeping for a random interval of up to 100 ms, and then we create a string
of the same format we saw in *Contributor Logging*, on page 242, which we output
by calling collector.emit().

These lines will be passed to the parser bolt, which we'll see next.

Parsing Log Entries

Our parser bolt takes tuples containing log lines, parses them, and outputs
tuples with four fields, one for each component of the log line:

LambdaArchitecture/WikiContributorsSpeed/src/main/java/com/paulbutcher/ContributionParser.java
```
Line 1 class ContributionParser extends BaseBasicBolt {
  2    public void declareOutputFields(OutputFieldsDeclarer declarer) {
  3      declarer.declare(new Fields("timestamp", "id", "contributorId", "username"));
  4    }
  5    public void execute(Tuple tuple, BasicOutputCollector collector) {
  6      Contribution contribution = new Contribution(tuple.getString(0));
  7      collector.emit(new Values(contribution.timestamp, contribution.id,
  8        contribution.contributorId, contribution.username));
  9    }
 10 }
```

We indicate that we're creating a bolt by deriving from BaseBasicBolt (line 1). As with our spout, we implement declareOutputFields() (line 2) to let Storm know how our output tuples are structured—in this case they have four fields, called timestamp, id, contributorId, and username.

The method that does most of the work is execute() (line 5). In this case, it uses the same Contributor as the batch layer to parse the log line into its components and then calls contributor.emit() to output the tuple.

These parsed tuples will be passed to a bolt that keeps a record of each contributor's contributions, which we'll see next.

Recording Contributions

Our final bolt maintains a simple in-memory database (a map from contributor IDs to a set of contribution timestamps) of each contributor's contributions:

LambdaArchitecture/WikiContributorsSpeed/src/main/java/com/paulbutcher/ContributionRecord.java

```
Line 1 class ContributionRecord extends BaseBasicBolt {
         private static final HashMap<Integer, HashSet<Long>> timestamps =
           new HashMap<Integer, HashSet<Long>>();

    5    public void declareOutputFields(OutputFieldsDeclarer declarer) {
         }
         public void execute(Tuple tuple, BasicOutputCollector collector) {
           addTimestamp(tuple.getInteger(2), tuple.getLong(0));
         }
   10
         private void addTimestamp(int contributorId, long timestamp) {
           HashSet<Long> contributorTimestamps = timestamps.get(contributorId);
           if (contributorTimestamps == null) {
             contributorTimestamps = new HashSet<Long>();
   15        timestamps.put(contributorId, contributorTimestamps);
           }
           contributorTimestamps.add(timestamp);
         }
       }
```

In this case we're not generating any output, so declareOutputFields() is empty (line 5). Our execute() method (line 7) simply extracts the relevant fields from its input tuple and passes them to addTimestamp(), which simply adds the timestamp to the set associated with the contributor.

Finally, let's see how to build a topology that uses our spout and bolts.

Building the Topology

Something might be worrying you about ContributionRecord—given that bolts have multiple workers, how do we ensure that we maintain only a single set

> ⌣/⌣ **Joe asks:**
> Ꙩ # Why Record a Set of Timestamps?
>
> The batch views we saw in *Day 2: The Batch Layer*, on page 237, just recorded per-day and per-month counts for each contributor. So why do our real-time views record full timestamps?
>
> Firstly, as we discussed earlier, our real-time views only need to record a few hours' worth of data, so the cost of storing and querying a full set of timestamps is relatively low. But there's a more important reason—adding an item to a set is idempotent.
>
> Recall that Storm supports "at least once" semantics (see *Fault Tolerance*, on page 255), so tuples might be retried. An idempotent operation gives the same result no matter how many times it's performed, which is exactly what we need to be able to cope with tuples being retried.

of timestamps for each contributor? We'll see how when we construct our topology.

LambdaArchitecture/WikiContributorsSpeed/src/main/java/com/paulbutcher/WikiContributorsTopology.java

```
public class WikiContributorsTopology {

  public static void main(String[] args) throws Exception {

    TopologyBuilder builder = new TopologyBuilder();

    builder.setSpout("contribution_spout", new RandomContributorSpout(), 4);

    builder.setBolt("contribution_parser", new ContributionParser(), 4).
      shuffleGrouping("contribution_spout");

    builder.setBolt("contribution_recorder", new ContributionRecord(), 4).
      fieldsGrouping("contribution_parser", new Fields("contributorId"));

    LocalCluster cluster = new LocalCluster();
    Config conf = new Config();
    cluster.submitTopology("wiki-contributors", conf, builder.createTopology());

    Thread.sleep(10000);

    cluster.shutdown();
  }
}
```

We start by creating a TopologyBuilder (line 5) and we add an instance of our spout with setSpout() (line 7), the second argument to which is a parallelism hint. As its name suggests, this is a hint, not an instruction, but for our purposes, we can think of it as instructing Storm to create four workers for our spout. For a full description of how to control parallelism in Storm, see "What Makes a Running Topology: Worker Processes, Executors and Tasks."[18]

Next, we add an instance of our ContributionParser bolt with setBolt() (line 9). We tell Storm that this bolt should take its input from our spout by calling shuffle-Grouping(), passing it the name we gave to the spout, which brings us to the subject of stream grouping.

Stream Grouping

Storm's *stream grouping* answers the question about which workers receive which tuples. The *shuffle grouping* we're using for our parser bolt is the simplest—it simply sends tuples to a random worker.

Our contribution recorder bolt uses a *fields grouping* (line 12), which guarantees that all tuples with the same values for a set of fields (in our case, the contributorId field) are always sent to the same worker. This is how we guarantee that we maintain only a single set of timestamps for each contributor, answering the question we posed at the start of this section.

A Local Cluster

Setting up a Storm cluster isn't a huge job, but it's beyond the scope of this book. And sadly, as it's a relatively young technology, nobody's currently providing managed Storm clusters that we can leverage. So we'll run our topology locally by creating a LocalCluster (line 17).

Our sample then allows this topology to run for ten seconds and then shuts it down with cluster.shutdown(). In production, of course, we would need to provide a means to shut our topology down when the real-time views it's handling are no longer necessary because the batch layer has caught up.

Day 3 Wrap-Up

That brings us to the end of day 3 and the end of our discussion of the Lambda Architecture's speed layer.

What We Learned in Day 3

The speed layer completes the Lambda Architecture by providing real-time views of data that's arrived since the most recent batch views were built. The speed layer can be synchronous or asynchronous—Storm is one means by which we can build an asynchronous speed layer:

---

18. http://storm.incubator.apache.org/documentation/Understanding-the-parallelism-of-a-Storm-topology.html

- Storm processes streams of tuples in real time. Tuples are created by spouts and processed by bolts, arranged in a topology.

- Spouts and bolts each have multiple workers that run in parallel and are distributed across the nodes of a cluster.

- By default, Storm provides "at least once" semantics—bolts need to handle tuples being retried.

Day 3 Self-Study

Find

- Trident is a high-level API built on top of Storm that, among other things, provides "exactly once" semantics as well as Storm's "at least once" default semantics. When does it make sense to use Trident and when the low-level Storm API?

- Which other stream groupings does Storm support in addition to shuffle and fields groupings?

Do

- Create a Storm cluster and submit today's example so that it runs distributed instead of locally.

- Create a bolt that keeps track of the total number of contributions that have been made each minute and a topology in which both it and ContributionRecord consume the output of ContributionParser.

- Today's example made use of BaseBasicBolt, which automatically acknowledges tuples. Modify it to use BaseRichBolt—you will need to acknowledge tuples explicitly. How could you create a bolt that processes multiple tuples before acknowledging them?

Wrap-Up

The Lambda Architecture brings together many concepts we've covered elsewhere:

- The insight that raw data is eternally true should remind you of Clojure's separation of identity and state.

- Hadoop's approach of parallelizing a problem by splitting it into a map over a data structure followed by a reduce should remind you of much of what we saw when we looked at parallel functional programming.

- Like actors, the Lambda Architecture distributes processing over a cluster to both improve performance and provide fault tolerance in the face of hardware failure.

- Storm's streams of tuples have much in common with the message passing we saw in both actors and CSP.

Strengths

The Lambda Architecture is all about handling huge quantities of data—problems where traditional data-processing architectures are struggling to cope. It's particularly well suited to reporting and analytics—the kinds of problems that might have been addressed with a data warehouse in the past.

Weaknesses

The Lambda Architecture's great strength—its focus on huge quantities of data—is also its weakness. Unless your data is measured in tens of gigabytes or more, its overhead (both computational and intellectual) is unlikely to be worth the benefit.

Alternatives

The Lambda Architecture isn't tied to MapReduce—the batch layer could be implemented with any distributed batch-processing system.

With that in mind, Apache Spark is particularly interesting.[19] Spark is a cluster computing framework that implements a DAG execution engine, allowing a number of algorithms (most notably graph algorithms) to be expressed more naturally than they can be with MapReduce. It also has an associated streaming API, meaning that both the batch and speed layers could be implemented within Spark.[20]

Final Thoughts

The Lambda Architecture is a fitting end to this book, leveraging as it does many of the techniques we've seen in earlier chapters. It's a powerful demonstration of how parallelism and concurrency allow us to tackle problems that would otherwise be intractable.

In the last chapter, we'll review what we've seen over the last seven weeks and examine the broad themes that have emerged.

---

19. http://spark.apache.org
20. http://spark.apache.org/streaming/

CHAPTER 9

Wrapping Up

Congratulations on making it through all seven weeks!

We've covered a great deal of ground, from the fine-grained parallelism supported by a data-parallel GPU to the massive scale of a MapReduce cluster. Along the way, we've seen not only how concurrency and parallelism allow us to exploit the power of modern multicore CPUs, but also many other benefits of moving beyond conventional, sequential code:

- We saw how Elixir, Hadoop, and Storm all distribute computation across a cluster of independent machines, allowing us to create solutions that can recover when hardware fails.

- When looking at core.async, we saw how concurrency could rescue us from the "callback hell" commonly associated with event handling.

- In the chapter on functional programming, we saw how a concurrent solution could be both simpler and easier to understand than its sequential equivalent.

Let's take a look at what this means for the future.

Where Are We Going?

More than two decades ago, I predicted that parallel and distributed programming were about to go mainstream, so I don't have a fantastic track record as a pundit. Nevertheless, I believe that the increasing importance of concurrency and parallelism have clear implications for the future of programming.

The Future Is Immutable

To my mind, one lesson shines through all others—immutability is going to play a much larger part in the code we write in the future than it has in the past.

Immutability is most obviously relevant to functional programming—avoiding mutable state is what makes parallelism and concurrency so easy in functional code. But we don't have to write functional programs for immutability to be beneficial. Let's look at the evidence from the last few weeks:

- Although Clojure isn't a pure functional language, its core data structures are immutable and therefore persistent (as we saw in *Persistent Data Structures*, on page 88). And persistent data structures allow Clojure to support mutable references that separate identity from state, avoiding the problems normally associated with mutable state.

- Although it's not typically constructed using functional code at the lowest level, immutability lies at the heart of the Lambda Architecture—by restricting the batch layer to eternally true (immutable) raw data, we can safely distribute that data across a cluster, process it in parallel and recover from both technical and human faults.

- Although Elixir is not a pure functional language, its lack of mutable variables is a key enabler for the impressive efficiency and reliability of the Erlang virtual machine upon which it runs.

- The messages sent by both actor and CSP applications are immutable.

- Immutability is even helpful when writing threads and locks–based programs—the more data that's immutable, the fewer locks we need and the less we need to worry about memory visibility.

It seems clear that, even if you're not using a functional language, the frameworks you use and the code you write are going to be increasingly influenced by functional principles. This is great news—not only will it make it easier for us to exploit parallelism and concurrency, but it will make our code simpler, easier to understand, and more reliable.

The Future Is Distributed

The primary reason for the current resurgence of interest in parallelism and concurrency is the multicore crisis. Instead of individual cores becoming faster, we're seeing CPUs with more and more cores. The good news is that we can exploit those cores by using the techniques we've seen over the last few weeks.

But there's another crisis coming our way—memory bandwidth. Current-generation machines with two, four, or eight cores can communicate effectively via shared memory. But what about when we have sixteen, thirty-two, or sixty-four cores?

If the number of cores continues to increase at the current rate, shared memory is going to become the bottleneck, which means that we're going to have to worry about distributed memory. The computer of the future may be contained within a single box, but from the programmer's point of view it's likely to look more like a cluster of independent computers.

This makes it inevitable, I think, that techniques based on message passing, like actors and CSP, will become more important over time.

You won't be surprised to hear that the last seven weeks haven't been a completely exhaustive exploration of your options when it comes to concurrent and parallel development. So what didn't we cover?

Roads Not Taken

One of the hardest decisions we had to make when creating this book was what to leave out. Here's a quick summary of the roads we didn't take, as well as some pointers if you want to investigate them yourself.

Fork/Join and Work-Stealing

Fork/Join is an approach to parallelism popularized by the Cilk language,[1] a parallel variant of C/C++, but implementations are now available for many environments, including Java.[2] Fork/Join is particularly suited to divide-and-conquer algorithms, such as those we saw in *Divide and Conquer*, on page 67 (indeed, Clojure's reducers make use of Java's Fork/Join framework under the hood).

Fork/Join implementations typically make use of work-stealing to share tasks across a thread pool, an approach very similar to Clojure's go blocks (see *Go Blocks*, on page 157).

---

1. http://www.cilkplus.org
2. http://docs.oracle.com/javase/8/docs/api/java/util/concurrent/ForkJoinPool.html

Dataflow

We briefly touched on dataflow in *Dataflow*, on page 73, but the subject really deserves more discussion. The primary reason why we didn't cover it further is that none of the attempts to create a general-purpose dataflow language have been particularly compelling. The best example is probably the multiparadigm programming language Oz (part of the Mozart Programming System).[3]

This doesn't mean dataflow isn't important, though—quite the opposite. Dataflow-based parallelism is extremely heavily used in hardware design—both VHDL and Verilog are dataflow languages.[4,5]

Reactive Programming

Closely related to dataflow is reactive programming, in which programs automatically react to the propagation of changes. Interest in reactive programming has increased recently thanks to Microsoft's Rx (Reactive Extensions) library and others.[6,7]

In this form, reactive programming has significant parallels with several of the technologies we've covered, including Storm's topologies and those based on message passing, such as actors and CSP.

Functional Reactive Programming

Functional reactive programming is a type of reactive programming that extends functional programming by explicitly modeling time. Elm runs in the browser and implements a concurrent version of FRP.[8] Like core.async, it provides a means to avoid the callback hell associated with handling events. Elm is one of the languages covered in the next book in this series, *Seven More Languages in Seven Weeks [TDMD14]*.

Grid Computing

Grid computing is a very loosely coupled approach to building a distributed cluster. Elements of a grid are typically very heterogeneous and geographically distributed, potentially even joining and leaving the grid on an ad hoc basis.

---

3. http://mozart.github.io
4. http://en.wikipedia.org/wiki/VHDL
5. http://en.wikipedia.org/wiki/Verilog
6. https://rx.codeplex.com
7. https://github.com/Netflix/RxJava
8. http://elm-lang.org

The best known example of grid computing is probably the SETI@Home project, which allows anyone to donate computing power to a number of projects.[9]

Tuple Spaces

A tuple space is a form of distributed associative memory that can be used to implement interprocess communication. Tuple spaces were first introduced in the Linda coordination language (which, incidentally, was the subject of my PhD thesis back in the early 1990s), and there are several tuple space-based systems under active development.[10,11,12]

Over to You

I'm a car nut, so the metaphors I've used at the start of each chapter have all been automotive. Like vehicles, programming problems come in a huge range of shapes and sizes. Whether you work on the computing equivalent of a lightweight bespoke racer, a mass-produced family sedan, or a heavy truck, the one thing I can say with confidence is that parallelism and concurrency will be increasingly important.

It's my sincere hope that, whether or not you use any of them directly, the different approaches and technologies we've seen over the last seven weeks will inspire you to tackle your future projects with confidence. Drive (thread-)safely!

---

9. http://setiathome.ssl.berkeley.edu
10. http://en.wikipedia.org/wiki/Linda_(coordination_language)
11. http://river.apache.org/
12. https://github.com/vjoel/tupelo

Bibliography

[Arm13]   Joe Armstrong. *Programming Erlang: Software for a Concurrent World*. The Pragmatic Bookshelf, Raleigh, NC and Dallas, TX, Second, 2013.

[Goe06]   Brian Goetz. *Java Concurrency in Practice*. Addison-Wesley, Reading, MA, 2006.

[HB12]   Stuart Halloway and Aaron Bedra. *Programming Clojure*. The Pragmatic Bookshelf, Raleigh, NC and Dallas, TX, Second, 2012.

[MD14]   Jack Moffitt and Fred Daoud. *Seven Web Frameworks in Seven Weeks: Adventures in Better Web Apps*. The Pragmatic Bookshelf, Raleigh, NC and Dallas, TX, 2014.

[MW14]   Nathan Marz and James Warren. *Big Data: Principles and best practices of scalable realtime data systems*. Manning Publications Co., Greenwich, CT, 2014.

[RW12]   Eric Redmond and Jim R. Wilson. *Seven Databases in Seven Weeks: A Guide to Modern Databases and the NoSQL Movement*. The Pragmatic Bookshelf, Raleigh, NC and Dallas, TX, 2012.

[Tat10]   Bruce A. Tate. *Seven Languages in Seven Weeks: A Pragmatic Guide to Learning Programming Languages*. The Pragmatic Bookshelf, Raleigh, NC and Dallas, TX, 2010.

[TDMD14] Bruce A. Tate, Fred Daoud, Jack Moffitt, and Ian Dees. *Seven More Languages in Seven Weeks*. The Pragmatic Bookshelf, Raleigh, NC and Dallas, TX, 2014.

[Tho14]   David Thomas. *Programming Elixir: Functional |> Concurrent |> Pragmatic |> Fun*. The Pragmatic Bookshelf, Raleigh, NC and Dallas, TX, 2014.

Index

More Seven in Seven

See what the rest of the world is doing with this introductions to seven different programming language approaches.

Seven Languages in Seven Weeks

You should learn a programming language every year, as recommended by *The Pragmatic Programmer*. But if one per year is good, how about *Seven Languages in Seven Weeks*? In this book you'll get a hands-on tour of Clojure, Haskell, Io, Prolog, Scala, Erlang, and Ruby. Whether or not your favorite language is on that list, you'll broaden your perspective of programming by examining these languages side-by-side. You'll learn something new from each, and best of all, you'll learn how to learn a language quickly.

Bruce A. Tate
(330 pages) ISBN: 9781934356593. $34.95
http://pragprog.com/book/btlang

Seven More Languages in Seven Weeks

Great programmers aren't born—they're made. The industry is moving from object-oriented languages to functional languages, and you need to commit to radical improvement. New programming languages arm you with the tools and idioms you need to refine your craft. While other language primers take you through basic installation and "Hello, World," we aim higher. Each language in *Seven More Languages in Seven Weeks* will take you on a step-by-step journey through the most important paradigms of our time. You'll learn seven exciting languages: Lua, Factor, Elixir, Elm, Julia, MiniKanren, and Idris.

Bruce Tate, Fred Daoud, Jack Moffitt, Ian Dees
(350 pages) ISBN: 9781941222157. $38
http://pragprog.com/book/7lang

Even More Seven in Seven

There's so much new to learn with the latest crop of NoSQL databases and web frameworks. Start here.

Seven Databases in Seven Weeks

Data is getting bigger and more complex by the day, and so are your choices in handling it. From traditional RDBMS to newer NoSQL approaches, *Seven Databases in Seven Weeks* takes you on a tour of some of the hottest open source databases today. In the tradition of Bruce A. Tate's *Seven Languages in Seven Weeks*, this book goes beyond your basic tutorial to explore the essential concepts at the core of each technology.

Eric Redmond and Jim R. Wilson
(354 pages) ISBN: 9781934356920. $35
http://pragprog.com/book/rwdata

Seven Web Frameworks in Seven Weeks

Whether you need a new tool or just inspiration, *Seven Web Frameworks in Seven Weeks* explores modern options, giving you a taste of each with ideas that will help you create better apps. You'll see frameworks that leverage modern programming languages, employ unique architectures, live client-side instead of server-side, or embrace type systems. You'll see everything from familiar Ruby and JavaScript to the more exotic Erlang, Haskell, and Clojure.

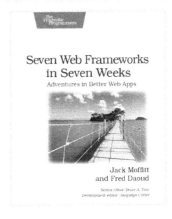

Jack Moffitt, Fred Daoud
(302 pages) ISBN: 9781937785635. $38
http://pragprog.com/book/7web

Clojure and Functional Patterns

Get up to speed on all that Clojure has to offer, and fine-tune your object thinking into a more functional style.

Programming Clojure (2nd edition)

If you want to keep up with the significant changes in this important language, you need the second edition of *Programming Clojure*. Stu and Aaron describe the modifications to the numerics system in Clojure 1.3, explain new Clojure concepts such as Protocols and Datatypes, and teach you how to think in Clojure.

Stuart Halloway and Aaron Bedra
(296 pages) ISBN: 9781934356869. $35
http://pragprog.com/book/shcloj2

Functional Programming Patterns in Scala and Clojure

Solve real-life programming problems with a fraction of the code that pure object-oriented programming requires. Use Scala and Clojure to solve in-depth problems and see how familiar object-oriented patterns can become more concise with functional programming and patterns. Your code will be more declarative, with fewer bugs and lower maintenance costs.

Michael Bevilacqua-Linn
(250 pages) ISBN: 9781937785475. $36
http://pragprog.com/book/mbfpp

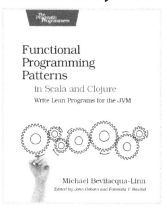

The Joy of Math and Healthy Programming

Rediscover the joy and fascinating weirdness of pure mathematics, and learn how to take a healthier approach to programming.

Good Math

Mathematics is beautiful—and it can be fun and exciting as well as practical. *Good Math* is your guide to some of the most intriguing topics from two thousand years of mathematics: from Egyptian fractions to Turing machines; from the real meaning of numbers to proof trees, group symmetry, and mechanical computation. If you've ever wondered what lay beyond the proofs you struggled to complete in high school geometry, or what limits the capabilities of the computer on your desk, this is the book for you.

Mark C. Chu-Carroll
(282 pages) ISBN: 9781937785338. $34
http://pragprog.com/book/mcmath

The Healthy Programmer

To keep doing what you love, you need to maintain your own systems, not just the ones you write code for. Regular exercise and proper nutrition help you learn, remember, concentrate, and be creative—skills critical to doing your job well. Learn how to change your work habits, master exercises that make working at a computer more comfortable, and develop a plan to keep fit, healthy, and sharp for years to come.

This book is intended only as an informative guide for those wishing to know more about health issues. In no way is this book intended to replace, countermand, or conflict with the advice given to you by your own healthcare provider including Physician, Nurse Practitioner, Physician Assistant, Registered Dietician, and other licensed professionals.

Joe Kutner
(254 pages) ISBN: 9781937785314. $36
http://pragprog.com/book/jkthp

The Pragmatic Bookshelf

The Pragmatic Bookshelf features books written by developers for developers. The titles continue the well-known Pragmatic Programmer style and continue to garner awards and rave reviews. As development gets more and more difficult, the Pragmatic Programmers will be there with more titles and products to help you stay on top of your game.

Visit Us Online

This Book's Home Page
http://pragprog.com/book/pb7con
Source code from this book, errata, and other resources. Come give us feedback, too!

Register for Updates
http://pragprog.com/updates
Be notified when updates and new books become available.

Join the Community
http://pragprog.com/community
Read our weblogs, join our online discussions, participate in our mailing list, interact with our wiki, and benefit from the experience of other Pragmatic Programmers.

New and Noteworthy
http://pragprog.com/news
Check out the latest pragmatic developments, new titles and other offerings.

Save on the eBook

Save on the eBook versions of this title. Owning the paper version of this book entitles you to purchase the electronic versions at a terrific discount.

PDFs are great for carrying around on your laptop—they are hyperlinked, have color, and are fully searchable. Most titles are also available for the iPhone and iPod touch, Amazon Kindle, and other popular e-book readers.

Buy now at *http://pragprog.com/coupon*

Contact Us

Online Orders:	*http://pragprog.com/catalog*
Customer Service:	*support@pragprog.com*
International Rights:	*translations@pragprog.com*
Academic Use:	*academic@pragprog.com*
Write for Us:	*http://pragprog.com/write-for-us*
Or Call:	+1 800-699-7764

Milton Keynes UK
Ingram Content Group UK Ltd.
UKHW012036270824
447508UK00009B/197